公共事务与国家治理研究丛书
Public Affairs and National Governance Series

公共项目的社会责任研究：
分析框架及其应用

Social Responsibility of Public Projects:
An Analytical Framework and Its Applications

林 雪◎著
Lin Xue

南京大学出版社
Nanjing University Press

图书在版编目(CIP)数据

公共项目的社会责任研究：分析框架及其应用 /
林雪著. — 南京：南京大学出版社，2020.5
（公共事务与国家治理研究丛书）
ISBN 978 - 7 - 305 - 23099 - 8

Ⅰ.①公… Ⅱ.①林… Ⅲ.①基本建设项目－社会责
任－研究 Ⅳ.①F284②C91

中国版本图书馆 CIP 数据核字(2020)第 046785 号

出版发行　南京大学出版社
社　　址　南京市汉口路22号　　　邮　编　210093
出 版 人　金鑫荣

丛 书 名　公共事务与国家治理研究丛书
书　　名　公共项目的社会责任研究：分析框架及其应用
作　　者　林雪
责任编辑　郭艳娟

照　　排　南京南琳图文制作有限公司
印　　刷　南京玉河印刷厂
开　　本　718×1000　1/16　印张16.5　字数259千
版　　次　2020年5月第1版　2020年5月第1次印刷
ISBN 978 - 7 - 305 - 23099 - 8
定　　价　60.00元

网　　址　http://www.njupco.com
官方微博　http://weibo.com/njupco
官方微信号　njupress
销售咨询热线　(025) 83594756

CONTENTS

PREFACE ·· ix

LIST OF FIGURES ·· xi

LIST OF TABLES ·· xiii

Chapter 1 Irresponsibility in Construction Projects ·················· 001

    1. 1 Irresponsible behaviors in construction practices ··············· 001

    1. 2 Complex stakeholder environment in construction projects ········ 003

    1. 3 Stakeholder power and influence ···························· 004

    1. 4 Theoretical foundation ·································· 005

    1. 5 Next steps ·· 007

Chapter 2 Corporate Social Responsibility (CSR) and Project Social

            Responsibility (PSR) ···································· 010

    2. 1 Corporate social responsibility (CSR) ···················· 010

    2. 2 Project social responsibility (PSR) ························ 033

    2. 3 Main obstacles to implementing PSR ···················· 042

    2. 4 Summary of the chapter ································ 045

Chapter 3 Construction Project Stakeholders: Theories and Models

            ··· 047

    3. 1 Classical stakeholder theories ·························· 047

    3. 2 Definition of stakeholders ···························· 049

    3. 3 Stakeholder analysis models ·························· 050

3.4　Project stakeholders in construction environment ·················· 052

3.5　Stakeholder collaboration on social responsibility tasks ············ 055

3.6　Summary of the chapter ·································· 058

Chapter 4　Stakeholder Power and Influence ·················· 059

4.1　Stakeholder power ······································ 059

4.2　Stakeholder influence ···································· 065

4.3　Limitations of current research ·························· 070

4.4　Summary of the chapter ································· 072

Chapter 5　Social Responsibility Tasks (SRTs) and the Investigation

　　　Process ·· 074

5.1　Identification of social responsibility tasks (SRTs) ·············· 074

5.2　Investigation process ······································ 078

5.3　Data analysis ·· 091

5.4　Summary of the chapter ································· 096

Chapter 6　Stakeholders' Power on the SRTs ·················· 098

6.1　Analysis of stakeholders' power over the SRTs ················ 098

6.2　Overview of stakeholder power ·························· 099

6.3　Stakeholder power across project stages and social responsibility

　　　dimensions ··· 104

6.4　Gaps between stakeholder power and interest ················ 108

6.5　Recommendations to improve project social responsibility ········ 112

6.6　Summary of the chapter ································· 119

Chapter 7　Stakeholders' Influence Strategies ·················· 120

7.1　How stakeholders use their power also matters ·············· 120

7.2　The concept map by Leximancer ·························· 121

7.3　Stakeholders' influences from the interviews ················ 123

7.4　Summary of the interview findings ······················ 129

7.5　Summary of the chapter ································· 137

CONTENTS

Chapter 8　Management Framework for PSR Implementation ············· 138

　　8. 1　Need for developing a PSR management framework ·············· 138

　　8. 2　Stakeholder power index ································· 139

　　8. 3　Stakeholder influence index ···························· 141

　　8. 4　Procedures of the management framework ···················· 145

　　8. 5　Characteristics of the management framework ·················· 152

　　8. 6　Comparisons with other stakeholder tools ·················· 153

　　8. 7　Summary of the chapter ····························· 158

Chapter 9　A Practical Case of the Management Framework ············· 160

　　9. 1　Background information of the case project ·················· 160

　　9. 2　Data collection process ····························· 162

　　9. 3　Identified social responsibility tasks ······················ 164

　　9. 4　Stakeholders related to the SRTs ························ 168

　　9. 5　Results and findings of the case study ···················· 169

　　9. 6　Participants' feedback ···························· 179

　　9. 7　Summary of the chapter ···························· 182

Chapter 10　Conclusion ································· 183

　　10. 1　Research is in need for PSR ························· 183

　　10. 2　Main conclusion ······························· 183

APPENDICES ····································· 192

　　Appendix A: Sample of preliminary questionnaire in the Delphi Method

　　　　·· 192

　　Appendix B: Sample of stakeholder power questionnaire ·············· 200

　　Appendix C: Sample of interview protocol ···················· 212

　　Appendix D: The case study plan ························· 215

　　Appendix E: Sample of the questionnaire used in case study ············ 216

　　Appendix F: Sample of the feedback forms in case study ············· 219

REFERENCES ···································· 220

PREFACE

The implementation of social responsibility of the public project is an imperative because of the adverse social and environmental impacts often made by construction activities. The construction process faces the problems of resource exploitation, pollution, and community hostility. In addition, the end products of construction have long-term impacts on people's lives and the environment. Therefore, besides the traditional objectives of time, cost, and quality, social responsibility must be incorporated in the public project life cycle as a routine goal. However, research at organizational level is ample, while research at project level is insufficient.

Collaboration among multiple stakeholders on social responsibility is essential but difficult to achieve because of the conflicting stakeholders' interests and unclarified responsibility distribution. Stakeholders are self-sufficient that they tend not to voluntarily share scarce resources in social responsibility tasks. In addition, the dynamic power structures and stakeholder interactions add complexity to any attempt at collaboration. The multiplicity and dynamics of stakeholders remain to be the major challenge and have been insufficiently addressed in existing research. In response to the current gaps, this book investigates the power and influences of multiple project stakeholders. Its aim is to facilitate stakeholder collaboration on implementing social responsibility tasks in construction projects. The book uses mixed-methods research strategies that combine quantitative and qualitative approaches.

First, through a literature review, the book shows that power and influence are two key factors that must be taken into account when facilitating stakeholder collaboration. Second, it uses a questionnaire and a two-mode social network analysis to reveal stakeholders' dynamic power to deal with various social responsibility tasks. Third, through in-depth interviews with practitioners and a computer-assisted qualitative analysis, it investigates heterogeneous strategies and tactics that stakeholders use to influence each other in social responsibility tasks. Fourth, it develops a managerial framework to facilitate the collaborative efforts of stakeholders on implementing social responsibility tasks in public projects. Fifth, it utilizes a case study in the Hong Kong-Zhuhai-Macao Bridge project to validate the applicability and effectiveness of the framework.

This book offers a better understanding of the dynamic power and heterogeneous influencing strategies of multiple project stakeholders including developers, contractors, consultants, governments, district councils, communities, NGOs, and end users. The valid framework also provides a tool for project practitioners to organize social responsibility collaboration within a complicated stakeholder environment.

This book makes an original contribution to the field in the following respects. First, it extends social responsibility theory from organizational level to project level. Second, it identifies power and influence as the perspective from which to explain stakeholder collaboration and endeavors to link stakeholder power with the corresponding responsibilities. Third, it supplements current stakeholder theories by addressing the further variables of stakeholder dynamics and multiplicity. Fourth, it enlarges the scope of stakeholder collaboration by involving multiple project stakeholders and exploring their different roles in improved levels of social responsibility.

LIST OF FIGURES

Figure 1-1   Theoretical framework of social responsibility in construction projects. ··· 007

Figure 2-1   The five main characteristics of social responsibility. ············ 018

Figure 2-2   The development of social responsibility research. ··············· 019

Figure 2-3   The framework for the analysis of social responsibility. ········· 024

Figure 2-4   The three-domain model of corporate social responsibility (CSR). ··· 025

Figure 2-5   The model of social performance. ·································· 028

Figure 2-6   The communication view on social responsibility. ················· 030

Figure 2-7   Social responsibility in construction project management. ······ 039

Figure 3-1   The development of stakeholder analysis model. ·················· 052

Figure 4-1   Three-attribute stakeholder salience model. ······················· 064

Figure 4-2   The process from power to influence. ···························· 066

Figure 5-1   The organizations' nature of the respondents. ···················· 082

Figure 5-2   The stakeholder groups of the respondents. ······················· 082

Figure 5-3   The distribution of respondents' work experiences. ·············· 083

Figure 5-4   The distribution of respondents' positions. ························ 084

Figure 6-1   The two-mode stakeholder-SRT power network. ·················· 100

Figure 6-2   Fluctuations of stakeholder power over the project life cycle. ·· 105

Figure 6-3   The profiles of stakeholder power on different dimensions. ··· 107

Figure 6-4   The comparison between stakeholders' average interest and
             power. ··· 109
Figure 7-1   Concept map generated by Leximancer. ························ 122
Figure 7-2   Stakeholder influence map in implementing PSR. ················· 132
Figure 8-1   The continuum of reactive-proactive stakeholder engagement.
             ·· 141
Figure 8-2   The continuum of cooperative-aggressive influence strategy.
             ·· 144
Figure 8-3   The stakeholder collaboration framework on social responsibility
             tasks. ·· 146
Figure 8-4   The stakeholder power/interest matrix. ························ 155
Figure 8-5   The sample of stakeholder circle. ···························· 156
Figure 9-1   The stakeholder collaboration network in the case project. ······ 178

LIST OF TABLES

Table 2-1   Summary of social responsibility definitions ···················· 011

Table 2-2   The comparison between social responsibility and shared value
            creation ··· 021

Table 2-3   Summary of current research on social responsibility in construction
            and building sectors ································· 035

Table 4-1   Summary of stakeholder influence strategies ················ 068

Table 5-1   The sources for identifying the social responsibility tasks ······ 076

Table 5-2   The list of social responsibility tasks over the construction project
            life cycle ··· 076

Table 5-3   Description of the interviewees ······················· 087

Table 6-1   The network centralities of the stakeholders ··············· 102

Table 6-2   Stakeholder power hierarchy ························· 103

Table 6-3   The paired t-test gaps between power and interest ··········· 112

Table 7-1   Themes and concepts generated from the concept map ·········· 121

Table 7-2   Stakeholder influencing strategies and tactics induced from the
            interviews ··· 131

Table 8-1   The organization strategies in Rowley's network model ········· 158

Table 9-1   The data collection process of the case study ·············· 164

Table 9-2   List of related stakeholders for PSR implementation ·········· 168

Table 9-3   The action plans for the HZMB authority ················· 170

Table 9-4   The action plans for the HZM committee ·············· 171

Table 9-5   The action plans for the CCCC ··· 172

Table 9-6   The action plans for the I & T project department ················· 173

Table 9-7   The action plans for the CRSD ··· 174

Table 9-8   The action plans for the ZLKR ··· 174

Table 9-9   The action plans for the maritime authority ························· 175

Table 9-10   The action plans for the CWD protection authority ·············· 176

Table 9-11   The action plans for the SPER institute ····························· 177

Chapter 1
Irresponsibility in Construction Projects

1.1 Irresponsible behaviors in construction practices

The concept of social responsibility has been increasingly recognized worldwide. It has received wide support and has been gradually embedded in business norms and practices in recent decades. Public sector is under pressure to fulfill its social responsibility, because apart from accelerating economic growth it also makes inevitable impacts on society and the environment (Othman, 2009). Construction activities have been associated with notorious reputations because of pollution, exploitation of nonrenewable resources, unhealthy and dangerous working conditions, and hostility of local communities (Barthorpe, 2010). The report of United Nations Environment Programme (UNEP) in 2014 reveals that, from the perspective of the whole life cycle, buildings are responsible for 10% of global energy consumption, 30%- 40% of greenhouse gas emissions, 40%- 50% of raw material use, and 12% of water use. Additionally, construction industry is widely regarded as a sector that is unethical and opaque (Ho, 2010; Oladinrin & Ho, 2014). Facing the growing pressures of taking up social responsibilities, construction sector is in imperative need to invest more resources in social responsibility implementation (Jones et al. , 2006).

However, Barthorpe (2010) points out that as a visible and high-impact sector that conducts most of its activities in public arena, construction industry has not yet established its formal social responsibility policies and procedures. Although some major construction companies report that they recognize the importance of social responsibility (Brown & Parry, 2009), very few of them practically embrace the idea and incorporate it into their business schemes (Myers, 2005). Due to the fragmented nature of the industry, there are obstacles to implementing social responsibility in construction sector. Nevertheless, research into the characteristics of social responsibility implementation in this specific sector is inadequate.

In addition, while social responsibility at organizational level has been extensively studied and practiced, social responsibility at project level is still in its infancy (Zeng et al., 2015). Traditional construction project management uses three criteria—time, cost and quality—to evaluate construction projects, neglecting the potential environmental and social impacts made by construction activities. This book argues that social responsibility should be incorporated as a criterion of construction project management. Considering social responsibility at project level is necessary because construction projects have widespread impacts. The public and future generations will have to live with the costs brought by and adverse impacts made by irresponsible projects. In addition, the process of construction also can cause high levels of pollution, resource consumptions, and health and safety risks (Othman, 2009). Implementing social responsibility at project level is also difficult because construction projects involve complicated and dynamic stakeholders, which are unlikely to voluntarily take part in social responsibility implementation because of limited critical resources. Therefore, the necessity of studying social responsibility in construction projects is unquestionable, and the key challenge is how to implement social responsibility in the dynamic and complicated stakeholder environment.

1.2　Complex stakeholder environment in construction projects

Roberts and Bradley (1991) define stakeholder collaboration as a temporary union of stakeholders that share their power and resources in order to achieve common goals. Project stakeholders from both public and private sectors need to collaborate on solving the "messy social problems" (Savage et al. , 2010). Bal et al. (2013) point out that the effective engagement of multiple stakeholders with required resources and expertise is critical to environmental protection, sustainable disclosure, and saving energy. Unlike individual organizations, the accomplishment of objectives in projects requires complicated stakeholder interactions and diverse exchanges of expertise and resources (Packendorff, 1995). The implementation of social responsibility tasks goes beyond individual organizations' abilities and requires efforts of various stakeholders.

　　Some major stakeholders like governments, developers and contractors are intensively claimed to practice social responsibility. However, the roles of other stakeholders, such as subcontractors, consultants, suppliers, NGOs, communities, and end users are often neglected. I argue that all internal and external project stakeholders have an indispensable role in social responsibility implementation. Cross-sector, interorganizational stakeholder collaboration has recently become a phenomenon and has been supported widely and internationally. It is also the result of an adaption to the increasingly dynamic, networked, and uncertain social environment (Savage et al. , 2010). Stakeholders can share resources and collaboratively seek solutions to the emerging issues (Bendell et al. , 2010). This way the ability of the project team to cope with emerging demands and risks can be enhanced (Peloza & Falkenberg, 2009).

　　Bryson et al. (2006) state that cross-sector collaboration is necessary and important, but hard to take place. Due to different organizational backgrounds and cultures, stakeholders tend to be self-sufficient and tend to put scarce resources on their own goals instead of making joint efforts to deal with social responsibility tasks (Cheng et al. , 2001). Collaboration is hard to take place due to conflicting stakeholder interests (Li et al. , 2012), lack of consensus-based communication (Cheng et al. , 2001), lack of trust (Karlsen et al. , 2008), and an unclear responsibility distribution (Loosemore, 1999).

The existing literature concentrates on the dynamic stakeholder collaborative relationships between companies and NGOs (Peloza & Falkenberg, 2009), policy makers (Doh & Guay, 2006), or mass media (Apostol & Näsi, 2013). Scant attention has been devoted to providing a better understanding of how multiple stakeholders with conflicting interests can collaborate with each other to implement social responsibility tasks in construction projects. This book addresses this gap by focusing on multi-stakeholder collaboration on social responsibility implementation.

1.3   Stakeholder power and influence

Power of social actors comes from their critical resources demanded by others (Emerson, 1962) and stands for their abilities to alter other social actors' behaviors regardless of resistance (Gaski, 1984). The capacity of stakeholders to influence project decision making comes from the amount of power they have (Mitchell et al. , 1997; Olander & Landin, 2005). Stakeholders with more resources have higher degree of power to propose initiatives, seek support, and achieve their objectives in construction projects (Leung et al. , 2013). According to Davis (1967), greater responsibility comes with greater power, because "those who do not take responsibility for their power ultimately shall lose it" (p. 49). Power and responsibility are twins. Powerful stakeholders have the abilities to implement social responsibility tasks, but this does not mean that they actually fulfill their responsibility. Loosemore (1999) reports that an overload of responsibilities is shifted away from powerful stakeholders to relatively weak stakeholders, because powerful stakeholders tend to avoid exposure to additional risks or resource demands. It is important that powerful stakeholders are aware of their responsibility and powerless stakeholders are empowered to safeguard their benefits (Kolk & Pinkse, 2006). According to Aas et al. (2005), the imbalance between power and responsibility is the main problem in stakeholder collaboration.

Stakeholders' influence is the manifestation of power, standing for the process of using critical resources to change other's behaviors to produce desired outcomes (Cook, 1977; Turner, 2005). Brass and Burkhardt (1993) point out that power represents the capacity to assert dominance over others, but is only visible when it is exercised with behavioral strategies and tactics. Project stakeholders have different strategies to influence social responsibility implementation in projects. The influence flowing among multiple stakeholders forms the original impetus to drive the diffusion of social responsibility values in construction projects. Powerful stakeholders can decide the allocation of project resources with which to achieve environmental and social goals. Nevertheless, secondary stakeholders can drive the implementation of social responsibility tasks by adopting proper strategies (Thijssens et al., 2015), and inappropriate strategies may lead to the failure of social responsibility efforts and even damage stakeholder relationships (Boyd et al., 2007).

1.4   Theoretical foundation

Aiming at facilitating social value creation in construction practices, three critical concepts including social responsibility, stakeholder management, and power theory are integrated. Because the concept of social responsibility is vague and lacks managerial implications, relational lens should be adopted as the preferable viewpoint. Based on relational lens, three new focuses including communication, coordination, and collaboration of social responsibility are required to be probed. Relational lens and the three new focuses imply the necessity to involve stakeholders in social responsibility of public projects.

Stakeholder management approach can provide important implications to implement social responsibility in organizations. Because social responsibility tasks in construction industry are created both within organizations and over the projects, an integrated stakeholder management framework needs to be developed to implement social responsibility at both organizational and project levels. Complex stakeholder networks need to be explored to identify important structures among stakeholders. Moreover, interorganizational power between stakeholders, which plays a significant role in tackling social and environmental issues, calls for further concern.

Power is a concept originated from sociology that could serve as a bridge between stakeholder management and social responsibility. Through evaluation of stakeholder power, implications could be obtained on stakeholders' capacities to resolve related problems through taking necessary actions or motivating other stakeholders to do so. Based on an analysis of stakeholder power and network, meaningful structures can be generated to guide the coordination of multiple stakeholders and their resources.

Therefore, by integrating social responsibility, stakeholder management, and power theory, a theoretical framework is developed to facilitate the implementation of social responsibility in public projects (see figure 1-1).

The left part shows three critical concepts, which form the fundamental theories for developing the framework. The middle part contains two levels of social responsibility: organizational level and project level. At organizational level, the primary task is to analyze stakeholders in order to facilitate the coordination of limited resources to maximize stakeholder satisfactions. Social responsibility at organizational level is often predetermined by organizational objectives, organizational culture and manager's preference. At project level, the emphasis changes to analyzing a complex stakeholder network and taking the stakeholders as knots and their relations as links. From the stakeholders' position and relational structure analysis of stakeholder network, the goal is to find stakeholder collaboration groups that can be used to guide collaboration among stakeholders. The right part shows the common goal of implementing social responsibility in construction projects as the designated targets of the framework.

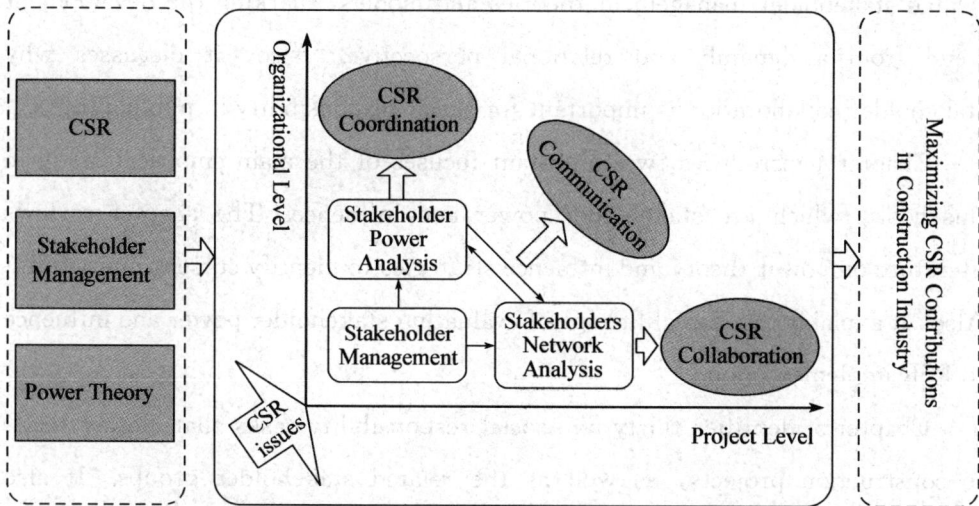

Figure 1-1　Theoretical framework of social responsibility in construction projects.

1.5　Next steps

The book contains ten chapters. This chapter is an introduction of current demands of and obstacles to practicing social responsibility (SR) in projects.

Also, it includes the theoretical framework on which the study in this book is based.

Chapter 2 elaborates the differences between corporate social responsibility and project social responsibility (PSR). The historical development of SR research is summarized. The concept of PSR is developed based on the discussions of related research and definitions, showing the main characteristics of PSR compared with traditional understanding of SR. Also, the main obstacles to practicing PSR are also identified. The following chapters focus on overcoming the obstacles in order to facilitate PSR implementation.

Chapter 3 focuses on project stakeholder theories. Project stakeholder is one of the important concepts in the theoretical foundation of this book. It reviews related stakeholder management theories and models, marking the development trend from a dynamic and relational perspective. Also, it discusses why stakeholder collaboration is important for social responsibility in public projects.

Chapter 4 introduces two important focuses of the main empirical study in this book, which are stakeholder power and influence. The chapter reviews literature on power theory and influence strategies to identify current limitations. Also, it explains the logical linkage of evaluating stakeholder power and influence to PSR implementation.

Chapter 5 identifies thirty-five social responsibility tasks that closely relate to construction projects, as well as the related stakeholder groups. It also illustrates in details two investigations.

Chapter 6 presents the empirical results of a questionnaire on stakeholder power. The findings are discussed to show how stakeholders' power and interest differ on the social responsibility tasks. The dynamics and heterogeneity of stakeholder power are discussed with empirical results.

Chapter 7 expounds the findings of the interview survey on stakeholder influence. It provides a summary of different strategies adopted by multiple stakeholder groups in driving PSR. Also, a stakeholder influence map is developed for depicting the diffusion of social responsibility values among project stakeholders and elaborated different roles of stakeholders in this chain.

Chapter 8 develops a management framework to facilitate social responsibility in projects. Based on previous findings, two quantifiable indexes including the stakeholder power index (SPI) and stakeholder influence index (SII) are developed. The detailed procedures and functionality of the framework are reported.

Chapter 9 presents a case study to perform the developed management framework in a real public project. The process and outcomes of implementing the framework in the project are described. The feedback from the participants is discussed for validating the performance of the framework.

Chapter 10 summarizes the main conclusions in this study. The initial research questions are revisited. The limitations and future research directions are concluded.

Chapter 2
Corporate Social Responsibility (CSR) and Project Social Responsibility (PSR)

2.1　Corporate social responsibility (CSR)

2.1.1　What is CSR?

According to Carroll (1999), the concept of social responsibility has a long and transformational history and has received a wide range of academic and industrial interests since it was first introduced in the 1950s. Then social responsibility research was expanded in the 1960s and proliferated in the 1970s. During this period, the debate was growing on whether business organizations should have the responsibility to contribute to tackling social issues beyond their narrow economic, technical, and legal requirements (Davis, 1973). Since the beginning of the 1990s, the debate over social responsibility has been subsided, following by the extension of the concept and derivation of alternative themes, e. g. , corporate citizenship (Matten & Crane, 2005), sustainability (Milne, 1996), and business ethics (Goodpaster, 1991).

Although most research under review uses the term CSR, this book proposes to adopt the term social responsibility to search and analyze the literature in order to broaden the scope from corporate to general types of organizations. Social responsibility has been a contestable construction since it was introduced. There have been no predominant and exclusive definitions till recently because social responsibility is a vague and intangible term that can mean anything to anybody (Frankental, 2001; Jamali & Mirshak, 2007). In addition, the dynamic social changes and uneven development of economy, culture, and politics decide social responsibility as an umbrella term that is applicable in different social environments. Sheehy (2015) argues that giving a certain definition to social responsibility is difficult and nearly impossible, but it is necessary to draw a clear boundary because of the expanded transnational initiatives and global government regulations. In order to provide a common ground for this book, a definition that can serve the research inquiry should be identified at first. The main definitions used in previous literature are listed in table 2-1.

Table 2-1　Summary of social responsibility definitions

No.	Source	Definition
1	(Bowen & Johnson, 1953)	The obligations of businesspeople to pursue those policies, to make those decisions, or to follow those lines of action, which are desirable in terms of the objectives and values of our society
2	(Davis, 1973)	The firm's consideration of, and response to, issues beyond the narrow economic, technical, and legal requirements of the firm
3	(Carroll, 1979)	The social responsibility of business encompasses the economic, legal, ethical, and discretionary expectations that society has of organizations at a given point of time.
4	(Jones, 1980)	Corporations have an obligation to constituent groups in society other than stockholders and beyond that prescribed by law or union contract.

(Continued)

No.	Source	Definition
5	(Epstein, 1987)	Social responsibility relates primarily to achieving outcomes from organizational decisions concerning specific issues or problems, which (by some normative standards) have beneficial rather than adverse effects upon pertinent corporate stakeholders.
6	(Carroll, 1991)	The total social responsibility of business entails the simultaneous fulfilment of the firm's economic, legal, ethical, and philanthropic responsibilities.
7	(Wood, 1991a)	Business is not responsible for solving all social problems. They are, however, responsible for solving problems that they have caused and helping to solve problems and social issues related to their business operations and interests.
8	(Frankental, 2001)	Social responsibility can only have substance if it embraces all the stakeholders of a company, if it is reinforced by changes in company law relating to governance, if it is rewarded by financial markets, if its definition relates to the goals of social and ecological sustainability, if its implementation is benchmarked and audited, if it is open to public scrutiny, if the compliance mechanisms are in place, and if it is embedded across the organization horizontally and vertically.
9	(McWilliams & Siegel, 2001)	Social responsibility is defined as action that appears to further some social good, beyond the interests of the firm and that which is required by law.
10	EU Commission, 2002 Green Paper, "Promoting a European Framework for Corporate Social Responsibility"	By stating their social responsibility and voluntarily making commitment that goes beyond common regulatory and conventional requirements, which they would have to respect in any case, companies endeavor to raise the standards of social development, protect the environment, respect fundamental rights and embrace an open governance, reconciling interests of various stakeholders in an overall approach of quality and sustainability.
11	(Garriga & Melé, 2004)	Social responsibility theories are focused on four main aspects: (1) meeting objectives that produce long-term profits; (2) using business power in a responsible way; (3) integrating social demands; (4) contributing to society by doing what is ethically correct.

(Continued)

No.	Source	Definition
12	(Simmons, 2004)	Organizations are expected to manage responsibly an extended web of stakeholder interests across increasingly permeable organization boundaries and acknowledge a duty of care to traditional interest groups as well as silent stakeholders, such as local communities and the environment.
13	(Sacconi, 2004)	A model of extended corporate governance whereby who runs a firm (entrepreneurs, directors, and managers) has responsibilities that range from fulfilment of their fiduciary duties to the owners to fulfilment of analogous fiduciary duties to the stakeholders
14	(Doh & Guay, 2006)	The notion that companies are responsible not only for their shareholders, but also for other stakeholders (workers, suppliers, environmentalists, communities, etc.)
15	(Enderle, 2006)	The contemporary morality to conduct right business
16	(Godfrey & Hatch, 2007)	Social responsibility represents actions that appear to further some social good, extend beyond the explicit economic interests of the firm, and are not required by law.
17	(Barnett, 2007)	A discretionary allocation of corporate resources toward improving social welfare that serves as a means of enhancing relationships with key stakeholders
18	(Basu & Palazzo, 2008)	The process by which managers within the organization think about and discuss relationships with stakeholders as well as their roles in relation to the common good, along with their behavioral disposition with respect to the fulfilment of these roles and achievement of these relationships
19	(Matten & Moon, 2008)	Social responsibility (and its synonyms) empirically consists of clearly articulated and communicated policies and practices of corporations that reflect business responsibility for some of the wider societal good.
20	(Freeman & Velamuri, 2008)	The main goal is to create value for multiple stakeholders simultaneously, through intensive communication with stakeholders, without trading off the interest of one against the other continuously.
21	(Vilanova et al., 2008)	Firms should interpret and apply issues that include five dimensions: vision, community relations, workplace, accountability, and marketplace.

No.	Source	Definition
22	(Barthorpe, 2010)	Social responsibility could be considered as an "umbrella" term, incorporating the tenets of environmental sustainability, business ethics, governance, public relations, stakeholder analysis and relationship marketing.
23	(Sheehy, 2015)	An international private business self-regulation, incorporating public and private international law norms seeking to ameliorate and mitigate the social harms and to promote public good by industrial organizations.
24	(Wilburn & Wilburn, 2014)	The term has an ethical responsibility focus; it focuses on doing right by the community and the environment, while also doing right by shareholders by making a profit.

Reviewing the existing definitions, I find that the endeavors on defining social responsibility decreased and became less intensive in the recent decade. Because the agreements haven't been achieved on the definition, this book includes several key arguments on social responsibility definition and defines social responsibility to be adaptive in the changing social environment.

(1) The subject of social responsibility should include general organizations instead of only focusing on big corporations.

A noticeable phenomenon is that most of the definitions are for corporations; however, social responsibility of other types of organizations lacks adequate attention (Farneti & Guthrie, 2009). Additionally, diverse types of organizations emerge along with the globalization and increasingly networked society, such as public sector institutions, temporary alliance, and joint venture (Schultz et al., 2013). ISO 26000 social responsibility guidance published by International Organization for Standardization in 2010 addresses that social responsibility should be generally applied in "all types of organizations regardless of their activity, size or location"[1]. Instead of only focusing on big corporations, all kinds of organizations should be included to meet the requirements of dramatically developing organizational environment (Freeman & Velamuri, 2008).

(2) The essence of social responsibility is the contemporary morality of doing business (Enderle, 2006).

Social responsibility has the sense of moral nature because it normally goes beyond the narrow economic, technical, and legal requirements at the given point of time (Davis, 1973). There are many reasons why organizations have the obligations or duties to society. Davis (1967) points out that due to their enormous resources, organizations have power to earn profits, as well as have the potential to harm social benefits. To maintain their power, organizations must take equivalent responsibilities to resolve the social problems by sharing their profits. In addition, as social citizens who are mutually dependent with the society, organizations have the responsibility to resolve the emerging social problems and safeguard the environment that their existence relies on (Matten & Crane, 2005). However, the core opposite view comes from Friedman (1970), who states that as long as business organizations are profitable, not deviating from the legal and ethical baseline, their responsibilities for the society can be accomplished. But such doctrine neglects that the isolation of profitability is unsustainable, leading to the loss of competence in the prospective market and failing as both profit-seeking entities and social citizens (Joyner & Payne, 2002). The increasing number of business ethical scandals that harm society and environment for individual benefits is a result of lacking moral obligations (Tievino & Blown, 2004). Therefore, the nature of social responsibility

---

1　http://www.iso.org/iso/home/standards/iso26000.htm.

addresses organizations' obligations to voluntarily and proactively respond to, put resources in, and seek solutions to contemporary social issues.

(3) Social responsibility is not pure altruism, while the intentions can be pluralistic.

Although social responsibility has its moral nature to contribute to wider social good, it does not mean it is pure altruism. Hemingway and Maclagan (2004) propose a framework for analyzing social responsibility. According to the framework, motivations for social responsibility initiatives can range from pure altruistic to pure strategic. As long as such actions can produce social benefits without harming other stakeholders' interests, the intentions of social responsibility endeavors will not necessarily be altruistic (Freeman & Velamuri, 2008). The instrumental view states that pursuing social responsibility can enhance the profitability of companies and bring more interests to their shareholders (Garriga & Melé, 2004). And the noted work published on *Harvard Business Review* by Porter and Kramer (2006) highlights that an important reason why organizations pursue social responsibility goals is that they are economically feasible without compromising profits. The intrinsic factors that lead to social responsibility actions range from pure morality of leadership, organizational culture of giving back to society, political effects, reputations, strategies to enhance competitiveness, to directly saving cost or extra profits in the long run.

(4) Social responsibility is for seeking a balance among economic, social, and environmental goals.

Some critics claim that because of the finite organizational resources, investments in social responsibility tasks are inevitably at the cost of shareholders' benefits (Munilla & Miles, 2005). Social responsibility is not asking business to give up or sacrifice their profitability; in contrast, it aims at seeking a balance between achieving organizational goals and social benefits (Carroll, 1979). Rather than investing in every social issue, social responsibility is the optimal allocation of limited organizational resources and generates most valuable outputs (Juscius & Jonikas, 2013). Therefore, organizations had better prioritize the social responsibility tasks that they have best abilities to cope with, such as those highly related to their business or those that can be easily influenced by organizational decisions (Wood, 1991b).

(5) Social responsibility is not constant. It is a changing term representing contemporary social requirements and dynamic stakeholder demands.

The vagueness of social responsibility definitions is mainly reflected in the scope of "social". It is noticeable that social issues that need to be responded to are changing along with the dynamic socialization process. Some definitions use unclear and broad words like "common good", "wider social good", and "social and ecological sustainability" (Basu & Palazzo, 2008; Garriga & Melé, 2004; Godfrey & Hatch, 2007). These vague descriptions lose efficacy for encompassing almost everything. The vague scope of social responsibility may cause ambiguity and lose its theoretical and practical implications. Carroll (1979) describes the boundary of social responsibility as "economic, legal, ethical, and discretionary expectations". Wood (1991a) argues that organizations should only be responsible for issues that relate to their business operations and interests, rather than solving every social problem. However, it is extremely difficult and nearly impossible to enlist every social issue to define social responsibility (Clarkson, 1995). The scope of social responsibility varies under different conditions, including particular social periods, legislations, political environments, national culture, etc. To clarify and operationalize the concept of social responsibility, Freeman (1984) proposes that organizations are allocating limited resources to meet the satisfaction of stakeholders. Dahlsrud (2008) finds that stakeholder theory is used in a large proportion of social responsibility definitions. Stakeholder perspective claims that organization's decision making should embrace the demands of its multiple stakeholders (Frankental, 2001) and create values for them (Freeman & Velamuri, 2008; Juscius & Jonikas, 2013). This stakeholder dimension is significant in social responsibility definition since the target of social responsibility became stakeholders instead of the whole society.

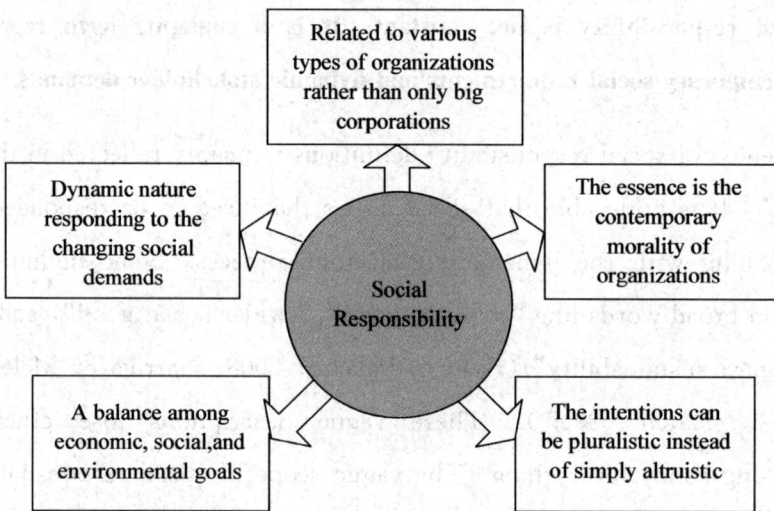

Figure 2-1 The five main characteristics of social responsibility.

2. 1. 2 Evolution of social responsibility research

Many researchers have devoted to social responsibility studies since the concept was expanded and prevalent. Some reviews on the existing social responsibility literature have been published. Carroll (1999) traces the history of social responsibility and identifies the milestones in the evolutionary stages of the concept. Dahlsrud (2008) systematically reviews the controversial social responsibility definitions. Garriga and Melé (2004) categorize four territories of social responsibility theories: instrumental, political, integrative, and ethical.

These reviews focus on finding out the development of social responsibility, but provide few implications of future directions. Currently, social responsibility practices in some major international companies have run advanced to the theories. Instead of looking into the history, it is worth finding out the demanded areas that future social responsibility research should aim at. This book attempts to provide a systematic understanding of the development of social responsibility research and seek new research directions from current research gaps.

Zwetsloot (2003) claims that the existing literature only focuses on "what are the right things" and "how to do the right things", while neglecting how to "continuously innovate and improve the effectiveness of the right efforts". This book proposes that there are three stages of the development of social responsibility: the consciousness-raising stage, the action-translating stage, and the effectiveness-improving stage. Along the development, the research focus has been changed from individual perspective to collaborative perspective. Figure 2-2 describes the three stages. The consciousness-raising stage lays solid theoretical foundation for the development of social responsibility research, which mainly originates from sociology and management studies. The action-translating stage provides productive managerial implications to transform social responsibility from a philosophical slogan to an operational scheme. The effectiveness-

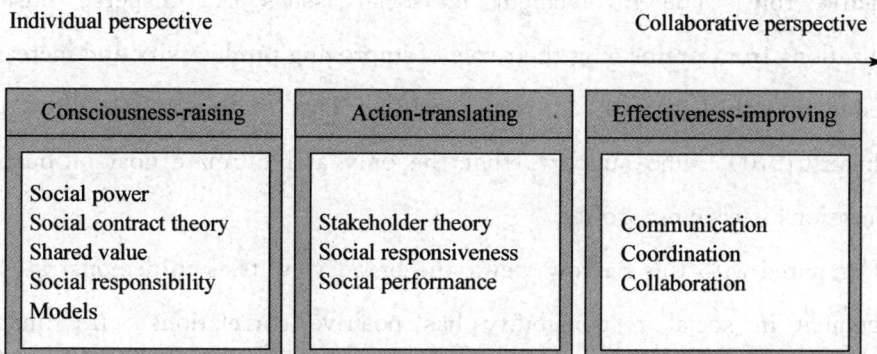

Individual perspective		Collaborative perspective
Consciousness-raising	Action-translating	Effectiveness-improving
Social power Social contract theory Shared value Social responsibility Models	Stakeholder theory Social responsiveness Social performance	Communication Coordination Collaboration

Figure 2-2   The development of social responsibility research.

improving stage stands for the shifting of focus from what and how to be socially responsible to improving the effectiveness of social responsibility efforts. Compared to the former two stages, this stage is currently in its infancy and lacks enough scholarly attention.

(1) Consciousness-raising stage

Consciousness-raising stage is the stage of transition of social responsibility from an unknown term to a generally accepted concept. The main question that is continuously asked at this stage is whether or not business organizations should have social responsibility. Davis (1973) claims that social responsibility is an eternal issue under debate. At this stage, diverse fields of knowledge are adopted to interpret the rationality of social responsibility, including economics, business, politics, law, and ethics (Sheehy, 2015). Three views are under extensive debate at this stage. We will choose three most dominant views to discuss: economic, political, and ethical views.

Economic view

Adam Smith's liberal doctrine denies the "ethical responsibility" of business organizations and claims that each type of organizations is designed for a distinctive role. The involvement in social issues can disperse business organizations from preforming their role of improving productivity and increasing economic growth (Apostol & Näsi, 2013). This statement is followed by Friedman (1970), who supports that the only and ultimate goal of business organizations is earning profits.

Compared with this narrow view, the broad view tries to demonstrate that engagement in social responsibility has positive correlations with financial performance. Considerable research attention has been devoted to testing this proposition. The findings show that although social responsibility investment may cause reductions of short time profits (Aupperle et al. , 1985; Davidson & Worrell, 1990; Hamid et al. , 2011; Spencer & Taylor, 1987), in the long run it can improve financial performance and profit premium by building favorable corporate reputations (Huang & Lien, 2012; Husted & Salazar, 2006; Klassen & McLaughlin, 1996; McGuire et al. , 1988; Spencer & Taylor, 1987; Zahra & Latour, 1987). The perceptions and attitudes of executives and managers towards social responsibility are altered by the positive profitable expectations from social efforts (Holmes, 1976; Ostlund, 1977).

Porter and Kramer (2006) propose the theory of creating shared value (CSV) that social responsibility is a strategy to enhance competitiveness in the market that achieves profitability and create values for society at the same time. And they described CSV as "a broader conception of Adam Smith's invisible hand" (p. 77) to manipulate the implementation of social responsibility in the market (Porter & Kramer, 2011). Table 2-2 shows the comparison between two concepts. The main difference between CSV and social responsibility is whether profit maximization is the ultimate goal.

Table 2-2   The comparison between social responsibility and shared value creation

Social responsibility (SR)	Creating shared value (CSV)
Value: Doing good	Value: Economic and societal benefits relative to cost
Citizenship, philanthropy, and sustainability	Joint company and community value creation
Discretionary or in response to external pressure	Integral to competing
Separate from profit maximization	Integral to profit maximization
Agenda is determined by external reporting and personal preferences	Agenda is company-specific and internally generated
Impact limited by corporate footprint and CSR budget	Realigns the entire company budget

(Source: Porter & Kramer, 2011, 76)

CSV is criticized by many researchers. Wilburn and Wilburn (2014) argue that CSV does not concern the ethical foundation of social responsibility, because the organizations will choose not respond to the problems when they think the actions will not bring extra profit. Crane et al. (2014) address CSV as "sophisticated strategies of greenwashing" rather than social responsibility. Additionally, the whole economic view has opposition due to the basic viewpoint that social responsibility should not simply rely on being market-driven (Doane, 2005; van Marrewijk, 2003).

Political view

Researchers who adopted a political view establish the foundations for the political ground of social responsibility. Davis (1960) advocates that organizations should not only be compliant with the legal and economic requirements. Social responsibility arises from the social resources held by business organizations (Davis, 1967). Organizations are constitutions of massive social resources. These resources generate power to make direct impacts on society and the environment. According to the "Iron Law of Responsibility" proposed by Davis (1967, p. 49), organizations will lose their power if they do not take the responsibility. Therefore, business organizations should take the responsibility to respond to social issues. Donaldson and Dunfee (1994) use social contract theory to explain the reason of the obligational connections between business organizations and society. To maintain the legitimacy in society and communities, business organizations should embed social responsibility philosophy in their decision making. Windsor (2006) identifies the relationships among political, economic, and ethical views of social responsibility, and the political view fills the theoretical gaps between purely ethical and economic approaches.

Ethical view

Ethical theories establish the original foundations for social responsibility to contribute to wide society good. This moral nature of social responsibility is corroborated by many scholars (Garriga & Melé, 2004; McWilliams & Siegel, 2001; Wilburn & Wilburn, 2014). When confronting ethical dilemma, Kantian deontology and utilitarianism tell what is right from wrong. But for business organizations with strongly bounded moral rationality, the classical theories tend to be unsuitable (Donaldson & Dunfee, 1994). It is hard to provide a universally ethical principle for business organizations because of the fickle environment. Power theory provides an approach to interpret the ethical view of social responsibility. Enderle (2006) claims that the ethical connotation of "responsibility" has received limited academic attention compared with its common and prevalent usage in daily language. He points out two types of responsibility: one comes with roles, and the other comes with power. Based on the traditional ethical principle of "ought" implies "can", the extent of responsibility should be allocated in accordance with the extent of power (Enderle, 2006). Following this principle, powerful social actors are supposed to bear more responsibilities, because greater power brings fewer constraints and more opportunities to abuse that power. Based on the discussion, the analysis of social responsibility can be viewed as a two-dimensional continuum (see figure 2-3). One dimension shows that the motivation behind social responsibility can be any point ranging from altruistic to strategic. The other dimension is the attitude ranging from reactive to proactive. This continuum shows that any static and absolute perspective on social responsibility is not flawless. Social responsibility research should start from an open and adaptive view to approach the concept.

Another important question remains to be answered at this first stage is what social responsibilities should be taken by companies. The most influential

Attitude
Proactive

Strategic ←——————————————————→ Altruistic
                                         Motivation

Reactive

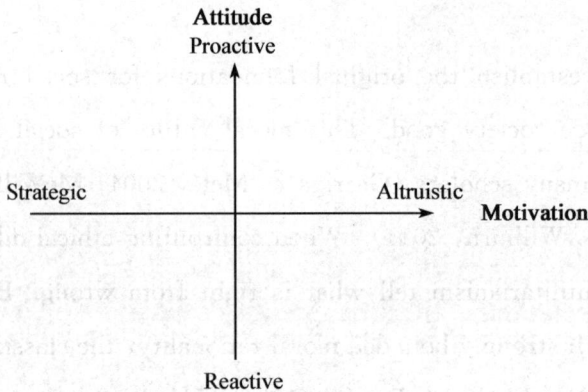

Figure 2-3   The framework for the analysis of social responsibility.

(Modified from Hemingway & Maclagan, 2004, 34)

and applicable typology was developed by Carroll and his team. Carroll (1979) initially categorizes social responsibility into four groups: economic responsibility, which is considered to be the most fundamental, followed by legal responsibility and ethical responsibility, and finally discretionary responsibility. Afterwards, he proposes another pyramid model depicting these four categories in a pyramid structure with being profitable as the base, obeying the law, being ethical, to the paramount of being a good corporate citizen (Carroll, 1991). Carroll's pyramid model has considerable merits on social responsibility research agenda; nevertheless, no metaphor is without its deficiency. Several criticisms generate: 1) there is no evidence of a hierarchical pattern among four groups of responsibilities; 2) four categories are not mutually exclusive as the pyramid model implicitly depicts; 3) philanthropic category may not be counted as responsibility, otherwise it could fall into ethical category. Considering these problems, Schwartz and Carroll (2003) propose a three-domain social responsibility model (see figure 2-4) with three equally significant domains: economic, legal, and social. They emphasize there are overlapping parts among these domains. This model shares the same Venn diagram with the model of "triple bottom line" (social, environmental and economic), but this three-domain model has a more general coverage with legal domain. Including the overlapping areas, seven distinctive categories of social responsibility can be sorted. Essentially, most social issues can hardly be defined as purely economic, legal, or social; on the contrary, they have a hybrid attribution combining two or three domains. It is the managerial decisions that organizations should make when encountering the conflicts in organizational goals; however, the central segment, which is beneficial to both society and organizations, is indispensable for organizations seeking to operate whenever possible.

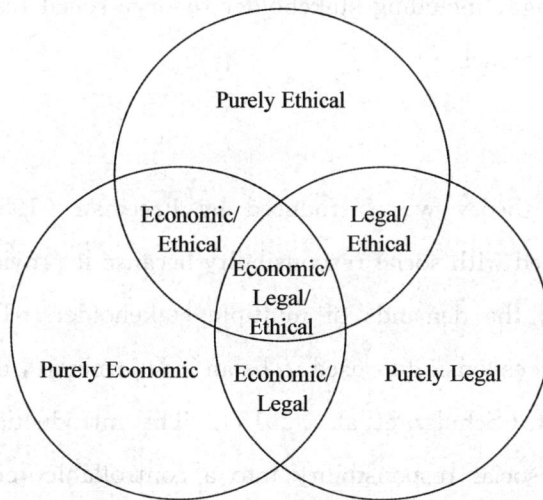

Figure 2-4   The three-domain model of corporate social responsibility (CSR).

(Source: Schwartz & Carroll, 2003, 509)

(2) Action-translating stage

At the action-translating stage, social responsibility has been transformed from an abstract concept to an operational scheme to manage organizational goals. The theoretical discussions on whether organizations should have social responsibility have subsided and have been replaced by how to translate social responsibility into actual policies, programs, and activities (Godfrey & Hatch, 2007).

Organizations only having the motivation or willingness to "do good things" is far from socially responsible; finding operational approaches to implement social responsibility initiatives and achieve social goals is the essential point (Jones, 1980). In practice, the "triple bottom line" and "people planet profit" principles are broadly used in social reporting by organizations. Moreover, detailed managerial principles of social responsibility are referred to in many global standards, including ISO 26000, the fourth generation of the GRI Sustainability Reporting Guidelines (G4), and Social Accountability International SA8000. From reviewing the literature, this chapter summarizes two significant research domains at this stage, including stakeholder theory, social responsiveness, and social performance model.

Stakeholder theory

Since stakeholder theory was introduced by Freeman (1984), it has been frequently associated with social responsibility because it provides an operational way by specifying the demands of multiple stakeholders. Due to the vague boundaries, social responsibility used to be an indeterminate, disintegrative, and conflictual concept (Schultz et al., 2013). The introduction of stakeholder perspective turns social responsibility into a controllable term by embedding stakeholder management. As Jamali (2007) indicates, stakeholder theory solves the problem of social responsibility with respect to vagueness and intangibility, and offers a practical way to implement social responsibility through managing relationships with key stakeholder groups.

Freeman and Velamuri (2008) propose "company stakeholder responsibility", addressing that the ultimate objective of social responsibility is to satisfy stakeholders' demands. Clarkson (1995) also advocates that stakeholder perspective is important in social responsibility because organizations are constituted by the relationships with multiple stakeholders. Organizations can implement their social responsibilities by identifying stakeholders, evaluating the salient stakeholder demands, and making strategies to meet their satisfactions (Zhuang & Wheale, 2004). In addition, the incorporation of good communications (Arvidsson, 2010), maintenance of stakeholder relationships (Kim & Reber, 2008), and stakeholder network management (Akiyama, 2010) also underline the significance of the stakeholder theory in social responsibility implementation.

Social responsiveness

Social responsiveness was introduced by Frederick (1994) as an advanced phase of social responsibility representing the process that organizations respond to social issues. Social responsiveness shifts social responsibility from a philosophical and conceptual term to the procedures to implement organizations' good will. The key argument is social responsibility should be implemented by organizational governance procedures rather than just being a philosophical slogan (Azzam, 2010; Nasi et al., 1997; Sturdivant & Ginter, 1977). Preston and Sapienza (1990) explain the procedural social responsiveness using a four-step social response model: 1) awareness or recognition of an issue; 2) analysis and planning; 3) response in terms of policy development; 4) implementation. Social responsiveness research has intersections with social issue management (SIM) division, which employs multi-disciplinary theories, such as management, economics, politics, business, and sociology, for developing organizational management models to respond to social demands (Carroll, 1994; Wood, 1991b). Social issue management is praised due to its diverse perspectives, practice relevance, and ethical focuses, and is criticized for lacking theoretical foundations and rigorous methodologies (Carroll, 1994).

Social performance model

Some scholars combine social responsibility and social responsiveness into an integrated social performance model (Carroll, 1979; Clarkson, 1995; Sethi, 1975; Wartick & Cochran, 1985; Wood, 1991a). Social performance incorporates social responsibility as the philosophical principle to motivate and guide good behaviors, social responsiveness as the processes and strategies to achieve social goals, and the measurements of outcomes of social endeavors (Clarkson, 1995). Wood (1991a) presents a model of social performance that embeds these three components (see figure 2-5). According to Wood (1991b), social performance can only be achieved by "examining the degree to which principles of social responsibility motivate actions taken on behalf of the company, the degree to which the firm makes use of socially responsive processes, the existence and nature of policies and programs designed to manage the firm's societal relationships, and the social impacts (i. e. , observable outcomes) of the firm's actions, programs and policies" (p. 693).

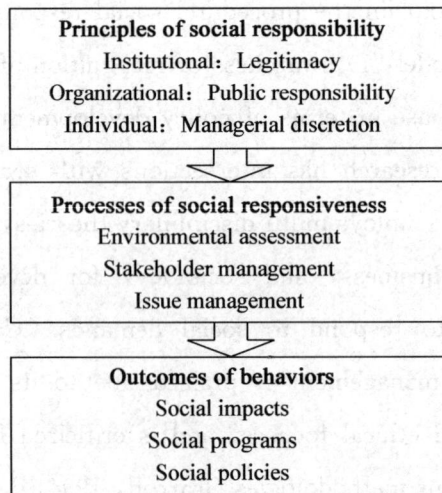

```
┌─────────────────────────────────────────┐
│   Principles of social responsibility     │
│       Institutional: Legitimacy           │
│   Organizational: Public responsibility   │
│   Individual: Managerial discretion       │
└─────────────────────────────────────────┘
                    ▽▽
┌─────────────────────────────────────────┐
│   Processes of social responsiveness      │
│       Environmental assessment            │
│       Stakeholder management              │
│       Issue management                    │
└─────────────────────────────────────────┘
                    ▽▽
┌─────────────────────────────────────────┐
│       Outcomes of behaviors               │
│           Social impacts                  │
│           Social programs                 │
│           Social policies                 │
└─────────────────────────────────────────┘
```

Figure 2-5   The model of social performance.

(Source: Wood, 1991a, 694)

In order to assess the outcomes of social endeavors, efforts have been made to develop measurement tools to evaluate social performance (Fernandes et al. , 2013; Gjolberg, 2009). Measuring social performance is difficult because of the unavailability of detailed information in quantitative terms (monetary and other forms) and the lack of methodology to measure the full impact on society. In general, there are two types of approaches for evaluating social performance: self-disclosure and objective benchmarking. Many transnational corporations worldwide publish annual social responsibility reports to disclose their social activities and achievements. Content analysis of these textual self-reflections has become a conventional and effective means for evaluation (Abbott & Monsen, 1979; Bhatia, 2012; Li et al. , 2013). However, these reports are based on self-evaluations, which may inevitably lead to bias in reliability. Several objective measurements, including scales (Isa & Reast, 2012), balance sheets (Saez-Moran et al. , 2008), scorecards (Spiller, 2000), and indicator systems (Fernandes et al. , 2013; Gjolberg, 2009; Tong & Wu, 2008; Zhao et al. , 2012a), have been developed to enhance the reliability of the evaluation.

(3) Effectiveness-improving stage

Due to the increasing specialization and complex market interactions, new demands on social responsibility research have emerged to consider the interrelations of multiple organizations in the highly networked society (Schultz et al. , 2013). Facing such challenges, social responsibility research should step further than accepting and implementing social responsibility, to a higher standard of discussing how to enhance the effectiveness of social responsibility efforts. Compared with the former two stages, research at this stage is evidently insufficient. Zwetsloot (2003) argues that social responsibility is not only about "doing the right things", but also about continuously improving and innovating social responsibility activities. Spena and Chiara (2012) also advocate that social responsibility should be combined with innovation, and be embedded in the supply chain management, because the isolated focus on focal organizations is no longer sufficient in the networked society. I conclude three prospective research focuses at this stage: communication social responsibility information, coordination of organizational resources, and collaboration among multiple organizations to deal with social issues.

Communication

Communication plays an important role in exchanging information and building relationships with stakeholders to maximize the returns of organizational social efforts (Manheim & Pratt, 1986). Besides the traditional normative, political, and instrumental view of social responsibility, a communication view is proposed by Schultz et al. (2013) (see figure 2-6). They argue that effective social responsibility implementation is very difficult, which requires adequate understandings of many concerns, voices, and demands. Therefore, communication view of social responsibility is worth valuing to be adaptive to the dynamic networked society (Schultz et al., 2013).

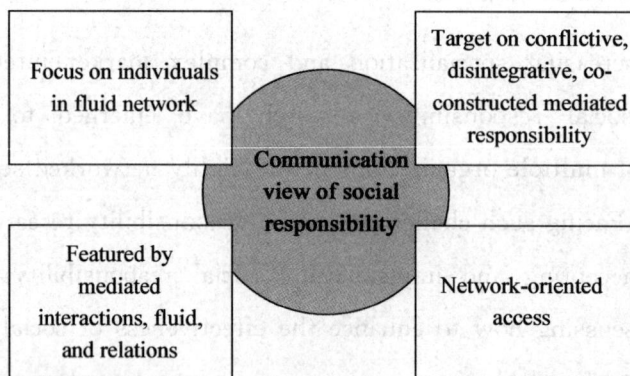

Figure 2-6 The communication view on social responsibility.

(Based on Schultz et al., 2013)

An increasing number of organizations around the globe have realized that they need to disclose their socially responsible activities and achievements to the public (Brown & Parry, 2009). Failure to communicate such information may reduce the expected returns of social responsibility because of customers' unawareness or incomplete information. Studies have been carried out to investigate the approaches that organizations use to communicate with the public (Grunig, 1979), communities (Manheim & Pratt, 1986), peers (Grafstrom & Windell, 2011), investors (Teoh & Shiu, 1990), and many other stakeholders. However, the lack of channels is an important obstacle to effective social responsibility communication (Capriotti & Moreno, 2007). It is safe to conclude that improving communications among organizations will be a significant focus of future social responsibility research.

Coordination

Coordination focuses on the optimal allocation of organizational resources to strategically respond to different social issues. Under conditions of finite resources and the conflicting demands of stakeholders, organizations cannot resolve all social issues and have to prioritize different goals (Freeman, 1984). Wood (1991a) notes that organizations are not responsible for all social issues, but only for the issues caused by their behaviors, and for the issues that relate to their business operations and interests. The stakeholder theory adds value to this point by advising organizations to put priority on the demands from the primary stakeholders, which can directly influence the existence and sustainability of organizations (Freeman & Velamuri, 2008). However, according to such principles, the difficult and nasty social issues may become the "hot potatoes" that are strategically avoided by most organizations. However, power theory provides the resolution that powerful organizations are trusted and vested to tackle the social issues they are capable with (Davis, 1967). Organizational resources should be first invested in the goals that organizations have higher abilities to achieve. Coordination of organizational resources aims at distributing resources strategically to dynamic social responsibility objectives to maximize the overall value. The coordination of resources on social responsibility tasks can also enhance reputations and amplify the level of social welfare delivered (Graafland et al. , 2003; Jamali et al. , 2008; Katavic & Kovacevic, 2011; Zwetsloot, 2003).

Collaboration

Debate continues over whether an internal management system within a single organization is sufficient, especially in a complicated environment (Akiyama, 2010). Research collaboration calls for joint efforts among multiple social actors towards a common goal instead of focusing on individual organizations (Dean, 1996). Because of specialization of societal divisions, organizations have distinctive expertise and resources to undertake different social missions (Cook et al. , 1983). Commonly, social responsibility tasks are "meta-problems" calling for an expanded framework of collaboration among organizations in various sectors. Each organization could make its own unique contribution, which is then pooled with those of others to promote sustainable social development in a united manner. Peloza and Falkenberg (2009) find that benefits from social responsibility initiatives can be enlarged by collaboration with other firms and NGOs. Jonker and Nijhof (2006) also note that a systematic method of collaboration among multiple participants becomes increasingly important, especially with regard to social issues. Without the effective collaboration among all essential parties, the total value of social responsibility efforts could be reduced (Peloza & Falkenberg, 2009). This statement also conforms to the challenge of current networked society (Boutilier, 2007), which is characterized by a dynamically changing environment, a high density of interactions, and high connectivity among organizations (Schultz et al. , 2013). The demands call for a shift from individual organization management to relational collaboration perspective on social responsibility (Peloza & Falkenberg, 2009; Ruan et al., 2013; Schultz et al., 2013). To sum up, research collaboration provides a holistic approach for organizations to exchange information, resources, and techniques on social responsibility implementation. Currently, collaboration has been inadequately addressed in current social responsibility literature. It is worth in future research enhancing collaboration amongst multiple organizations and thereby implementing social responsibility more effectively and efficiently.

2.2   Project social responsibility (PSR)

2.2.1   Social responsibility research in construction sector

Compared with the burgeoning research in general management field, studies on social responsibility specific in construction industry are currently fragmented and lack rigor in terms of methodology. Table 2-3 summarizes the list of formally published literature on social responsibility in construction and building sectors. Among the little available research, most is conceptual and qualitative analyses. They started from the late 2000s and about half of them are from conference proceedings. Therefore, it is worth noting that the research on social responsibility in construction environment is at a very preliminary stage.

The majority of the existing research focuses on constructing conceptual framework for bringing in social responsibility concept from general management to construction context. Construction activities are associated with irresponsible behaviors including numerous onsite accidents, jerry-built projects, delay in payment, and pollution (Lu et al., 2007). Wang et al. (2008) attempt to provide a behavioral model to respond to social responsibility tasks. Ye and Xiong (2011) report the dissatisfactory social responsibility performance in construction industry and call for future attention to change this situation. Liu (2011), Zhao et al. (2011), and Zhao et al. (2012a) endeavor on establishing indicator systems for assessing social performance of construction industry, and interestingly, all research uses stakeholder perspective. Most of the literature focuses on construction organizations. Zeng et al. (2015) propose a novel social responsibility framework at construction project level by considering the project life cycle dynamics, stakeholders' heterogeneity, and interactivity. Their research highlights the extension of social responsibility research from organizational level to project level.

Several journal articles have adopted empirical approaches to explore the current situations of social responsibility report and implementation in local construction industry. Jones (1980) analyzes the annual reports of large UK construction companies. His study shows that although companies claim they have recognized the importance of social responsibility, it is found they fail to incorporate it in practices and executions. Later, another study by Brown and Parry (2009) finds that UK construction industry actually makes significant commitments to social responsibility. According to their social responsibility reports, the focused issues are community, health and safety, environmental performance, energy and resources, and workforce. Petrovic-Lazarevic (2008) conducts interviews with Australian practitioners and finds that social responsibility in construction requires "applying a corporate governance structure that takes into consideration working environment concerns; improving their sustainability, occupational health and safety measures, relationships with suppliers and commitment to local community protection and engagement". The research of Huang and Lien (2012) shows that construction companies can benefit from social responsibility activities. Current problems of social responsibility implementation include lack of internal governance, limited government incentives, and negative perceptions of time, cost and energy constraints

(Othman, 2009).

Table 2-3   Summary of current research on social responsibility
in construction and building sectors

No.	Author and year	Source	Research approach	Research focus
1	(Jones et al., 2006)	*Journal of Corporate Real Estate*	Documentary analysis	Exploration of social responsibility implementation and reporting of major UK construction companies
2	(Kolk & Pinkse, 2006)	*European Management Journal*	Case study	Social responsibility scandals in Dutch construction industry
3	(Ma & Zhai, 2006)	*Proceedings of 2006 International Conference on Construction & Real Estate Management*	Conceptual study	Implementing social responsibility to cope with migrant worker shortage in China
4	(Lu et al., 2007)	*Proceedings of 2007 International Conference on Construction & Real Estate Management*	Conceptual study	Reasons for the unsatisfactory social responsibility of construction industry of China
5	(Petrovic-Lazarevic, 2008)	*Construction Management and Economics*	Interview	Social responsibility tasks addressed by construction industry in Australia
6	(Wang et al., 2008)	*Proceedings of 2008 International Conference on Construction & Real Estate Management*	Conceptual study	Social responsibility implementation in large Chinese construction enterprises
7	(Brown & Parry, 2009)	*Proceedings of the Institution of Civil Engineers*	Documentary analysis	Identification of the prominent topics and waves of social responsibility reported by large UK construction companies
8	(Othman, 2009)	*Architectural Engineering and Design Management*	Questionnaire and interview	Investigation into social responsibility implementation of South African architecture firms

(Continued)

No.	Author and year	Source	Research approach	Research focus
9	(Wang et al., 2009)	*Proceedings of 2009 International Conference on Construction & Real Estate Management*	Conceptual study	Social responsibility motivations of Chinese construction companies
10	(Akiyama, 2010)	*Asian Business & Management*	Case study	The best practices of social responsibility management in Sekisui House Group of Japan
11	(Barthorpe, 2010)	*Property Management*	Case study	The development of social responsibility in construction industry and the current implementation
12	(Liu, 2011)	*Proceedings of the 7th Euro-Asia Conference on Environment and Construction*	Conceptual study	Social responsibility evaluation index for real estate companies
13	(Sardinha et al., 2011)	*Journal of Cleaner Production*	Comparative study	Social responsibility benchmarking in real estate companies
14	(Ye & Xiong, 2011)	*Proceedings of the 16th International Symposium on Advancement of Construction Management and Real Estate*	Conceptual study	Social responsibility implementation in major Chinese construction companies
15	(Zhao et al., 2011)	*Proceedings of the 16th International Symposium on Advancement of Construction Management and Real Estate*	Conceptual study	Social responsibility indicators combining social responsibility tasks and related stakeholders
16	(Huang & Lien, 2012)	*Construction Management & Economics*	Empirical study	The relationship between social responsibility and financial performance of construction companies in the Taiwan region, China

(Continued)

No.	Author and year	Source	Research approach	Research focus
17	(Zhao et al. , 2012a)	*Journal of Cleaner Production*	Conceptual study	Social responsibility indicator framework for construction organizations from stakeholders perspective
18	(Zeng et al. , 2015)	*International Journal of Project Management*	Conceptual study	Conceptual framework for social responsibility of major infrastructure projects

The literature review above shows that the development of social responsibility research in construction industry remains in infancy. On the one hand, literature on social responsibility in construction can only be found after 2006, and the number of literature is considerably poor. On the other hand, in construction management field, the research focuses on fragmented and branched topics in social responsibility, including construction sustainability (Bal et al. , 2013; Shen et al. , 2010; Yao et al. , 2011), ethical conduct (Ho, 2013; Ho, 2011; Oladinrin & Ho, 2014; Oladinrin & Ho, 2015), green building (Jing & Qin, 2011), environmental management (Johansson & Svane, 2002), and health and safety (Lingard & Rowlinson, 1998; Ringen et al. , 1995). These studies are fragmented and focus on different social aspects, therefore lacking common ground to communicate with each other. The reason why social responsibility is irreplaceable is that it can offer a theoretical foundation encompassing different social issues and integrate them into one body of knowledge. Construction industry features multi-disciplines, multi-techniques, and complex stakeholders' relationships. General social responsibility research findings may not be applicable in construction context, since social responsibility without considering industrial background can be fatally deficient (Cottrill, 1990). Under this condition, how social responsibility can be constructed in a specific context, construction industry, requires broader attention (Dahlsrud, 2008). Given that the significance of social responsibility in construction industry has been recognized, this book emphasizes on answering how to implement social responsibility more effectively in a complicated stakeholder environment, how to balance multiple goals within construction projects, and how to promote stakeholder collaboration on social responsibility tasks.

2. 2. 2 Defining project social responsibility

The current social responsibility literature mainly focuses on individual organizations. However, for construction projects, implementing social responsibility becomes more difficult due to the complex project stakeholders. Unlike traditional organizations, projects are temporary unions for completing unique tasks through interactions between various project stakeholders with different expertise and resources (Packendorff, 1995). Although social responsibility at organizational level has been extensively studied, social responsibility at construction project level is still an undeveloped field (Zeng et al. , 2015). There are several reasons for bringing social responsibility from organizational level to project level.

(1) **Social responsibility should be incorporated in project management besides time-cost-quality goals, because of the adverse impacts made by construction project life cycle.**

Construction projects consume tremendous physical resources and have harmful impacts on the environment over project life cycle, from project construction process to the operation of the end product (Othman, 2009). The construction process is associated with exploitation of non-renewable resources and neighborhood hostility, and the disturbance on communities and environment is inevitable (Moodley et al. , 2008). Compared with the construction process, the end products of construction projects, the artificially built environments, have longer-lasting and more significant impacts on the society and the environment. The life cycle assessment of building energy analysis shows that the operating stage of buildings has the largest share (80%–90%) of the overall energy demand (Ramesh et al. , 2010). Carbon dioxide emission per square meter at the operation stage is nearly 12 times higher than that at the construction stage for a life span of 50 years, about 23 times higher for a life span of 100 years. It is nearly 105 times higher than that at the demolition stage for a life span of 50 years, 209 times higher for a life span of 100 years (Gustavsson et al. , 2010).

The traditional construction project management only concentrates on the triangle of time, cost, and quality. Because of the potential social and environmental impacts and the increasing pressures from the society, social responsibility should be incorporated in project management as the ultimate goal of successful projects. As shown in figure 2-7, the traditional triangle of time-cost-quality is compassed in the general scope of social responsibility. However, it also shows that most of the other issues in the scope, such as environmental protection, human rights, community issues, and philanthropy, have been ignored.

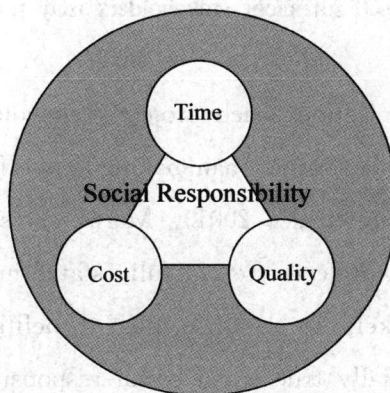

Figure 2-7   Social responsibility in construction project management.

(2) Construction industry features multi-level operations (intra-organizational and intra-project management). A separate management system should be implemented at project level to cope with social issues.

Construction projects contain interactions and resource exchanges both within and between organizations. Besides organizational governance, social issue management at project level is also indispensable for achieving social responsibility goals. Packendorff (1995) redefines construction projects as temporary organizations that are well-organized for producing a non-routine product. Since the early 1990s, project companies have been established at project conception stage for some long-span infrastructure projects as independent business entities that are vested to take both financial and social responsibility like normal business organizations do. According to the definition of social responsibility in section 2.2.1, social responsibility should be taken by all types of organizations, including construction projects. Therefore, construction projects are also expected to embrace social responsibility and respond to the social demands of employees, communities, and the general public.

(3) Construction projects lack pre-agreed framework for dealing with social issues collaboratively, while self-sufficient stakeholders may not take the responsibility voluntarily.

As a self-sufficient organization, each project stakeholder tends to devote its resources to its primary goals rather than making joint efforts to implement social responsibility tasks (Cheng et al., 2001). Moreover, stakeholders' obligations to social responsibility in projects are not fully stated in contracts and policies; stakeholders are less likely to sacrifice their benefits or share competitive resources. This is especially true when social responsibility tasks bring extra costs and risk exposure. Stakeholders avoid taking responsibility and often shirk the responsibility to others when the social issues arise. One example is the pollution of the Pearl River in Guangdong Province, China. According to the

2009 *Poisoning the Pearl River Report* by Greenpeace [1], the rate of qualified drinking water in Guangdong was only 67.8% among the samples. In addition to the polluting factories, many construction projects including dam and power stations along the bank caused the pollution. No controlling measures were taken before the pollution was found. This was because the powerful stakeholders, including the developer and the government, transferred the risk and responsibility to relatively powerless taxpayers at the expense of the health of current and future generations. In construction projects, it is common that powerless stakeholders take responsibility that goes beyond their capacity, while powerful stakeholders take less (Loosemore, 1999). This imbalance between power and responsibility calls for the management framework at project level to explicit stakeholders' roles and responsibilities in social issues.

(4) The last reason why social responsibility should be extended to project level is that construction projects are highly uncertain and dynamic in nature (Missonier & Loufrani-Fedida, 2014).

Compared with general organizations, construction projects are conducted in the uncertain and complicated stakeholder environment over life cycle (Aaltonen, 2011). Emerging social issues like ecology habitat conservation, land use, resettlement of the local residents, relationship with neighbors, construction waste, energy efficiency, dust environment need the immediate reactions and proper solutions of relevant stakeholders. Under the challenges of such emergent and dynamic project environment, implementing social responsibility at project level provides a novel approach to redefine project goals and pursue improved social performance. However, implementing social responsibility in construction projects is not an easy practice; an integrative framework that enables the

---

1   Greenpeace(2009), "Poisoning the Pearl River", available at http://www.greenpeace.org/international/en/publications/reports/poisoning-the-pearl/.

effective communication and collaboration among stakeholders is required to achieve that goal.

From the literature review, it is found that the existing research on social responsibility in construction environment is still in its infancy. To address this issue, this book attempts to focus on social responsibility in a construction project, which is characterized by a dynamic and complex stakeholder environment. Based on the discussions above, the definitions of project social responsibility and project social responsibility tasks adopted in this book are as follows:

Project social responsibility (PSR) is that, besides focusing on quality, time, and cost, construction stakeholders have the obligations to respond to broader social, environmental, and ethical issues involved in the overall project life cycle.

Project social responsibility tasks (SRT) are measures, policies, and activities that are implemented by construction stakeholders to generate broader values for the society.

2.3   Main obstacles to implementing PSR

Based on the arguments, research on social responsibility should concentrate on sharing information, optimizing resource allocation, and facilitating stakeholder collaboration to improve the effectiveness of social responsibility efforts. Stakeholder collaboration on social responsibility is not only the theoretical gap in general social responsibility research, but also the bottleneck of construction practices. The main obstacles to implementing project social responsibility are as follows:

(1) Construction stakeholders need to collaboratively build and maintain reputations of construction projects; otherwise, projects will have a negative impact on all project stakeholders.

Construction projects are unique and temporal unions of different project participants, and therefore the social influences on these projects will not be attributed to any single organization (Packendorff, 1995). However, irresponsible behaviors and outcomes like on-site accidents, environmental pollution, and community conflicts can influence the credits of all project stakeholders. All stakeholders including developers, contractors, consultants, government departments, and subcontractors should be aware of this risk and try to improve the social performance of the project collaboratively.

(2) Social issues involved in construction projects are "mega problems" that call for resource sharing and actions of multiple stakeholders.

Similar to achieving many project goals, achieving social responsibility objectives relies on the effective interaction between multiple stakeholders (Missonier & Loufrani-Fedida, 2014). Social and environmental issues related to construction practices like air pollution, unsafety, unsustainability, energy inefficiency, unemployment, and ecological disturbance are all "wicked problems", which need the engagement of various sectors (Bendell et al., 2010; Savage et al., 2010). It is impossible for individual organizations to respond to all these issues due to the scarcity of resources (Jamali, 2007). Stakeholders from the private sector, government, and civil society all have specific roles. For example, to implement green construction, governments must enact regulations to force developers to require green materials in tenders. Developers, in turn, must encourage contractors to adopt green features during procurements. End users can drive the developers and contractors to use green products via green purchase or increasing demand for green buildings. Therefore, stakeholder collaboration is essential in pursuing social responsibility in construction projects.

(3) Stakeholders have heterogeneous interests, so it is difficult for them to share critical resources and information to collaborate on social responsibility tasks.

Construction projects currently face such diverse social responsibility tasks as labor issues, sustainable construction, and green building, and challenges are increasing, including resource inefficiency, climate change, and housing issues (Martinuzzi et al., 2011). The discretion and heterogeneity of stakeholders determine that stakeholders' emphases are different due to their varied organizational backgrounds and values (Jonker & Nijhof, 2006). Lindgreen et al. (2009) find that organizations have different focuses on stakeholders' demands, putting varying emphases on customers and suppliers, employees, financial investors, philanthropy, and environment. And such difference may relate to the organizations' size, nature, history, culture, leadership, etc. In addition, construction projects involve an extensive scope of stakeholders, representing conflicting interests and demands (Aaltonen, 2011). Driven by self-interest, project stakeholders tend to invest resources in their own goals instead of showing concerns for a project's overall social performance (Cheng et al., 2001). A lack of consensus and joint efforts among stakeholders may lead to the failure of a project's social performance (Li et al., 2012). Therefore, the complexity of stakeholder environments is the main obstacle to stakeholder collaboration in construction projects.

(4) Another obstacle is the dynamic stakeholder power and complex interactions in construction projects.

Because of resource differentiation and specialization, stakeholders have different power and abilities to deal with social issues (Cook, 1977). But it cannot be guaranteed that the powerful stakeholders are aware of their abilities and voluntarily take the corresponding responsibilities. In addition, in construction projects, the power that determines the flow of resources for implementing project social responsibility is changing constantly (Aaltonen & Kujala, 2010).

This dynamic nature of construction projects makes it even more difficult for stakeholders to collaborate on social responsibility tasks. The failure of empowerment of important stakeholders brings ineffective social engagement and bad social performance of the projects (Dainty et al. , 2002). The unbalanced power and responsibility is also one of the consequences that let the powerless stakeholders bear more pressures than they can cope with (Loosemore, 1999). And more importantly, the power of stakeholders is dynamically changing in construction life cycle (Aaltonen & Kujala, 2010). For different social responsibility tasks, the stakeholders that should take leading responsibility are different. The dynamic power structures and complicated interactions cause essential obstacles to the collaboration of project stakeholders on implementing project social responsibility.

Accordingly, an effective approach is needed to assist project teams to identify dynamic power in order to ensure proper engagement of capable stakeholders in implementing social responsibility in construction projects. Although the demands of stakeholder collaboration on social responsibility implementation in construction projects are urgent, there is limited research that contributes to the theory and practice of how stakeholders with different interests and resources can collaborate.

2.4   Summary of the chapter

This chapter firstly reviewed the existing definitions of corporate social responsibility and discussed the five important characteristics of the concept, which are: 1) relate to all types of business organizations rather than only big corporations; 2) contemporary morality of doing business; 3) plural instead of simple intentions; 4) a balance of multiple objectives; 5) dynamically changing environment. Later, it reviewed the research, including the awareness-raising

stage, action-translating stage, and effectiveness-enhancing stage. Through
exploring the social responsibility research in the construction industry, I found
that improving stakeholder dynamic power and complex collaboration is the key
to implementing social responsibility in construction environment. Also, general
definitions of project social responsibility and social responsibility tasks were
proposed at the end of this chapter to identify the fundamental scope of this
study.

Chapter 3
Construction Project Stakeholders:
Theories and Models

3.1　Classical stakeholder theories

Stakeholder theories are found prevailing in the management of social issues. They have been integrated into research on sustainability (Bal et al. , 2013; Sharma & Henriques, 2005), social performance (Clarkson, 1995; Valackiene & Miceviciene, 2011; Xun, 2013), environmental management (Onkila, 2011; Reed, 2008), risk management (Deng & Zhou, 2009; Jing & Qin, 2011), and business ethics (Jones, 1995; Moodley et al. , 2008). Stakeholder and social responsibility theories both speak for the extension of organizational objectives to create broader social and environmental good. Stakeholder theories become dominate in resource and objective management of corporations. Nevertheless, they have different emphases with the concept of social responsibility: stakeholder theories focus on providing managerial and strategic solutions, while social responsibility tends to focus on the dilemmas of multiple financial, social, environmental, and ethical objectives (Phillips et al. , 2003). General stakeholder theories contain various aspects of assumptions and models. To clarify the integrating point of this book, I try to draw the boundaries between general stakeholder theories.

The notion of stakeholder is introduced by Freeman (1984) in his book *Strategy Management: A Stakeholder Approach*. Stakeholder theory aims at explaining and improving the operation of organizations and becomes prevailing in both academic and managerial practices (Mitchell et al. , 1997). The proliferation of stakeholder theory in management field has been praised for enlightening the way to achieve organizational objectives through analyzing and managing stakeholder relationships. Donaldson and Preston (1995) propose that stakeholder theories can be used in three different aspects: descriptive, instrumental and normative perspectives. Descriptive aspect depicts organizations' characteristics and behaviors by using a perspective of stakeholders. Using this aspect, organizational success and sustainability can be described as creating desired values to all important stakeholders who can influence the operations and survival of organizations (Clarkson, 1995; Jawahar & McLaughlin, 2001). Instrumental stakeholder offers managerial tools for organizations to achieve organizational goals through analyzing and managing the demands of their stakeholders (Brugha & Varvasovszky, 2000). This view is frequently used in empirical studies that try to evaluate the correlations between organizational performance and stakeholder management. Normative aspect is the core of stakeholder concept, which addresses the basic philosophy that stakeholders are persons or groups having intrinsic interests in organizational activities. Descriptive, instrumental, and normative aspects address different perspectives of stakeholder theories. This study also adopted hybrid aspects of normative, descriptive, and instrumental, by accepting the basic concept of stakeholders, admitting that the nature of construction projects is to meet the demands of stakeholders, and seeking management framework for stakeholder collaboration on implementing project social responsibility tasks.

3.2   Definition of stakeholders

The initial step to employ stakeholder theories is to answer the question "who are the stakeholders" and draw a boundary by defining stakeholders with distinctive features. These particular features depend on the meaning of "stake", reflecting the influences, claims, or interests of stakeholders with respect to the focal organization (Clarkson, 1995). One of the most recognizable definitions is proposed by Freeman: "Any group or individual who can affect or is affected by the achievement of the organization's objectives." (Freeman, 1984) Following this definition, stakeholders mean those who hold influences on organizations or their activities. Clarkson (1995) describes organizations as systems of primary stakeholders who can directly influence the survival of focal organizations like shareholders, investors, employees, customers, and suppliers. The secondary stakeholders are defined as those who do not participate in core business activities and thus cannot influence the survival of focal organizations. Mitchell et al. (1997) argue that stakeholders must include individuals or groups having either claims or abilities to influence. According to the statement of Mitchell et al. (1997), some organizations or individuals have claims, interests, or risks that relate to the organizations' activities but not necessarily have enough power to influence the decision making. Vice versa, the powerful stakeholders may not have interests to perform their influences.

The existing definitions are criticized as too broad and almost include every group and individual, leading to the loss of focuses and lending no reference to management (Aaltonen & Kujala, 2010). Because stakeholders are changing under different conditions, stakeholder definition in specific context can provide more operational and managerial implications (Weber & Marley, 2012). This book used influences as the "stake" held by stakeholders, thus specifying the definition for stakeholders to deal with social responsibility tasks. Those who have power to influence project objectives are the ones that needed to be identified to take certain responsibilities. Also, those who lack enough power but are to some extent influenced by projects activities also need to be focused to find out what issues or problems need to be dealt with.

Based on the discussions, establishing a specific boundary for identifying stakeholders is the important precondition. Thus, stakeholders in the context of this book are defined as "groups, organizations or individuals that can influence or be influenced by the overall life cycle of construction projects".

3.3 Stakeholder analysis models

The development of stakeholder analysis model is depicted in figure 3-1. It shows that classical view takes organizations as focal positions and stakeholders are individuals or groups having a one-direction relation with the organization (Freeman, 1984). In the early input-output model, the focal firm was taken as a black box, which creates products to meet customers' demands. Afterwards, Donaldson and Preston (1995) propose the interacting model, indicating stakeholders and the focal firms have mutual influences. Both input-output model and interacting model put the focal organizations as the core. The main aim is to design strategical approaches for focal organizations to cope with different stakeholders' demands by analyzing stakeholders' salience. This viewpoint of focal organizations has been adopted by many stakeholder research (Jensen, 2002; Mitchell et al. , 1997; Polonsky & Scott, 2005; Yang et al. , 2008).

The introduction of network model of stakeholder analysis is inspired by Rowley's work in 1997. Rowley (1997) argues that "stakeholder relationships do not occur in a vacuum of dyadic ties, but rather in a network of influences". Stakeholder relationships are dependent on each other, so one relationship can be influenced by the change of network structures. As it is shown in figure 3-1, in the network model, each stakeholder can have interactive relationships with other stakeholders (Rowley, 1997). This model changes the focus from organization-stakeholder relationship to stakeholder-stakeholder interactions. The focus of stakeholder analysis has changed from focal organizations to the holistic view of stakeholders (Co & Barro, 2009; Peloza & Falkenberg, 2009; Roberts & Bradley, 1991).

However, Rowley's network model has no consideration of the dynamics and heterogeneity of stakeholders. Stakeholders and their interactions change significantly in different issues. Because stakeholders and issues are two different concepts with different analyzing focuses, it is demanded to involve both dynamic stakeholders and issues in the analyzing model. Luoma-aho and Vos (2010) point out that stakeholder management should move forward to "issue arenas", by which both issues and stakeholders can be analyzed to assist stakeholder management more efficiently. The latest work of Van Offenbeek and Vos (2016) asserts current research neglect the linkages between stakeholders and issues. This study adopted the stakeholder-issue model to study stakeholder collaborations on social responsibility tasks. The dynamics of stakeholders' characteristics in different social responsibility tasks were highlighted in this model. The identification of stakeholders and their salience were after the identification of issues, and were based on these identified issues. The analysis of stakeholder-issue network structures shows the characteristics of stakeholder interactions, issue clusters, as well as the stakeholder-issue relationship.

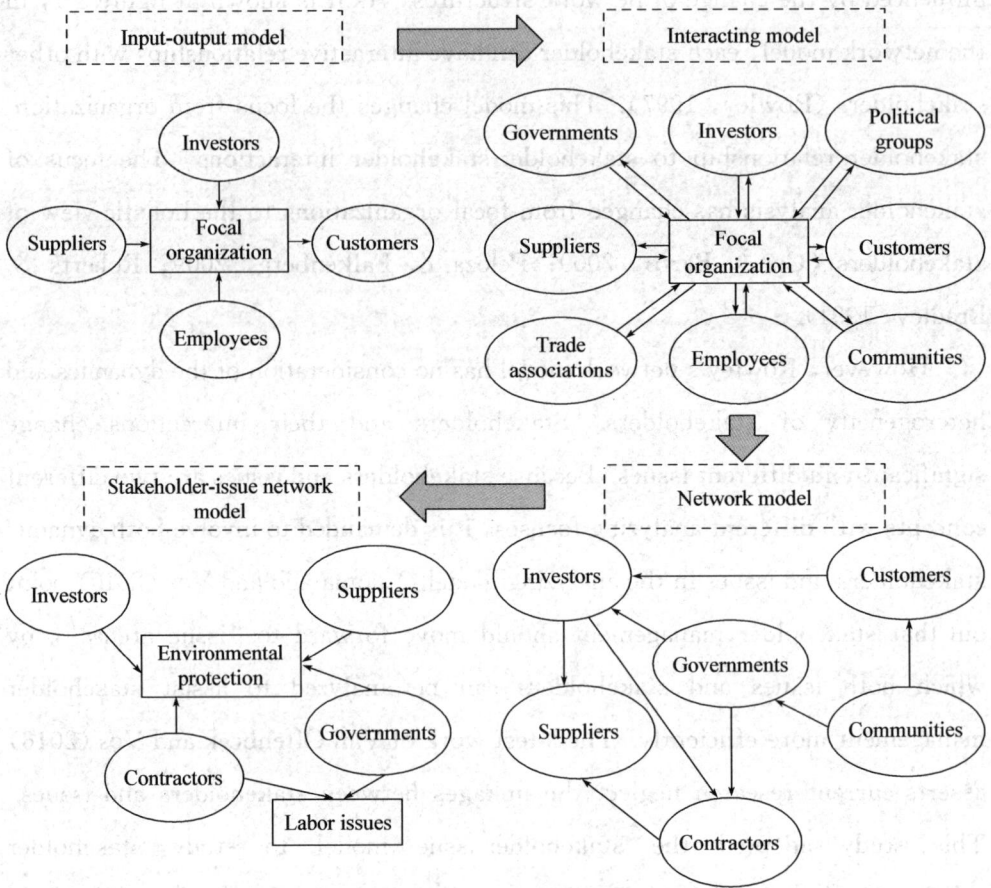

Figure 3-1   The development of stakeholder analysis model.

3.4   Project stakeholders in construction environment

3.4.1   Who are the construction project stakeholders?

The application of stakeholder theories has been spreading from its original strategic management field to project management research and practice since 1980s (Littau et al. , 2010). Project Management Institute (PMI) defines construction project as "a temporary endeavor undertaken to create a unique product or service". Because the construction projects are unique in location, time, and scope, project stakeholders involved in project implementation are also distinguished. Achterkamp and Vos (2008) claim that although stakeholder theory has been extensively used in project management literature, the identification of project stakeholders in different project environments is still unclarified. Li et al. (2012) define project stakeholders as individuals or organizations "who can influence the project process and/or final results, whose living environments are positively or negatively affected by the project, and who receive associated direct and indirect benefits and/or losses of project execution or project completion" (pp. 4 – 5). Considering the life cycle perspective, construction projects involve a changing profile of stakeholders including but not limited to client, project management team, consultant and designer, contractor, subcontractor, supplier, employees, local communities, financial institutions, government authorities, end users, NGOs and NPOs (Heravi et al. , 2015).

The categorization of project stakeholders continues to use the typology in classical stakeholder theories (Clarkson, 1995; Freeman, 1984). Freeman (1984) classifies stakeholders into internal and external stakeholders based on their proximity of relationships with focal organizations. In view of project, stakeholders also usually are separated into two categories (Aaltonen & Kujala, 2010; Winch & Bonke, 2002). Internal stakeholders are those who have formal, official, or contractual relationships regarding and within the project. External stakeholders are those who do not have formal connections with the project, but can potentially influence or be influenced by project activities.

Rather than only focusing on internal stakeholders like shareholders and key developers, an increasing stream is to include external groups and find out invisible project stakeholders. It is noted that there are more literature focusing on internal stakeholders, while limited attentions have been addressed on external stakeholders that do not directly relate to the project (Davis, 2014).

Implementing project social responsibility requires the input of both internal and external stakeholders. They have different roles, which are determined by their different positions in the project, diverse relationships embedded in the whole project network, as well as different resources they possess to carry out the social responsibility tasks.

3. 4. 2 Dynamics and heterogeneity of project stakeholders

Projects feature highly dynamic and uncertain environment (Aaltonen, 2011; Karlsen, 2002), represented by the highly complicated stakeholder interactions and conflicting demands, dynamic and increasing uncertainty in project life cycles, and the severe public hostilities and controversies (Mok et al. , 2015). General stakeholder management theories cannot be employed directly in construction project management because the dynamic context requires continuous adjustments (Cuppen et al. , 2016). Stakeholder dynamics and heterogeneity are significant natures that need to be taken into consideration in project stakeholder research.

Project stakeholders often have different and conflicting interests (Atkin & Skitmore, 2008). Li et al. (2012) identify the conflicts among the external stakeholders' concerns on infrastructure projects. They find that the general public care most about land use and environmental issues, governments focus mainly on economic growth, while NGOs value the green and sustainable techniques. Bryde and Robinson (2005) reveal the conflicts between contractors and developers. They find that contractors put more emphases on saving cost and shortening durations, while developers show higher interests in meeting needs of end users and communities. The differences in stakeholder interests are caused by the intrinsic nature of stakeholders (Donaldson & Preston, 1995) and the different perceptions of project successes (Davis, 2014). The conflicting stakeholder interests have been revealed by many researchers and marked as the primary problem in project management practices (Bourne & Walker, 2005;

Olander & Landin, 2005; Sutterfield et al. , 2006; Winch & Bonke, 2002).

Also, stakeholders' salience is not static but changing in different issues and at different project stages. The role of stakeholder power and influences is essential to achieving project goals for driving exchanges of critical resources among project stakeholders (Bal et al. , 2013). Bourne and Walker (2005) address the complexity and dynamics of stakeholder influences on project decision making. Because of the changing conditions and variations of materials, techniques, skills, knowledge, and information, stakeholders' power and influences vary throughout the project life cycle (Aaltonen & Kujala, 2010). Stakeholders have different power to control resource flows, so they play unique roles in dealing with social responsibility tasks. Understanding stakeholders' changing power and influences can help to manage resources and relationships in a highly dynamic and uncertain environment in the process of projects.

3.5   Stakeholder collaboration on social responsibility tasks

Stakeholder collaboration between the public and private sectors on addressing social and environmental issues is extolled as having many advantages, including sharing competency and resources, enhancing innovation, and promoting partnerships (Savage et al. , 2010). It becomes a recent phenomenon and receives widespread governmental support for private and public sectors to seek resolutions collaboratively for contemporary social challenges (Bendell et al. , 2010). Stakeholder collaboration is also the result of adaption to the increasingly complex, uncertain, and turbulent environment (Savage et al. , 2010).

Social responsibility tasks emerging in projects cannot be accomplished by individual organizations and important stakeholders need to collaborate in responding to these issues (Peloza & Falkenberg, 2009). Stakeholder collaboration brings positive effects to social responsibility implementation, such as enhanced commitments, higher degree of consensus, and shared ownership by involving all stakeholders with shared goals and continuous communications (Aas et al. , 2005). Stakeholder collaboration is also an operational way to implement social responsibility tasks by setting out common goals, communicating and negotiating, finding out innovative resolutions, and achieving desirable outcomes. How stakeholders can take collaborative actions to respond to the emerging social demands needs further explorations (Bendell et al. , 2010).

Roberts and Bradley (1991) illustrate collaboration by five sociology elements: 1) a temporary arrangement; 2) explicit understanding about participants' capacities in collaboration process; 3) consistent interactions for dealing with the emerging difficulties and conflicts; 4) elaborate planning and coordination; 5) a common goal of the improvement of the current situations. The definition of stakeholder collaboration proposed by Roberts and Bradley (1991) is that "collaboration is a temporary social arrangement in which two or more social actors work together toward a singular common end requiring the transmutation of materials, ideas, and/or social relations to achieve that end" (p. 212).

Given the importance of stakeholder collaboration, it is not a simple end to achieve. Barriers remain to hinder the effectiveness of collaborative endeavors. The current stakeholder research and practices reveal two main problems that need to be overcome.

(1) **The ignorance of the imbalanced power and responsibility is the primary problem for current stakeholder collaboration research and practices (Hardy & Phillips, 1998; Loosemore, 1999).**

The most important criticism of collaboration theory is that all interested stakeholders are assumed to have equal capability to discharge their different levels of responsibilities, which neglects the basic constraint of power distribution and resource variation (Aas et al. , 2005). Obviously, not every stakeholder has the same resource and capability to accomplish social responsibility tasks. Some stakeholders with claims or interests may not have the corresponding power to influence (Mitchell et al. , 1997). The imbalanced power and responsibility can threaten the success of collaboration. Powerless stakeholders have difficulties in raising their voice, while powerful stakeholders form coalitions to marginalize the legitimate demands of weak stakeholders (Arnaboldi & Spiller, 2011). Some powerful stakeholders may be reluctant to collaborate due to the fear of uncertain costs, time-consuming procedures, and the loss of control in decision making (Arnaboldi & Spiller, 2011; Jamal & Getz, 1995). Thus collaboration is not a simple gathering of interested parties; stakeholders' different power should be identified and should be commensurate with corresponding responsibility (Aas et al. , 2005). This imbalance between power and responsibility has been demonstrated by empirical studies and needs to be addressed in stakeholder collaboration research (Aas et al. , 2005; Arnaboldi & Spiller, 2011; Loosemore, 1999).

(2) An operational framework is needed to assist collaborative interactions and facilitate joint decision making in implementing social responsibility tasks.

Many researchers have found that setting common goals alone is not enough for stakeholder collaboration; structural features that facilitate stakeholder interactions is one of the most important factors (Savage et al. , 2010). The literature reveals positive correlations between the clarification of group structures and the performance of group work. Aviv et al. (2003) find that a structural group has higher levels of group learning than a nonstructural group. The group structures include newfound accountabilities, active mutual communications, and appropriate responses (Valentine & Edmondson, 2014). Group structures should be designed with a strong form of collective responsibility, which means all stakeholders should jointly share the consequences (Valentine, 2014). In construction projects in particular, "team scaffolds" can be built to clarify role boundaries in order to enhance stakeholder collaboration by assigning roles to different stakeholders and enabling stakeholders to interact like an actual team. By establishing roles and structures, a complex task with unclear responsibilities can be transformed into an explicit working procedure with clear accountabilities, thereby facilitating collaborative implementation of social responsibility in project teams.

Although stakeholder collaboration on social issues has been added considerable merits, a collaborative framework considering imbalanced power and responsibility of facilitating stakeholder collaboration on implementing social responsibility tasks is still undeveloped.

3.6   Summary of the chapter

This chapter firstly reviewed the classical stakeholder theories and defined project stakeholders as "groups, organizations or individuals that can influence or be influenced by the overall life cycle of construction projects". Along with the increasing complexity of corporate governance, stakeholder analysis approach has evolved from conventional input-output model, to the "spoke and hub" model, to stakeholder-stakeholder network and to current stakeholder-issue network model. In the project environment, it is important to take into consideration both internal stakeholders who have official connections with the focal project and the external stakeholders who do not have connections but potentially influence or be influenced by project activities. Considering the dynamic and heterogenous nature of stakeholders, the key obstacles to stakeholder collaboration on implementing common social responsibility tasks were discussed in the last part of this chapter. How to overcome the constraints and facilitate the collaborative endeavors is the key question that this book answers.

Chapter 4
Stakeholder Power and Influence

4.1 Stakeholder power

4.1.1 Power theories

Power is a concept in sociology derived from a psychological term, permeating into social, political, and organizational research (McGuirk, 2001). As familiar as in academic and daily language, power is often confused with many terminologies, such as control, influence, dominance, authority and status, due to the bias in understanding. It is the primary task to answer "what exactly is power" before using power theory. This section elaborates the nature of power by reviewing relevant literature.

According to the notable definition of Max Weber, power is one's capacity to perform his or her own will against resistance representing the control of resources in particular domains, such as economic power, social power, legal or political power. Another distinguished sociologist Lenski (1966) interprets power as the ability to govern the distribution of surplus and determine the prestige. This view to conceptualize power as a property of individual social actor is shared by many other scholars (French Jr. & Raven, 1959; Pfeffer, 1992).

The basis of power is control of different resources, such as coercion, reward, legitimacy, expertise, and information (French Jr. & Raven, 1959). To sum up, power can be understood as the potential of one social actor to change other actors' behaviors in order to achieve one's own intentions (Gaski, 1984).

Power is not an evil term. It can be acted in coercive approaches, but it can also be acted in moderate manners. The manipulative character of power is over-stressed in daily usage of the word, because powerful actors can coercively alter others' behaviors to the favorable direction regardless of resistance (Gaski, 1984). Overcoming rejection is addressed in many definitions of power (Pfeffer & Fong, 2005), so power is labeled with the property of going against others' wills (Emerson, 1962). On the contrary, not all of the power works through coercively pressuring others. Turner (2005) reveals two distinctive approaches through which power can work. On the one hand, power through affecting is to persuade others to voluntarily perform in accordance with power holders' intentions through changing people's attitude, value and beliefs, for instance by rewards, culture, or leaderships. On the other hand, power through controlling means manipulating people's behaviors by conducting coercion, threat, or punishment regardless their original initiatives (Turner, 2005).

Power exists and is exercised within interactions between social actors. Therefore, power needs to be associated with social relations (Blau, 1964; Emerson, 1962; Hickson et al. , 1971). According to Oxford English Dictionary [1] , relation is defined as "social interactions that occur and feelings that exist between two or more people or groups of people". Motivated by the contingencies including asymmetry, reciprocity, efficiency, stability and legitimacy, social actors tend to establish multiple forms of relations with other social actors (Oliver, 1990). As it is indicated in social exchange theory,

---

[1] Refer to "relation", item 3c, in Oxford English Dictionary, Third Edition, December 2009.

resources flow through exchanges between social actors (Emerson, 1976). Different social actors are bonded together by relations to cope with uncertainties. Because power is the key driving force of the resource exchanges, as well as the key adhesive of stakeholder relations, the effective exercise of power is essential to successful functioning of the society.

This book focuses on interorganizational power rather than interpersonal power, since the targets are project stakeholders that are organizations, institutions, and groups of individuals with similar interest in construction projects (Brass & Burkhardt, 1993). There are two important theories of interorganizational power: power-dependence theory (Emerson, 1962) and resource exchange theory (Blau, 1964; Cook, 1977; Cook et al. , 1983; Emerson, 1976). According to the power-dependence theory of Emerson (1962), actor A's power over actor B is equal to the dependence of actor B on actor A. This theory indicates that power relation is the reflective relation of resource dependency. The degree of power depends on the criticality of A's resources to actor B, and the substitutability of those resources. Trigos (2007) points out that in organizational settings, power can emanate from diverse sources, including coercive, utilitarian, or normative resources. In resource exchange theory, Cook (1977) defines interorganizational relations as exchanges of resource between two or more organizations for mutual benefits. The resources that flow from one actor to the other include material and non-material resources (Blau, 1964). Power in resource exchanges stands for the ability to determine what and how many resources to be exchanged (Cook et al. , 1983).

According to the two classical theories, stakeholder power comes from the possession of resources that is demanded by other stakeholders in projects. The degree of stakeholders' power is directly determined by the criticality of the resources and inversely determined by the substitutability of the resources. As the consequence of stakeholder power, necessary resources flow among stakeholders driven by power for implementing social responsibility tasks in construction projects.

4. 1. 2 Linking power with responsibility

An important argument in this book is that power should be linked with responsibility of stakeholders to deal with social and environmental issues. Referring to the political view of social responsibility, powerful stakeholders should take the corresponding responsibilities to respond to social issues, otherwise they will lose their power (Davis, 1967, p. 49). As in policy making, power of citizens determines the participatory levels of their engagement in the policy making process (Arnstein, 1969). Enderle (2006) claims that the term "responsibility" has received limited attention compared with its common and prevalent usage. There are two types of responsibilities: one comes with roles, and the other comes with power. Because power can bring additional freedom to the decisions and actions of social actors, as an antecedent, an equal scope of responsibility should be allocated to social actors to constrain their behaviors (Enderle, 2006).

Therefore, powerful stakeholders are supposed to accept and take important roles to implement project social responsibility, because they are more capable of accessing scarce resources and obtaining support from other stakeholders. With sufficient power, stakeholders can "alter social and political forces, as well as their capacity to influence project objectives, obtain resources from the community, and maintain social relationships" (Leung et al. , 2013, p. 2). The use of power can drive the diffusion of social responsibility values along the construction supply chain (Jones et al. , 2006). More values can be produced given the effective resource flows among stakeholders (Cook, 1977).

However, investigations in construction projects show an imbalanced distribution of stakeholder power and responsibility, which inevitably causes pressures on stakeholders with limited power (Loosemore, 1999). If powerful stakeholders are unaware of or intentionally avoid taking their responsibilities, the influenced stakeholders may suffer from undesirable outcomes. Linking responsibilities with power can help stakeholders to clarify and to become more aware of their responsibilities (Aas et al. , 2005).

Despite the moral nature of social responsibility, there are no moral standards for business organizations to judge what is right and what is wrong. Therefore, it is important to introduce power theory to social responsibility research to bring constraints to businesses to create public goods instead of expanding power unrestrictedly for private profits. In construction practices, social responsibility needs to be initiated and led by powerful stakeholders. The existing research on social responsibility has shown limited attentions on balancing stakeholder power and responsibilities. In general stakeholder management research, stakeholder power is assessed for suggesting focal firms with strategies to cope with stakeholder risks; however, whether stakeholders' responsibilities are balanced with their power is currently neglected. It may lead to the powerless stakeholders taking responsibilities beyond their capacity, but powerful stakeholders can increase their profit unrestrictedly. The theories of social responsibility and power theory have not linked enough. Following the discussion above, this research integrates "power comes with responsibility" as a basic philosophy, that is, stakeholders' responsibilities are assigned based on the evaluation of their power.

4. 1. 3　Defining stakeholder power

In traditional stakeholder theories, power is regarded as one of the attributes to evaluate stakeholder salience. Organizations are unlikely to satisfy every stakeholder's interests because of finite organizational resources (Jawahar & McLaughlin, 2001). Thus, there come the demands for evaluation of stakeholders' levels of salience before making decisions on allocating organizational resources to meet stakeholders' demands (Harrison & Freeman, 1999).

Mitchell et al. (1997) propose a three-attribute model to depict stakeholder salience, including power, legitimacy, and urgency (see figure 4-1). This three-attribute model has been extensively used and receives wide reputations (Eesley & Lenox, 2006; Friedman & Mason, 2004; Sharma & Henriques, 2005). Among the three salience attributes, stakeholder power is the most effective in evaluating stakeholders' potential influence (Roome & Wijen, 2006). And it is stated as the best predictor in stakeholder prioritization for organizational management (Parent & Deephouse, 2007). It determines "the degree to which managers give priority to competing stakeholder claims" (Mitchell et al. , 1997,

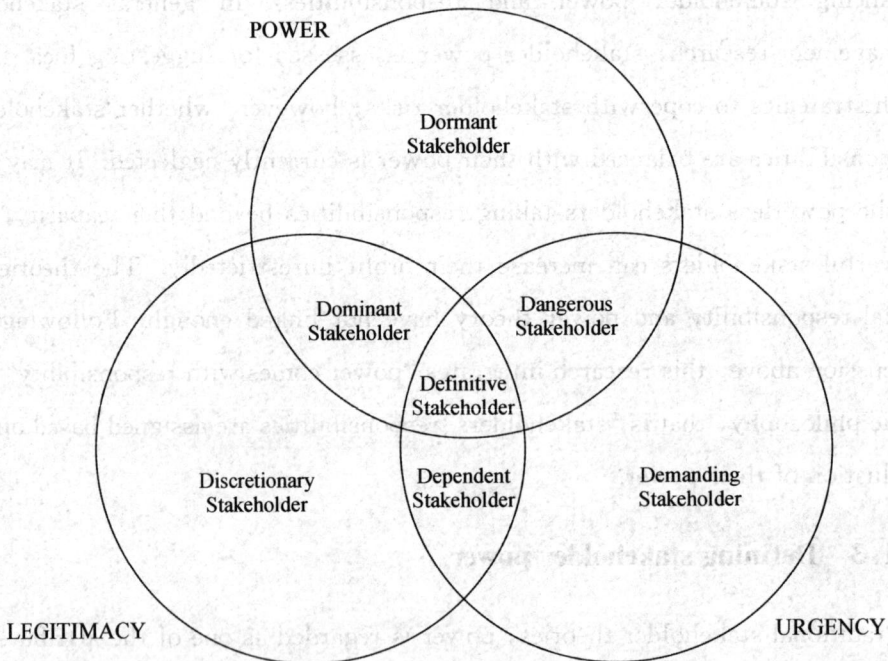

Figure 4-1   Three-attribute stakeholder salience model.

(Source: Mitchell et al. , 1997, 872)

p. 854). Therefore, in traditional stakeholder management research, power is taken as a criterion by managers for giving priorities to conflicting stakeholder demands. However, in this study, power is extended to a vested property of stakeholders that determines responsibilities in dealing with social issues.

In the context of implementing social responsibility tasks, power performs as an indispensable attribute of stakeholders to obtain necessary resources and the engagements of other stakeholders to fulfill their projects or plans, in exchange for the compliance with others' power simultaneously. Stakeholder power does not only represent manipulations and coercions for individual favorable results, in contrast it is an approach through which stakeholders with different resources could collaborate to accomplish common social responsibility goals. With legitimate intentions, stakeholder power can be defined as:

Stakeholder power evaluates the capacity of stakeholder A to coordinate necessary resources and engage with key stakeholders to collaboratively implement their social responsibility tasks.

4.2　Stakeholder influence

4.2.1　Relationship between power and influence

Although power has been extensively studied in sociology and management science for decades, research on stakeholder influence as the manifestation of power is in its infancy (Somech & Drach-Zahavy, 2002). Power and influence have interrelationship. Power is the ability to influence, and influence is the exercise of power (French Jr. & Raven, 1959; Pfeffer, 1992). Brass and Burkhardt (1993) argue that power with no manifestations should not be taken into consideration, because power has no impacts on targets if they are not aware of it. Influences can be exercised in different strategies to alter the behaviors of targets. The definition of stakeholder influence is "stakeholders use their power to drive others to achieve their desired outcomes" (Frooman, 1999).

The general argument is that influence is the manifestation of potential power held by social actors. The power process includes the causal relation between power and influence (Pfeffer & Fong, 2005). Power, as the capacity to influence, is just one of the multiple steps. Besides, actions and results of power are also included. According to Turner (2005), the casual relation between potential power and influence is displayed in figure 4-2. The starting point is the power holder, actor A's intentions to exert power, which is often motivated by the pursuit of its goals at others' resources. French Jr. and Raven (1959) proposes the classical five bases of power including legitimate, referent, expert, reward and coercion. More power bases were gradually raised by researchers, for instance, the size of social entities (Snyder, 1996), social status (McGuirk, 2001), cope with uncertainty (Hickson et al., 1971), positions in networks (Cook, 1977). Then actor A can choose strategies to either aggressively or cooperatively influence actor B. When actor B perceives the power actions,

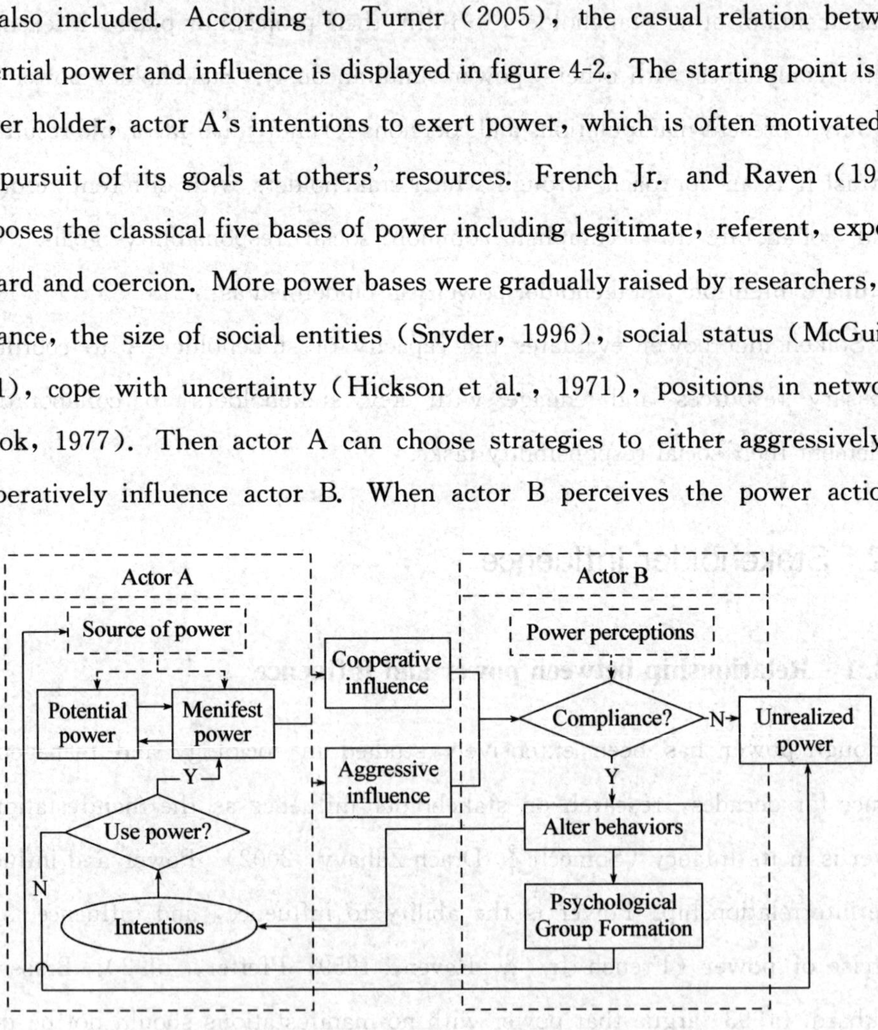

Figure 4-2   The process from power to influence.

(Based on Turner, 2005)

decisions on whether to comply or not is carried out (Dahl, 1957). Actor B either chooses to change its behavior in conformity with A's intentions, otherwise actor B does not yield to actor A's influence considering evaluation of costs and benefits of such changes. Additionally actor B will form shared social identity after submission to actor A, and this will in return enhance actor A's power.

4. 2. 2   Influence strategies in literature

Table 4-1 lists the existing research on stakeholder influence strategies. Stakeholder influence research has two separate branches. One stands on the perspective of corporate decision makers and tries to craft strategies to cope with stakeholders' demands. The other one stands on the view of stakeholders to investigate the strategies and tactics that stakeholders can use to achieve their interests. Based on resource exchange theory of Emerson (1976), Frooman (1999) proposes a stakeholder influence model including four strategies: direct usage, indirect usage, direct withholding, and indirect withholding. He argues when stakeholders are at the powerful status and hold resources desired by organizations, they tend to use directly withholding strategy to influence target organizations by threatening to discontinue supply of resources. After six years, Frooman and Murrell (2005) extend the theory by experiments showing powerful stakeholders mostly choose coercive strategy (decrease benefit or increase cost), while stakeholders with little power choose compromise (increase benefit or decrease cost). According to the existing literature, the determinant of stakeholder influence strategies is the relative power between stakeholders and focal companies (Co & Barro, 2009; Somech & Drach-Zahavy, 2002).

Previous literature shows a focus on maximizing self-benefits or minimizing costs by taking the perspective of either stakeholder or focal companies. However, limited research is found to address stakeholder influence on maximizing collective goals. In addition, upon the review on stakeholder influence strategy research, the majority of research focuses on single stakeholders' strategies, while the holistic view of multiple influence flows can generate different structures and patterns of stakeholder influence.

Table 4-1 Summary of stakeholder influence strategies

Author (year)	Determinants	Strategies
(Etzioni, 1975)	Compliance	Coercive Utilitarian Normative
(Mendelow, 1981)	Dynamism/power	Continuous scanning Irregular scanning Periodic scanning NIL
(Savage et al., 1991)	Potential to threaten or cooperate	Mix blessing Involve Defend Monitor
(Rowley, 1997)	Stakeholder network density/centrality	Compromise Subordinate Command Solitarian
(Somech & Drach-Zahavy, 2002)	Relative power	Hard strategy Rational strategy Soft strategy
(Frooman, 1999)	Resource dependence	Direct withholding Direct usage Indirect withholding Indirect usage
(Maignan et al., 2002)	Resource dependence/communication skills/coordination ability	Normative (letter writing campaigns, protests, and negative publicity) Utilitarian (boycotts, lawsuits, new regulations) Coercive
(Tsai et al., 2005)	Resource dependence/legitimacy of decisions	Direct withholding Direct usage Indirect withholding Conformity

(Continued)

Author (year)	Determinants	Strategies
(Frooman & Murrell, 2005)	Resource dependence	Coercive strategy Compromise strategy Indirect strategy Direct strategy
(Hendry, 2005)	Experiences and opportunity	Blockade Partnership Multi-stakeholder dialogue Boycott, litigation, lobbying Letter-writing campaign Shareholder resolution
(Olander & Landin, 2005)	Power and interests	Key players Keep satisfied Keep informed Minimal effort
(Polonsky & Scott, 2005)	Relative threatening potential/ relative cooperative potential	Change the rules/collaborate Exploit/involve Defend Hold current position/monitor
(Co & Barro, 2009)	Trust level/sense of urgency/ legitimacy	Aggressive strategy Cooperative strategy

4. 3. 2   Stakeholder influences on social responsibility tasks

Because power does not definitely lead to effective influence, stakeholders' choices of influence strategies are also essential to getting desired outcomes. However, the general stakeholder influence theories are deficient in predicting choices of influencing strategies regarding social responsibility tasks. Instead of selecting one strategy, stakeholders often adopt mixed strategies simultaneously in order to impose their social responsibility advocacy. For example, NGOs and environmental organizations use lobby to concert with all other strategies rather than only relying on individual strategies (Hendry, 2005). According to Frooman (1999), coercive strategies are more likely to be adopted if stakeholder is at powerful status to exert influences. But with regard to social responsibility tasks, hard or coercive strategy adopted by powerful stakeholders is more like a bully rather than a collaboration, and tend to receive negative impacts (Boyd et al. , 2007).

According to the special characteristics of stakeholder influence on implementing social responsibility tasks, it can be assumed that stakeholders' choices of strategies are not simply determined by stakeholder power (Maignan et al. , 2002; Olander, 2007). This is because not only powerful stakeholders can influence, stakeholders with little power can also take actions to influence social responsibility tasks. In fact, every stakeholder has the indispensable role in promoting social responsibility tasks. External stakeholders can set out problems, and internal stakeholders have ideas and knowledge to solve those problems (Roome & Wijen, 2006). Compared with powerful stakeholders, influences of stakeholders with limited power also have significant functions in organizational decision making (Thijssens et al. , 2015; Zietsma & Winn, 2007).

If stakeholders can adopt proper influencing strategies, the target organization would like to proactively involve in advanced social responsibility tasks beyond simple compliance (Sharma & Henriques, 2005). However, inappropriate influencing strategies may lead to unintended effects. For example, buyer companies' monitoring program on their suppliers did not necessarily increase compliance with incorporate social responsibility, but damage stakeholder relationships (Boyd et al. , 2007). Therefore, research on choices of stakeholder influence strategies is significant and needs extensive focuses.

4.3 Limitations of current research

Stakeholder power on social responsibility tasks is the ability to define common goals and to influence other stakeholders to engage in these initiatives (Onkila,

2011; Tang et al. , 2012). The more power stakeholders hold, the more likely they can successfully resolve the social problems, and the more likely the other stakeholders will reply to their advocates (Azzam, 2010). There are some gaps that need to be further addressed in stakeholder power research:

(1) Stakeholder power is regarded as an attribute for managers to prioritize stakeholders; however, it is neglected that stakeholders as individuals should take the corresponding responsibility that equals to their power.

(2) The usage of power in Mitchell's model is at an all-or-nothing stance; a stakeholder either has or does not have power, giving no distinction between one with a lot of power and the other one with little power (Mainardes et al. , 2012).

(3) Most literature analyzes stakeholder power as a constant attribute, but the dynamics of stakeholder power have not been adequately addressed.

Although stakeholder power has been taken as an important attribute in stakeholder salience model, research addressing the connections between power and responsibility is still scarce. Stakeholder power, as a vested property of stakeholders, needs to be associated with the responsibility that stakeholders should take in dealing with social responsibility tasks.

For stakeholder influence, it is important for stakeholders to choose proper strategies to exercise their power. Current research has gaps in selecting stakeholder strategies adopted regarding social responsibility tasks.

(1) The majority of literature focuses on stakeholder strategies in commercial environment that need precise evaluations of individual benefits and costs; however, research is scarce on investigating influencing strategies on social responsibility collaboration, where collective benefits are addressed.

The motivation of stakeholders' influence on social responsibility tasks is promoting collaborative efforts to improve overall social value output. Under such conditions, hard strategies as often adopted in commercial environment are unlikely to receive desirable performance, because such strategies are too aggressive and hostile, which is against the principle of collaboration. Further research is needed to address how stakeholders choose their strategies when they aim at increasing social benefits instead of maximizing individual benefits.

(2) **Stakeholder influence research mainly focuses on individual stakeholders, but the holistic view of influence structures among multiple stakeholders has not received enough attention.**

Because social responsibility collaboration is an "emergent organizational arrangement through which organizations collectively cope with the growing complexity of their environments" (Gray, 1989, p. 236), forces are needed from different stakeholders to facilitate such arrangement. The existing research only focuses on individual stakeholders, such as NGOs (Jamali & Keshishian, 2009; Jonker & Nijhof, 2006), policy makers (Doh & Guay, 2006), and mass media (Apostol & Näsi, 2013). But no studies have explored, especially in construction project context, how the whole internal and external stakeholders can influence social responsibility collaboration and what strategies and tactics they use to influence (Elijido-Ten et al. , 2010). The research question arises as to investigate how different stakeholders use their power to influence each other in order to achieve social responsibility collaboration on construction projects.

4.4   Summary of the chapter

This chapter introduced related theories of social power and influence to explain why and how to enable powerful stakeholders to implement project social responsibility tasks. The power-dependence and resource exchange theories on which the inter-organizational power is based. Then, the bridge between power and responsibility was discussed as the fundamental assumption of the entire book. Combining classical stakeholder salience theories, a definition of stakeholder power was proposed as to "evaluate the capacity of stakeholder A to coordinate necessary resources and engage with key stakeholders to collaboratively implement their social responsibility tasks".

The selection of influence strategies can lead to different outcomes in seeking collaborative endeavors. Therefore, besides analyzing stakeholders' power, there is also a need to understand how the power can be exercised. The second half of the chapter focused on stakeholder influence. It reviewed stakeholder influence strategies and key determinants in existing literature and proposed how stakeholder influence on social responsibility tasks can be different. It concluded the current limitations of stakeholder power and influence research.

Chapter 5
Social Responsibility Tasks (SRTs)
and the Investigation Process

5.1   Identification of social responsibility tasks (SRTs)

Based on previous discussions, the diverse tasks that stakeholders perform in construction project environment in dealing with current environmental or social issues are the bricks and tiles of project social responsibility implementation. There are diverse types of construction projects including infrastructures, commercial buildings, public housing, hospitals, renovations, etc. The specific social responsibility tasks that stakeholders perform in these different types of projects can be various. From a general perspective, considering the nature of construction projects, there are some general issues in all types of projects, including environmental pollution, noises, and disturbances on local residents. These tasks are occurred at different project stages from project inception to demolition, and led by different project stakeholders. Because of the diverse interests, stakeholders tend to perceive these with different levels of importance. This chapter attempts to identify a list of project social responsibility tasks that occur generally in all types of construction projects over the project life cycle. Based on the list, a series of investigations were carried out to look into how stakeholders perceive these tasks, who are the powerful stakeholders that should lead in different tasks, how stakeholders influence each other in different situations.

The identification of project social responsibility tasks followed two steps by using literature review and questionnaire. Firstly, eighty social responsibility tasks that are closely related to construction projects activities were extracted through reviewing the literatures. As shown in table 5-1, the sources of the literatures fell into three categories: academic literature, publications by international organizations, and corporate reports. During reading the literatures, the practices, measures, programs that fell into the scope of project social responsibility were identified and recorded.

Secondly, I invited twenty experts (thirteen construction management scholars and seven industrial project managers, all with more than ten-year experiences in construction project management) to filter the identified social responsibility tasks. A questionnaire (see appendix A) was used for the refining of the list. The experts were asked to evaluate whether the identified issues are important tasks in implementing project social responsibility. According to the questionnaire results, some items were combined or removed from the list as they considered as overlapping or unimportant. In the questionnaire, the invited experts were also asked to nominate the stakeholders they think are related to the implementation of the tasks. A final list of the thirty-five social responsibility tasks was identified (see table 5-2), as well as seven related stakeholders including main contractors, developers, end users, governments, consultants, NGOs, and district councils.

Table 5-1   The sources for identifying the social responsibility tasks

Categories	Sources
Academic research into social responsibility in construction context	(Barthorpe, 2010), (Petrovic-Lazarevic, 2008), (Jones et al., 2006), (Shen, Tam, et al., 2010), (Brown & Dacin, 1997), (Zhao et al., 2012b), (Martinuzzi et al., 2011)
Publications by the international organizations	GRIG4 sustainability reporting guidelines launched by Global Reporting Initiative in 2013 ISO 26000 social responsibility guidance launched by International Standard Organization in 2010 UNEP greening the building supply chain launched by United Nation Environmental Planning in 2012 CSR guidelines launched by Construction Excellent in 2004 BRC project building responsible competitiveness launched by European Commission in 2010 CSR index reports launched by Hong Kong Quality Assurance Agency in 2008
Annual reports of world leading construction companies	Annual sustainability/CSR reports publicized by Gammon Ltd., Leighton Ltd., and AECOM Ltd. from the year of 2005 to 2014

As shown in table 5-2, the thirty-five social responsibility tasks can be categorized into three project life cycle stages: initiating and planning stage, execution stage, and controlling and closing stage. Also, the tasks fall into seven categories according to the ISO 26000 Social Responsibility Guidelines, including organizational government (OG), human rights (HR), labor protection (LP), environment (En), fair operation (FO), customer issues (CI) and community involvement and development (Co).

Table 5-2   The list of social responsibility tasks over the construction project life cycle

Project stage	Project social responsibility task	ISO26000 category
Initiating and planning Stage	Disclosing social and environmental impacts of new project	OG
	Establishing stakeholder (including public) engagement platform	OG
	Discussing human rights policies during project planning	HR

(**Continued**)

Project stage	Project social responsibility task	ISO26000 category
	Identifying H & S[1] risks for employees during planning	LP
	Minimizing adverse impacts of land use plan on ecosystems	En
	Evaluating project feasibility considering environmental impacts	En
	Prioritizing life cycle environmental performance in design	En
	Preventing anti-competitive behaviors in bidding and procurements	FO
	Establishing codes of ethics for new projects	FO
	Identifying H & S risks to project users during design	CI
	Compensating and resettling relocated household	Co
	Making development plan for local community	Co
Execution stage	Meeting stakeholders regularly to discuss conflicts during construction	OG
	Protecting the rights of migrant labors	HR
	Protecting employees from H & S risks	LP
	Promoting H & S culture in project	LP
	Protecting living habitat for both human beings and animals	En
	Controlling construction dust, gas, sewage, waste and noise	En
	Using green materials, plants, technologies and services	En
	Implementing environmental management system[2]	En
	Implementing transparency management and promoting trust climate	FO
	Ensuring healthy in-door environment	CI
	Considering local suppliers for procurements	Co
	Reducing adverse impacts on local transportation, work and life	Co
	Protecting local residents from H & S risks during construction	Co
Controlling and closing stage	Monitoring and reporting project sustainable performance	OG
	Avoiding discrimination and providing equal opportunities during operation	HR

---

1   Health and safety.

2   For example, ISO14000 environmental management systems and ISO26000 guidance on social responsibility.

Project stage	Project social responsibility task	ISO26000 category
	Protecting employees from risks of demolition	LP
	Resettling involuntarily dismissed employees because of the end of project	LP
	Providing training programs of green facilities	En
	Promoting environmental protection and energy saving culture	En
	Alleviating disturbance on eco-system and neighborhoods by demolition	En
	Avoiding bribe and corruptions during operation	FO
	Reviewing project users' complaints and making responses	CI
	Rehabilitating damaged local environment	Co

This list shows a general standard of what a socially responsible project should be like. The listed tasks are conducted in most types of projects ranging from large infrastructures to private constructions. By using this list as a benchmark, the project managers and related stakeholders could conduct self-checking to identify what tasks should be carried out in the project at different project stages. Also, the public sector and third-party organizations could use it as an instrument for assessing project social performance. In this book, the list is a starting point to further investigate how diverse stakeholders hold different power and influence in implementing these tasks and how the responsibility can be clarified to facilitate collective actions towards project social responsibility.

5.2 Investigation process

5.2.1 Questionnaire

The questionnaire is to investigate interests and capacity of multiple stakeholder groups towards the identified SRTs. In order to obtain a realistic image, a small-scale questionnaire was carried out to look through the practitioners' eyes to get a clearer understanding of the diversity of stakeholders in project social responsibility. Through the investigation, I collected data on how practitioners, who have work experiences in construction projects, perceive multiple stakeholders in terms of interests and power in implementing different SRTs.

(1) Instrument design

The instrument was designed based on the identified social responsibility tasks and the related stakeholders. The widely adopted 5-point Likert scale was used for measuring stakeholders' perceptions of the degree of power and the degree of interests towards the listed tasks. For each social responsibility task, respondents were asked to evaluate their organizations' interests from 1 (not interested) to 5 (extremely interested) and their perceptions of the seven stakeholders' power from 1 (not at all influential) to 5 (extremely influential). The word "influence" was substituted for "power" due to their similarity in daily usage and the negative connotation associated with the word "power" (Brass & Burkhardt, 1993).

The questionnaire contained three parts. The first part was a letter to the respondents. The second part asked about respondents' background information. And the third part, which was the main body of the questionnaire, was a matrix evaluating stakeholders' power over thirty-five SRTs. The wording was modified in a clear and simple way to specify related definitions in order to avoid misleading, ambiguous, or threatening feelings (Sudman & Bradburn, 1982). The questionnaire was designed in the form of a matrix using the thirty-five social responsibility tasks as row titles and the seven stakeholders as column titles. The final questionnaire had three versions: traditional Chinese, simplified Chinese, and English (see appendix B).

(2) Pilot study

All the three versions of questionnaire were pre-tested with a small group of pilot samples containing native speakers of English, Cantonese, and Putonghua. The respondents in the pilot study were invited from my network of professionals in the construction industry in Hong Kong. They were asked to examine whether the questions were easy to understand, clear and unambiguous in wording. Based on the feedback from the pilot study, some changes on the wording were made to improve the intelligibility. In addition, one problem reported by the respondents was that "writing numbers in all blanks in the matrix was too time-consuming". In order to reduce the time that respondents use to finish the questions, the strategy was changed to ask respondents to writing numbers only in blanks that have certain levels of influences. If the targeted stakeholder group is not influential at all towards the SRT, the place can be left blank. Since many of the SRTs involve only a few influential stakeholders, this strategy can save time notably.

(3) Distribution and collection

Questionnaire distribution can be conducted through many approaches, including self-report (Internet/mail) and face-to-face (Robson, 2011). The choice of approaches depends on various criteria, such as cost, complexity of questionnaire, data quality requirement, response rates, and sensitivity of questions. Due to the complexity of the concepts involved in the questionnaire and the requirements for high quality data, face-to-face questionnaire was used in this study. The paper-based questionnaires were distributed to construction practitioners in Hong Kong in 2015. The questionnaire distributions and collections were conducted face-to-face. To ensure the quality of the data, I first explained the purpose of the questionnaire. When the respondents were completing the questionnaires, I kept standby for clarifying any confusion and query that the respondents may come across. The invalid questionnaires were filtered and disposed after collected. The data in the valid questionnaires were inputted for analysis. All questionnaires were anonymous without identifications of respondents' personal information.

(4) Sample description

A non-probability sampling was employed for the condition that it was impossible for all construction practitioners to be selected with a same probability considering the diversity and large population. The respondents were from the construction practitioners in Hong Kong. In order to ensure the variety of sample from diverse stakeholder groups, a stratified sampling was adopted for selecting units from different sub-populations of construction organizations, such as developer companies, contractor companies, design and consulting companies, subcontractor companies, government departments, NGOs, and professional organizations. Different types of organizations involved in construction projects were included as sources of respondents. When inviting participants, it was addressed that representatives of different sectors were involved, including public and private, to avoid potential sample bias. The final valid sample size was 132, at valid return rate of 66. 67%. The Cronbach's alpha was 0. 98, indicating the questionnaire adopted has high reliability, but it also indicated some questions might be redundant for an acceptable reliability of the compounded concept. However, since the items represent social responsibility along different project stages and ISO categories, they were all kept in the final questionnaire for the analysis of diversity and multiplicity of stakeholder power.

Figure 5-1 shows the diverse nature of respondents' organizations. 57. 58% came from private companies, whose social responsibility was the most demanded to be improved. 22. 73% of the respondents were from the public listed companies. These companies were required to publicize their social responsibility performance annually and were under great pressures from shareholders. 12. 88% were from the government department. The rest came from educational/ professional/public institutions and other organizations.

To improve the overall representativeness, the respondents' background included diverse stakeholder groups. According to figure 5-2, the stakeholder

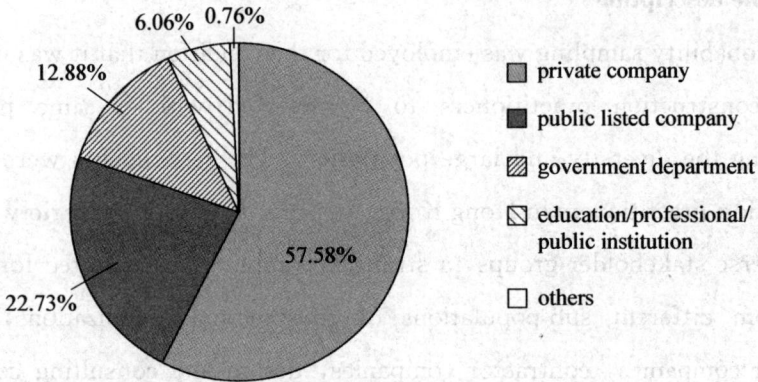

Figure 5-1   The organizations' nature of the respondents.

groups of representatives included main contractors ($n = 52$, $p = 39.39\%$), developers ($n = 15$, $p = 11.36\%$), project end users ($n = 2$, $p = 1.52\%$) government departments ($n = 15$, $p = 11.36\%$), subcontractors/suppliers ($n = 10$, $p = 7.58\%$), consultants ($n = 35$, $p = 26.52\%$), and others ($n = 3$, $p = 2.27\%$). Since the sample size from each stakeholder group was not equally distributed, which may cause over-representation of several groups, and under-representations of the others. To alleviate potential over- or under-representiveness, the collected data were reweighed to balance the opinions from different stakeholder groups before data analysis.

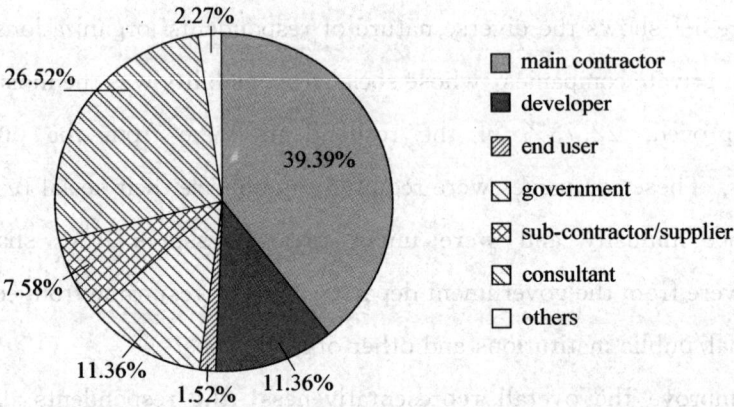

Figure 5-2   The stakeholder groups of the respondents.

   Respondents' work experience in construction projects can affect the quality
and reliability of the collected data. Practitioners with longer experience have
richer observations of stakeholder inter-influences and are more likely to be
involved in project social responsibility tasks. Therefore, the work experience of
respondents was an important criteria under consideration. Figure 5-3 shows
that, in the valid sample, 21. 21% of the respondents had more than 6 years'
work experience in construction projects. The 4. 55% of the respondents were
with over 16 years' related work experience. The positions of respondents also
affect what kind of information we can get from the respondents. Since the data
related the relationships with other organizations, the higher the position of the
respondent, the more accurate the answer could be. As it is shown in figure 5-4,
0. 76% of the respondents were senior managers, 18. 94% were project
managers, and 27. 27% were site supervisors. The work experience and positions
of the respondents can to some extent improve the reliability of the collected
data.

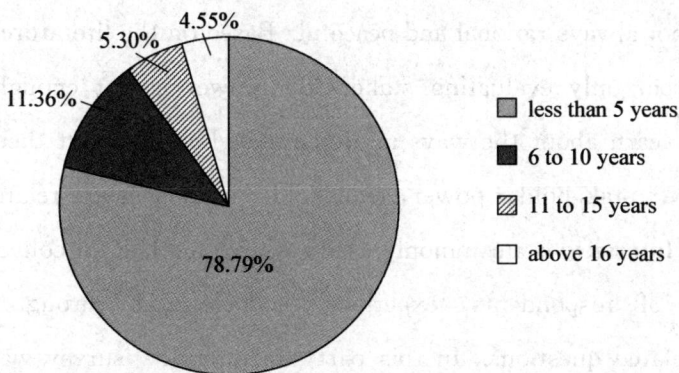

Figure 5-3   The distribution of respondents' work experience.

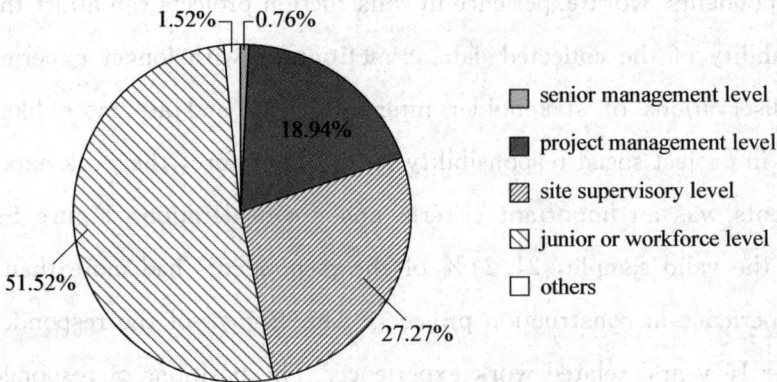

Figure 5-4   The distribution of respondents' positions.

5. 2. 2   Interview survey

The questionnaire was to find out how many interests and how much power multiple stakeholders have towards implementing the SRTs. However, having power does not necessarily mean effective influence. Also, from the construction practices, we have noticed the behaviors of stakeholders to express that their appeals are not always rational and peaceful. Based on the literature review, it is also found that only evaluating stakeholder power is not enough. It is also necessary to learn about the ways in which stakeholders exert their influences. Compared with stakeholder power, stakeholder influences are relatively difficult to quantify. Interview is a commonly used research method for collecting in-depth descriptions of respondents' experience and feelings through asking and answering related questions. In this part, an interview survey was adopted to investigate what strategies each stakeholder group usually uses to influence others in terms of the implementation of social responsibility in construction projects.

(1) Development of the interview protocol

Based on the degree of fixation of questions, interview survey can be classified into fully-structured interview with designed questions, semi-structured interview with a planned list of topics but does not limit the questions, and unstructured interview that allows themes and concepts to emerge from interview process (Robson, 2011). Project stakeholders have heterogeneity and dynamics, so I couldn't list all of the stakeholder relationships in questions. For flexibility, this study adopted a semi-structured interview method for collecting qualitative data on stakeholder influence strategies and tactics. A protocol (see appendix C) was developed for implementing the interviews. The first part of the interview protocol is a brief introduction of the interview purpose, process, estimated time period, and ethical considerations. The second part consisted of a set of questions, probes, and a proposed sequence for the questions. In this part, the starting five questions were about the interviewees' basic background information and their organizations' social responsibility policies. Next, the rest fifteen questions are about how their organizations influence and are influenced by other stakeholders on social responsibility. According to the different responses of interviewees, the investigator will use some probes to ask further and more detailed questions based on the provided information. For example, when the respondents mentioned the reaction of employees about corporations' SR policy, the investigator would ask follow-up questions about the measures they use to drive employers' motivation. In order to ensure the logic flows of the interviews, the questions were designed in two part: one was about influences on and by the supply chain stakeholders, and the other was about external stakeholders' groups. The supply chain stakeholders can be further divided into upper echelons (builders, suppliers, subcontractors, consultants, advisors, etc.) and lower echelons (developers, property management, end users, facility management companies, etc.). The external stakeholders include governments, NGOs, communities, unions, public media, or other pressure groups.

(2) Pre-test of the interview protocol

In order to improve the content validity of the interview protocol, a pre-test of the questions was conducted before the formal survey. Two industrial practitioners who work in the construction industry for years were invited from my personal network. They were asked to look at the questions listed in the protocol to evaluate whether they were clear, easy to understand, and can recall their related experiences, whether the list of stakeholders was completed, and how the questions addressed the research objectives. Based on their feedback, the interview protocol was further revised and modified.

(3) Interview processes

The interviews were conducted from March to May 2015. The interviewees were invited by email and/or telephone calls from the leading construction organizations, including contractor companies, developer companies, consulting companies, NGOs, government departments, project investment companies, and urban planning authorities. This part adopted a non-probability sampling method. The potential interviewees were contacted through emails and telephone calls. Confirmed interviewees were sent an invitation letter that introduced research background and confidential considerations. Most interviews were conducted face-to-face (e. g., in a meeting room or private office) upon appointments. Only two interviews were conducted over telephone calls because of the distant locations of the interviewees. For some of the interviews, a supermarket coupon valued at 50 HKD was presented to the interviewee after interviews as an incentive. At last, a total of 17 interviews were conducted. The interview processes lasted from 22 minutes to 49 minutes. All interviews were recorded in high audio quality for further examinations and transcriptions under the permissions of the interviewees. Also, the investigators kept notes during each interview.

(4) Interview sample

Unlike quantitative survey, the interview survey adopted a non-probability sampling strategy (Trost, 1986). Instead of being statistically representative, interview sample should have variations in terms of backgrounds, positions, culture, age, sexuality, and experiences. The more diverse the sample, the less bias the collected data have. When selecting interviewees, construction practitioners with different characteristics and experiences were purposefully invited, such as different genders, ages, positions, and backgrounds. Also, considering the specialty of the construction practitioner group, it is difficult to conduct a truly random sampling. Therefore, a convenient sampling strategy was used to invite interviews with higher probability to provide related information from the working networks.

The final sample contained 17 practitioners with diverse backgrounds. The details of the interviews were shown in table 5-3. It shows that the interviewees were from different organizations: governments ($n=1$), planning authority ($n=1$), NGOs ($n=1$), developer ($n=5$), investor ($n=1$), main contractor ($n=6$), consultants ($n=2$). The interviewees' average work experience in construction industry was 12 years. Among all interviewees, 9 out of 17 had worked for more than 16 years in construction industry. The rich experiences of the interviewees to some extent ensure the richness and quality of the qualitative data.

Table 5-3 Description of the interviewees

No.	Region	Background of the interviewees	Work experience (years)	Position	Time (DD/MM/YY)	Period (mins)
1	HK	Government	6. 5	Site supervisor	08/04/15	22
2	HK	Planning authority	16	Committee member	04/05/15	38
3	HK	NGO	4	N/A	28/05/15	27
4	HK	Investor	25	Investment director	29/04/15	33

No.	Region	Background of the interviewees	Work experience (years)	Position	Time (DD/MM/YY)	Period (mins)
5	HK	Contractor	4	Assistant engineer	07/03/15	37
6	HK	Contractor	16	Project manager	28/03/15	46
7	HK	Contractor	5	Vice project manager	24/03/15	29
8	HK	Contractor	20	Senior manager	13/04/15	24
9	HK	Consultant	4	Safety supervisor	30/05/15	22
10	HK	Contractor	18	Senior manager	14/04/15	30
11	HK	Consultant	6	N/A	13/04/15	23
12	HK	Developer	20	Commercial manager	08/05/15	22
13	HK	Developer	2	Planning officer	08/05/15	24
14	HK	Developer	20	Project manager	09/05/15	49
15	HK	Developer	20	Safety manager	08/05/15	25
16	HK	Developer	2	Designer	08/05/15	23
17	HK	Contractor	16	Quantity surveyor	28/04/15	46

(5) Transcription of interview recordings

With regard to the language usage, 13 interviews were conducted in English and the other 4 were conducted in Putonghua. Upon the examinations of the audio records, all interviews were translated into English, transcribed into texts and saved as Microsoft Word documents. The data collection and storage procedures strictly followed the ethical procedures, which exactly kept the interviewees' personal information confidential and unidentified. To accelerate the analyzing procedures, the transcriptions were then went through and were cleansed to eliminate the meaningless greetings and small talks. After data cleansing, the full corpus contained 50,345 English words.

(6) Semantic analysis by Leximancer

The final corpus was imported and analyzed by a computer-assisted qualitative data analysis (CAQDA) tool Leximancer. Qualitative data analysis is a flexible analytical method for analyzing text data in form of verbal, print, or electronic document obtained from narrative responses, open-ended survey questions, interviews, focus groups, observations, or print media. It aims at interpreting "the content of text data through systematic classification process of coding and identifying themes or patterns" (Hsieh & Shannon, 2005). The outcomes of qualitative data analysis are concepts or categories that could describe the phenomenon, for the purpose of "providing knowledge, new insights, a representation of facts and a practical guide to action" (Elo & Kyngäs, 2008). Using computer-assisted tools has become a trend in qualitative analysis. The adoption of appropriate software can increase both the rigor and efficiency of qualitative research. Leximancer is a text-mining software developed by a team led by Dr. Andrew E. Smith at the University of Queensland. Leximancer uses unsupervised machine learning algorithms to automatically generate concepts and themes based on word frequency and co-occurrence (Smith & Humphreys, 2006). Compared with other CAQDA tools like Nvivo and Atlas. ti, Leximancer can automatically identify concepts and interrelationships from the unified data without the premise of manual interventions, which decreases the subjectivity of analysis process (Sotiriadou et al. , 2014).

A three-stage semantic analysis was adopted in this study. At the first stage, a concept map was generated by Leximancer to reveal important stakeholders and their interconnections. In order to improve the meaningfulness of the concept map, some adjustments were made in the concept seeding. Since Leximancer has limits in differentiating daily use languages, I manually deleted seven concepts from the seeding due to the lack of semantic meanings for the research topic ("things", "terms", "look", "guess", "example", "doing", and "probably"). Eighteen pairs of concepts with similar meanings were merged, which bear the same meanings ("issue/issues", "project/projects", "developer/

developers/client/clients", "contractor/contractors", "company/companies",
"client/clients", "building/buildings", and "environment/environmental"). Two
concepts "main" and "contractor" were compounded into "main contractor" to be
more specific. In order to include all stakeholders mentioned in the interviews,
some concepts that refer to important stakeholders of construction projects were
manually defined. They are "consultants", "consumers", "employees",
"investor", "manager", "NGOs", "representative", "planning authority",
"residents", "subcontractors", "suppliers", "tenants", and "workers". The
thesaurus of each concept was coded manually, for example, the concept of
NGOs includes six items including the names of NGOs and their abbreviations.

The second stage was to further explore and interpret the influence
strategies and tactics adopted by pairs of stakeholders. The interactive concept
map was used to extract the textual segments that contain two stakeholders. By
clicking one stakeholder concept on the map and selecting the other stakeholder
concept on the associated concepts list, the text segments that contain the two
stakeholders' concepts and their interactions were extracted from the transcripts.
Then I interpreted the extracted segments based on the original contexts to
identify the strategies and tactics adopted by stakeholders in that context. At this
stage, not only the segments that contained the words of stakeholder names were
retrieved, but also those contained the thesaurus that embedded under each
concept. All textual segments were extracted with no interventions and analyzed
based on the original contexts. Strategies and tactics that adopted by
stakeholders were identified one by one at this stage.

At the third stage, along with the identification of strategies and tactics, the
potential determinants that may cause stakeholders to adopt aggressive influences
were also recorded and analyzed. When the excerpts contain an aggressive
strategy, which contains coercive usage or withdrawal of resources, the excerpts
were then marked and analyzed in a deeper way focusing on what maybe the

reasons behind. At last, all strategies and tactics used by each stakeholder were summarized. The influences were summarized in a network flow depicting how different stakeholders influence each other to implement project social responsibility. What the roles of the internal and external stakeholders in project social responsibility were were further discussed based on the results.

5.3   Data analysis

(1) Reweighing data

From the sample description, the numbers of representatives from different stakeholder groups were imbalanced. In order to reduce the over- and under-representations resulting from the disproportionate numbers from the different stakeholder groups, the data were reweighed using the adjusted coefficients before analysis. To get impartial results, it was assumed the number of representatives from these stakeholder groups should be the same in the target population. The data from end users and other groups did not change because their numbers were too small and may cause bias after reweighing. Apart from end users and other groups, there were five stakeholder groups whose response data need to be reweighed: main contractor ($n = 52$), developer ($n = 15$), government ($n=15$), subcontractor/supplier ($n=10$), and consultant ($n=35$). The formula for the reweighed coefficient is

$$\pi_k = \frac{\dfrac{N_k}{N}}{\dfrac{n_k}{n}}$$

In this formula, the $\dfrac{N_k}{N}$ represents the proportion of the stakeholder group k in the target population, which equals to $1/5$. And the $\dfrac{n_k}{n}$ represents the proportion of this stakeholder group k in the sample. The overall sample size n is

127, excluding the end user and other groups. If the coefficient is smaller than 1, it means that the stakeholder group was over-represented. If it is larger than 1, it means that the stakeholder group was under-represented.

Therefore, the reweighed coefficients for each stakeholder groups were main contractor ($\pi = 0.488$), developer ($\pi = 1.693$), government ($\pi = 1.693$), subcontractor/supplier ($\pi = 2.540$), consultant ($\pi = 0.726$). After reweighed, the average stakeholder power over the social responsibility tasks was calculated for further analysis.

After reweighed, using the 7 stakeholders and the 35 social responsibility tasks (SRTs) as nodes, and the average perceived power of the stakeholders over the social responsibility tasks as the weighted links, a stakeholder-SRT network was built for analyzing the complex stakeholder power structures of diverse social responsibility tasks. This study employed the concepts, measures, and analyzing tools from two-mode social network analysis (SNA), as potential methods for network analysis.

SNA was introduced as a graph theory for linking micro and macro levels of sociological theory (Granovetter, 1973). It has been broadly used as an effective tool of mapping complicated stakeholder relations (Boutilier, 2007; Rowley, 1997; Vance-Borland & Holley, 2011). The focuses of SNA are the interdependence of actors and how their positions in networks influence their opportunities, constraints, and behaviors (Wasserman & Galaskiewicz, 1994). This systematic analyzing method has various measures, such as centrality, density, benevolence, structure holes, transitivity, reciprocity of ties and brokerage (Freeman, 1978), and multiple analysis levels, including actor level, dyadic level, triad level, sub-group level, and network level analysis (Prell, 2012). SNA has been taken as a promising research instrument for construction project management, with which many fruitful insights are produced from the perspective of network structures (Ruan et al. , 2013). Emerson (1962) indicates that "through treating both persons and groups as actors in a power network, the door is opened for meaningful analysis of complex power structures". New characteristics can emerge from the macro view on the whole power network.

However, most SNA methods are designed for simple binary situations, with only one set of vertices, and ties are either present or absent (Opsahl et al., 2010). In this study, the network is a typical two-mode weighted network, which consists of two sets of nodes, and between which are links attached with values. This type of network is considerably complicated, so general SNA methods are mostly inappropriate. The analysis of weighted two-mode networks is merely noted in the existing literature.

The analysis of two-mode networks, also known as affiliation networks, describes relations between two different groups of entities, such as actor-movie network, company-board network, and author-paper network (Latapy et al., 2008). Generally there are two approaches for analyzing two-mode network data (Borgatti & Everett, 1997). One is to convert two-mode to one-mode using projection or bipartite matrix, after which all the fundamental measures designed for one-mode network are available to use. However, it may lead to the loss of information because there are only links between nodes in separate groups, but no links between nodes within one group in a two-mode network. The other approach is to find some measures that can be directly used in a two-mode network. Borgatti and Everett (1997) contribute to this approach. They designed direct measures for two-mode networks. This study integrated the measures from Borgatti's work from weighted networks and built the measures that can be directly used in a two-mode weighted network, as in the stakeholder-SRT network.

The network centralities are mainly used for evaluating stakeholders' power status. The three centralities proposed by Freeman (1978)—degree centrality, closeness centrality and betweenness centrality—were used for analyzing stakeholder power status on the social responsibility tasks. These three network centralities have received many academic credits (Borgatti, 2005; Faust, 1997; Freeman et al. , 1991; Opsahl et al. , 2010). However, some modifications need to be done before they can be employed in the two-mode weighted network. Degree centrality was originally defined as the number of the adjacent links to a node (Freeman, 1978). For weighted network, it is extended to the sum of weights of the adjunct edges (Opsahl et al. , 2010). For two-mode network, because nodes can only be connected to the other set of nodes, the sum of weights should be normalized by the number of nodes in the opposite set. Therefore, the degree centrality in two-mode weighted network, which stands for stakeholder power status on social responsibility tasks, was calculated using the following formulas:

$$d_i^* = \frac{d_i}{n_2} \quad i \in V_1$$

$$d_j^* = \frac{d_j}{n_1} \quad j \in V_2$$

d_i^* and d_j^* stand for the degree centralities of node i and j; d_i and d_j stand for the sum weights of edges connected to nodes i and j; n_1 and n_2 are the sizes of node sets V_1 and V_2.

In weighted network, closeness centrality is the inverse sum of shortest paths from one node to all other nodes (Opsahl et al. , 2010). Carter and Jennings (2002) propose the shortest path algorithm. The length of each edge is inversely to the edge strength, because the stronger links mean shorter distance between two nodes (Newman, 2001). According to the definitions of closeness centrality, high closeness centralities of a stakeholder not only means that the sum of power over all the social responsibility tasks is high, but also shows that the stakeholders have closer relationships with other powerful stakeholders. Based on the work of Borgatti and Everett (1997), the closeness centrality in two-mode weighted network was normalized in this study:

$$c_i^* = \frac{n_2 + 2n_1 - 2}{c_i} \quad i \in V_1$$

$$c_j^* = \frac{n_1 + 2n_2 - 2}{c_j} \quad j \in V_2$$

c_i^* and c_j^* stand for the closeness centralities of node i and j; c_i and c_j are the sum of lengths of shortest paths from node i and j to all other nodes.

Betweenness centrality is designed for revealing how many shortest paths pass through a given node originally. It represents the important intermediary role of the stakeholders because high betweenness centrality means that the stakeholders are at the core positions that other stakeholders may seek support from. In two-mode weighted network, according to Borgatti and Everett (1997), the normalization of betweenness centrality was (in this case $n_1 < n_2$):

$$b_i^* = \frac{b_i}{\frac{1}{2}n_2(n_2-1) + \frac{1}{2}(n_1-1)(n_1-2) + (n_1-1)(n_2-1)} \quad i \in V_1$$

$$b_j^* = \frac{b_j}{2(n_2-1)(n_1-1)} \quad j \in V_2$$

b_i^* and b_j^* stand for the betweenness centralities of node i and j. b_i and b_j are the shares of shortest paths that pass-through node i and j.

For the visualization of the stakeholder-SRT network, the spring embedding graph layout algorithm proposed by Kamada and Kawai (1989) was adopted. It is designed for generating large-scale network visualization with the optimal layout of nodes and links, while the distance between nodes is uninterpretable.

The visualization of the network was performed by the Netminer 4, a well-reputed SNA software tool praised by network researchers (Maloni & Brown, 2006). Because currently Netminer 4 has limited functions on calculating centralities for two-mode weighted network, this study also chose R project to calculate the network centralities. The data set of tnet package produced by Cruz (2009) was employed in R project for calculating two-mode and weighted networks. The centralities results output by tnet were normalized by the author using the formulas described in this section.

(2) Paired t-test analysis

Besides stakeholder power, the questionnaire also measured the interests of the respondents' organizations over the social responsibility tasks. Because the stakeholder interest was subjective evaluation of the respondents, the subjectivity bias can be significant if the stakeholder representative numbers are too small. Therefore, only four subgroups of stakeholders were targeted for power-interest comparison analysis, including main contractors ($n=52$), developers ($n=15$), governments ($n=15$), and consultants ($n=35$). This part of analysis compared the subjective evaluation of their organizational interests towards the SRT with the objective power of this stakeholder group perceived by the respondents. The average interest of the four targeted groups of stakeholders was calculated for the comparative analysis. Paired t-test is a commonly used method for testing differences between two observations in a group of subjects (Hsu & Lachenbruch, 2007). In this part of the analysis, the paired t-test was adopted to identify any gap between stakeholders' power and interest in implementing the SRTs.

5.4 Summary of the chapter

This chapter identified the thirty-five social responsibility tasks (SRTs) that were commonly conducted in a construction project. There is a commonly observed phenomenon that most of the construction practitioners do not know project social responsibility and what they should do for a socially responsible project. Although it is a nearly impossible mission to provide a complete and universally accepted list of what should be included in project social responsibility, this list of SRTs can still be a starting point for benchmark or as a check list. In practice, project social responsibility is more likely to involve improvisational decisions and tasks that respond to ad hoc instead of pre-prepared problems. However, it is useful for practitioners to understand the abstract concept of social responsibility by using some concrete, solid, and real-life examples.

The discussions of stakeholder power and influence in this book were primarily based on empirical analysis. Therefore, this chapter also reported the investigation process where the main conclusions of this book came from. It introduced in details how the author designed and conducted the questionnaire and interview survey, how the quantitative and qualitative data was collected and processed to collectively serve for the investigation purpose. The investigation data provided a fundamental basis for the following analysis and discussion of the power and influences of stakeholders. Also, the descriptions can provide an example for scholars on how mixed method research could be designed and used for a stakeholder-related research.

Chapter 6
Stakeholders' Power on the SRTs

6.1 Analysis of stakeholders' power over the SRTs

The literature review revealed that stakeholder power structures need to be firstly clarified for identifying stakeholders' diverse roles in implementing project social responsibility. A questionnaire was conducted among construction practitioners for investigating stakeholders' power over the thirty-five social responsibility tasks across project life cycle. This chapter elaborates the findings from analysis of the questionnaire data for illustrating the stakeholders' power distribution on different social responsibility tasks.

Initially, the results on the overall power status of seven stakeholders were reported by two-mode social network analysis. The stakeholder-SRT network was visualized as a mapping of stakeholder power distributions on different social responsibility tasks. Degree centrality shows the direct power status possessed by stakeholders; closeness centrality shows the appealing power to seek support from all other stakeholders; and betweenness centrality stands for the intermediate between other stakeholders. By combining three centralities, the seven stakeholders were categorized into five power hierarchies. Next, based on the categorization of SRTs in terms of project stages and ISO 26000 categories, the dynamics and heterogeneity of stakeholder power were analyzed. This part of results showed the fluctuation of each stakeholder's power across different project stages and the variations on different ISO social responsibility dimensions. At last, the gaps between stakeholders' power and interest on the social responsibility tasks were identified and discussed.

6.2   Overview of stakeholder power

6.2.1   Visualization of the stakeholder-SRT network

The stakeholder-SRT network (see figure 6-1) was generated using the spring embedding graph layout algorithm of Netminer. The layout of the links and nodes was produced for optimal visualized presentation. The links were bundled to reduce the overlapping lines and enhance readability. The network displays a global view of power distribution of the seven stakeholders on the thirty-five social responsibility tasks. The node sizes show degree centralities. The round nodes are social responsibility tasks. The larger sizes of the nodes mean that the seven stakeholders have more control over them. The square nodes are the stakeholders. The larger sizes show that the stakeholders have stronger power status. The lines linking stakeholder and social responsibility tasks are present when the power is greater than the average.

According to figure 6-1, governments, developers, and main contractors have high power with almost all the social responsibility tasks, which means that all the social responsibility tasks require the involvement of at least one of these three stakeholders. Among these three core stakeholders, government was exclusively associated with two social responsibility tasks, which were developing human right policies and anti-discrimination. It shows that governments have exclusive power over human right issues in projects. Apart from the three core

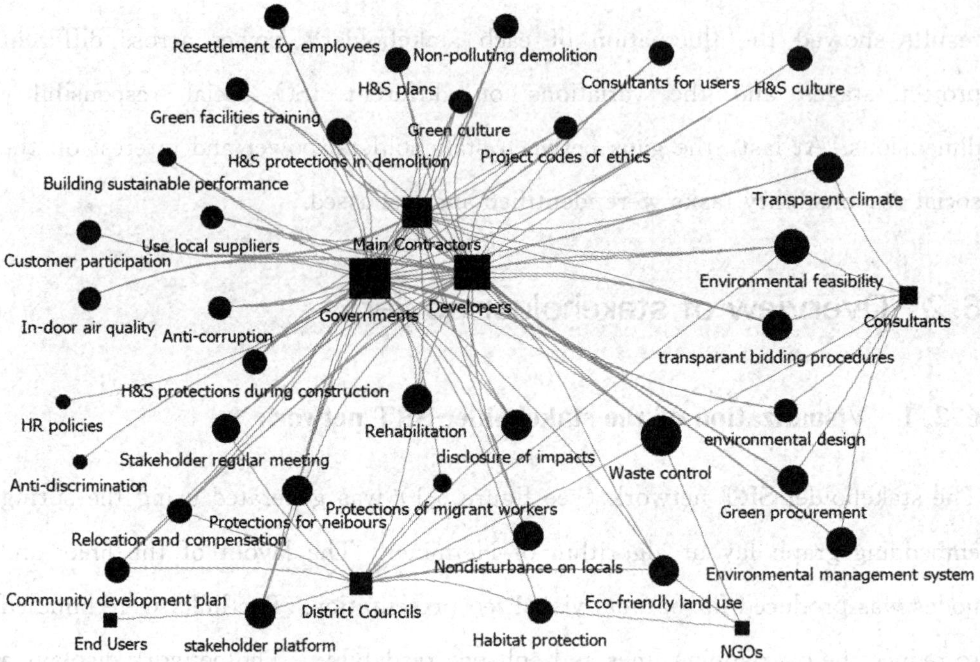

Figure 6-1   The two-mode stakeholder-SRT power network.

(Generated by Netminer based on my data analysis)

stakeholders, the rest stakeholders also have unique roles in specific social responsibility tasks. For example, waste control in projects was controlled jointly by the three core stakeholders, consultants, district councils, and NGOs. These stakeholders have responsibility and resources to reduce construction wastes. Habitat protection was linked with governments, district councils, and NGOs. It means that the collaboration among these stakeholders is essential for successful protection of natural habitat from the damage of construction projects.

Some of the social responsibility tasks have higher stakeholders' control compared with the others, such as waste control, environmental feasibility, transparent climate, stakeholder platform, green procurement, environmental management system, eco-friendly land use, disclosure of impacts, and rehabilitation. This result shows that these social responsibility tasks require collaborations between multiple stakeholders rather than a single organization's job. By contrast, some tasks are only controlled by a few key stakeholders or a single stakeholder, for example, the protection for migrant workers, the sustainability performance of buildings, and the human right issues.

6. 2. 2 Network centralities of the stakeholders

According to the two-mode weighted network centrality formulas introduced in Section 5. 3, the centralities of the seven stakeholders on the thirty-five social responsibility tasks were calculated based on stakeholder-SRT network (see table 6-1). In the table, the stakeholders are ranked from the highest degree of centrality to the lowest. According to the classification of the internal and external stakeholder groups, the seven stakeholders can be divided into internal stakeholders (developers, main contractors, consultants, and end users) and external stakeholder group (governments, district councils, and NGOs).

The centralities show that governments had the highest scores in all three centralities. This means that governments have highest direct power (d. c. 3. 850), the most power to call for cooperation from other stakeholders (c. c. 1. 195), and the center role in intermediating between other stakeholders (b. c. 1. 373). Among the external stakeholders, district council had the second highest centralities (d. c. 3. 072). The rest of the external stakeholders all had low power over social responsibility tasks, including NGOs (d. c. 2. 927) and end users (d. c. 2. 732).

Among the internal stakeholders, the network centralities of developers and main contractors were the first and second highest (d. c. 3. 494 and 3. 353), implying they have considerable power over implementing social responsibility tasks in construction projects. Compared to them, consultants have relatively weak power (d. c. 3. 001). Compared with the closeness and betweenness centralities, degree centrality is easier to interpret as stakeholder's direct power over all the social responsibility tasks. Therefore, the following analysis used degree centrality to discuss the dynamic changes of stakeholder power status.

Table 6-1   The network centralities of the stakeholders

Stakeholder	Degree centrality (d. c.)	Closeness centrality (c. c.)	Betweenness centrality (b. c.)
Government	3. 850	1. 195	1. 373
Developer	3. 494	1. 101	0. 044
Main contractor	3. 353	1. 056	0. 044
District council	3. 072	0. 984	0
Consultant	3. 001	0. 963	0
NGOs	2. 927	0. 943	0
End user	2. 732	0. 889	0

6. 2. 3   The stakeholder power hierarchy

The stakeholder-SRT network shows not only the global view of stakeholder power distribution, but also a hierarchy of stakeholders' power status. The three most powerful stakeholders in the center of the network—governments, developers, and main contractors—formed the core authority and had high power over almost all of the social responsibility tasks. The remaining stakeholders, with relatively small nodes, had power with regard to limited scopes of the social responsibility tasks. Table 6-2 shows the hierarchical power status of the stakeholders. The three core stakeholders constitute the first tier of powerful stakeholders, and they had power over all of the social responsibility tasks. The second tier contains district councils only. As representatives of communities, district councils have power over most of the community issues, including making community development plan, relocation and compensation, protections for neighbors, non-disturbance on locals, and rehabilitation after demolition. They also have power and obligations over some environmental and human right issues like stakeholder platform, regular meetings, project impact disclosure, waste control, protection of migrant workers, and habitat protection. Consultants belonged to the third tier of stakeholder power. They possess both technical and professional knowledge to engage in environmental design of projects, environmental management system, environmental feasibility, and green procurements. Meanwhile, consultants also have power over controlling transparent bidding procedures, and develop the transparent climate in projects by using their professional management knowledge and experiences. NGOs, at the fourth tier, are less powerful stakeholders in implementing project social responsibility compared with the above-mentioned stakeholders. The tasks that NGOs have power over were related to environment and ecology, including habitat protection, eco-friendly land use, and waste control. End users were at the fifth tier, who were the least powerful stakeholders on social responsibility tasks. Among the identified tasks, they hold power only over driving the development of stakeholder platforms. The end users have right and responsibility to ask other stakeholders to disclose and consult projects' environmental and social influence.

Table 6-2　Stakeholder power hierarchy

Hierarchy	Stakeholders	The social responsibility tasks that under the stakeholder's power
1st tier	Governments; developers; main contractors	All the issues
2nd tier	District councils	Community development plan; relocation and compensation; protections for neighbors; non-disturbance on locals; rehabilitation; stakeholder platform; stakeholder regular meeting; protections of migrant workers; disclosure of impacts; waste control; habitat protection
3rd tier	Consultants	Transparent climate; environmental feasibility; transparent bidding procedures; waste control; environmental design; green procurement; environmental management system

(Continued)

Hierarchy	Stakeholders	The social responsibility tasks that under the stakeholder's power
4th tier	NGOs	Habitat protection; eco-friendly land use; waste control
5th tier	End users	Stakeholder platforms

6.3 Stakeholder power across project stages and social responsibility dimensions

6.3.1 Dynamics of stakeholder power over project life cycle

From the life cycle perspective, stakeholders' power status fluctuated over projects' different stages (figure 6-2). Mitchell et al. (1997)'s stakeholder salience theory supports the proposition that stakeholder power is not a constant variable. This changing power adds credibility to the arguments of Missonier and Loufrani-Fedida (2014) that the influence of stakeholders is emergent and dynamic over the life cycle of a project. The social responsibility tasks identified in this research were divided into three project stages, including project initiating and planning stage, execution stage, and at last, controlling and closing stage. The fluctuations of stakeholder power were found by analyzing the stakeholders' degree centralities over the social responsibility tasks that fell into these three project stages.

According to the results, governments and developers had highest power at the project initiating and planning stage. This result corroborates the conclusion of Shen et al. (2010) that governments and owners play significant roles at a project's inception and design stage. Governments have authorized legislative power in project approvals and establishments. Developers have the financial power to decide whether to include social responsibility requirements at the design and tendering stages. Although these are the two most powerful

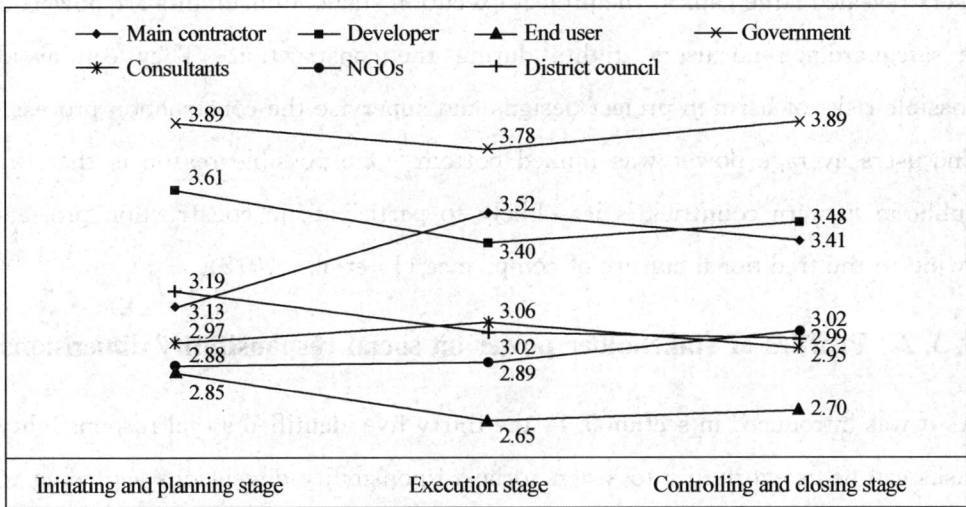

Figure 6-2　Fluctuations of stakeholder power over the project life cycle.

stakeholders at the early stage, governments' and developers' power gradually decreased after construction work began, while main contractors became the most dominant stakeholders. Main contractors are the commanders in the construction process and they control the operations on site, executing the project and coordinating many of the most important resources. Therefore, at the project execution stage, main contractors are the responsible party for project social responsibility. Among the powerless stakeholders, district councils held relatively more power than the others at project execution stage because they act as the communication bridge between governments, companies, and local residents. District councils are able to effectively raise demands on behalf of their voters at project stages. It is interesting to note that the power of NGOs gradually increased as the power of the district councils decreased, thereby showing a complementary effect between formal and informal community power along the project life cycle. This complementary relationship also disproves the proposition that the power of all the weak external stakeholders decreases as the project proceeds (Aaltonen & Kujala, 2010). The curves of consultants and end users revealed large gaps at the project execution stage. Consultants are powerful in safeguarding end users' rights during the construction. They can avoid possible risks of harm in project designs and supervise the construction process. End users average power was ranked bottom. One possible reason is that the public in Eastern countries is less likely to participate in construction projects owing to the traditional culture of compliance (Li et al. , 2012).

6.3.2   Profiles of stakeholder power on social responsibility dimensions

As it was introduced in section 5.1, the thirty-five identified social responsibility tasks can be categorized into seven social responsibility dimensions according to the ISO 26000, including organizational government (OG), human rights (HR), labor protection (LP), environment (En), fair operation (FO), customer issues (CI), and community involvement and development (Co). The stakeholders all have their specialties and weaknesses in implementing the tasks on different dimensions. Such profiles of stakeholder power can be revealed by analyzing the stakeholders' network centralities over the social responsibility tasks on each dimension (see figure 6-3). According to figure 6-3, governments had an exclusive power over human rights dimension, which is a weak spot for all the other stakeholders. Except for governments, only district councils and NGOs have slight advantage on the human right related issues. Because district councils are responsible for protecting the benefits of communities, they hold relative power advantages on the community issues dimension. As the defender of the public and natural environment, NGOs' power profile shows a strength on environmental protection dimension.

Among the internal stakeholders, contractors exhibit prominently strong power advantage on labor protection dimension. Compared with other stakeholders, developers had superior power on almost all dimensions, particularly on community development and organizational governance, fair

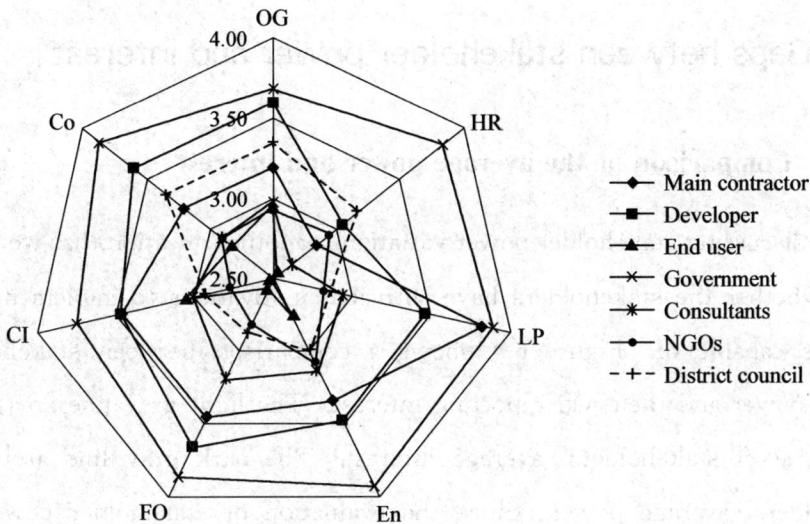

Figure 6-3   The profiles of stakeholder power on different dimensions.

operation, and environmental issues. As the provider of technical knowledge, consultants had higher power on the environment issues, fair operation, and organizational governance. At last, as the end consumers, end users have power advantage on customer issues.

Comparing the power profiles with the stakeholder interest matrix built by the World Business Council for Sustainable Development (WBCSD), several gaps were detected between stakeholders' interests and the areas they have power over. For example, government interest in business operations was weak; however this study revealed it had supreme power on organizational governance dimension. By contrast, NGOs had an interest in all social issues, but from the questionnaire data they had limited power on all the seven dimensions. The substantially powerful stakeholders, namely, developers, showed no interest in areas that they had power over, such as the environment, human rights, and governance. These gaps between stakeholders' interests and their power attracted my attention, which also informed the further explorations on comparison analysis in the next section.

6. 4   Gaps between stakeholder power and interest

6. 4. 1   Comparison of the average power and interest

Besides discussing stakeholder power variations, another question that we should ask is whether the stakeholders have sufficient motivations to implement what they are capable of. Figure 6-4 shows a comparison between stakeholders' average power and their self-reporting interest. The light gray line area shows the degree of stakeholders' average interest. The dark gray line are shows stakeholders' average power. Since the evaluation of stakeholder power and interests did not use the same benchmark, we only compare the differences.

From the profile of stakeholder interests, there shows an overview of stakeholders' preferences in diverse SRTs. The profile in the figure reveals that much attention has been devoted to the labor protection, environment issues, customer issues, and community development, whereas limited attention has been devoted to the organizational governance, fair operation, and human right. This result corroborates that of a study about UK construction companies, where health/safety and environmental issues are currently the social responsibility hotspots in construction organizations, whereas less concern are devoted to internal governance (Jones et al. , 2006). The disparities between interest and power varied significantly among the seven social responsibility dimensions. The issues about labor protection, environment, fair operation, and customers had a significant gap between higher interest and lower power. The result is reasonable because China's Hong Kong SAR government put construction health and safety as the top focus of industrial legislation. Moreover, China's Hong Kong SAR is one of the leading transparent markets in the world (ranked 17th out of 175 markets in corruption perception index in 2014). This shows that the legislation

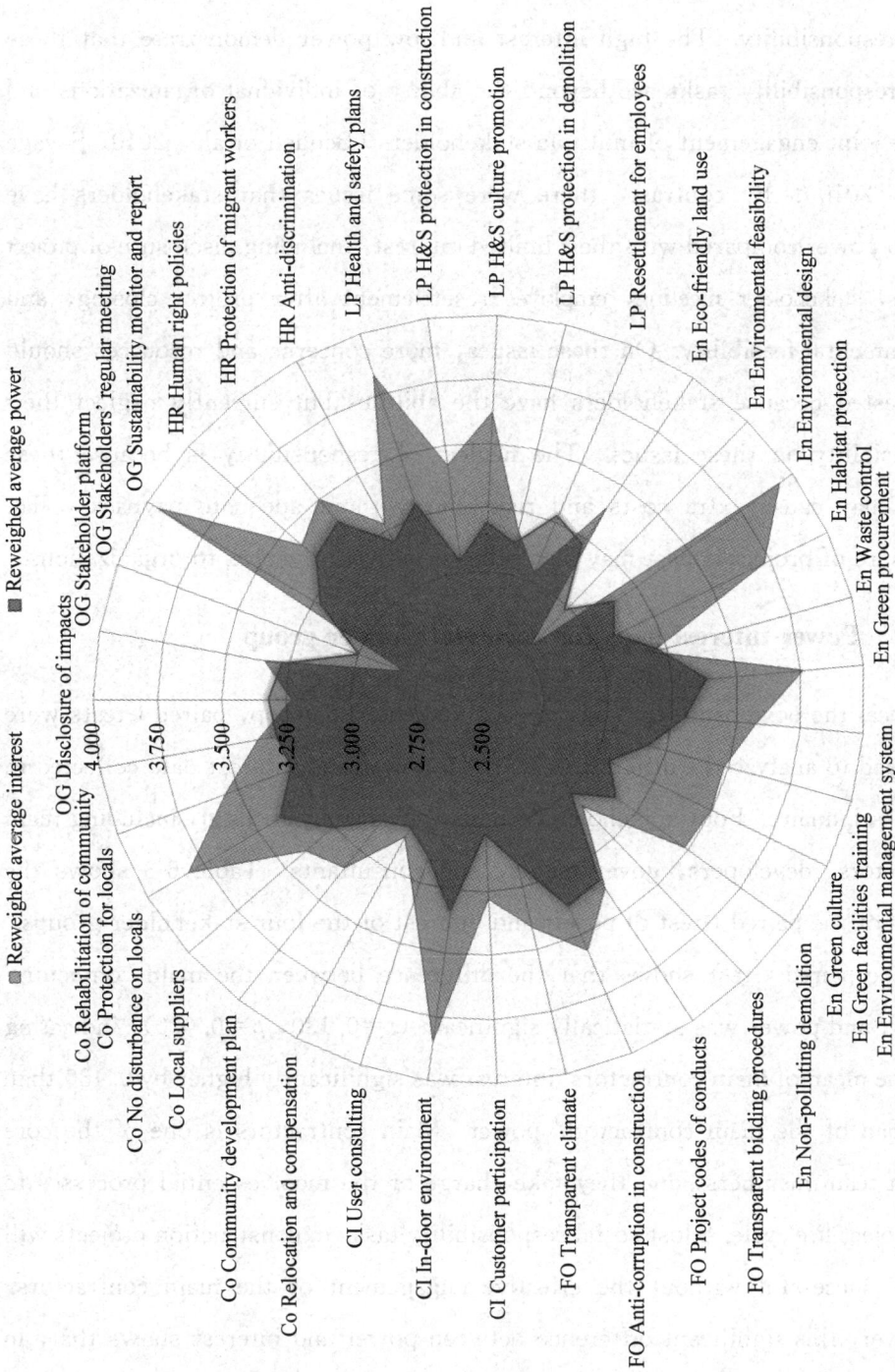

Figure 6-4　The comparison between stakeholders' average interest and power.

of local government highly influences the construction organizations' emphasis on social responsibility. The high interest and low power demonstrate that these social responsibility tasks are beyond the ability of individual organizations and require joint engagement of multiple stakeholders (Bendell et al. , 2010; Savage et al. , 2010). By contrast, there were some issues that stakeholders have enough power compared with their limited interest, including disclosure of project impacts, stakeholder meeting, employee resettlement after project closing, and environmental feasibility. On these issues, more concerns and resources should be invested because stakeholders have the abilities but currently neglect their responsibility on these issues. The neglect of responsibility is because these issues may cause extra costs and risks but without adequate paybacks, like disclosure of project impact may also bring negative influences to organizations.

6. 4. 2 Power-interest gaps for each stakeholder group

To reveal the power-interest gaps of each stakeholder group, paired t-tests were employed to analyze the differences between power and interest data collected in the questionnaire. Four stakeholder groups were mainly focused, including main contractors, developers, governments, and consultants. Table 6-3 shows the results of the paired t-test of power and interest of the four stakeholder groups.

The paired t-test shows that the difference between the main contactors' interest and power was statistically significant ($t=0.130$, $p=0.000$), indicating that the mean of main contractors' interest was significantly higher by 0.130 than the mean of the main contractors' power. Main contractors is one of the core project team members, and they take charge of the most essential processes in the project life cycle. Most social responsibility tasks in construction projects will not be successful without the effective engagement of the main contractors. However, this significant difference between power and interest shows that, in Hong Kong, although main contractors are interested in improving project social responsibility, their power is not enough to initiate and implement the social responsibility tasks that they are interested in.

The result of the paired t-test on developers shows that the mean of developers' interest is not significantly different from the mean of their power ($t=-0.027$, $p=0.574$). The developers' power is slightly higher (mean $=$ -0.027) but not statistically significant. Developers generally play a powerful role in construction projects because they can directly raise their demands in bidding documents or contracts, as well as the social requirements of the construction outcomes. This finding indicates that developers' interest in social responsibility tasks and their power are approximately consistent, which means developer companies are aware of their responsibilities and try to put efforts to fulfil them.

There exists a significant gap between the governments' interest and power ($t=-0.653$, $p=0.000$). The mean of governments' power is higher by 0.653 than the governments' interest, indicating that the Hong Kong government currently has insufficient concerns on social responsibility in construction projects compared to their authorized power. Government departments normally set the baseline for social responsibility; therefore, if they were not sufficiently motivated, the bottom lines will be the ignored or used by the private sector at the cost of public benefits. This lack of interests of governments on social responsibility legislation possibly results in the lagging development of construction market in Hong Kong.

A significant gap is detected between consultants' interest and power ($t=0.216$, $p=0.000$). Consultants' interest is greater by an average of 0.216 than their power, implying that consulting companies are very proactive in promoting project social responsibility. These companies possess advanced knowledge and techniques in improving project social performance. However, because consultants are normally under the command of their clients, implementing social responsibility initiatives without support from developers or governments can be very difficult or even impossible. Consultants can only provide some socially responsible alternatives for their client to decide whether to implement or not, such as green building design or resource efficiency construction techniques.

Table 6-3   The paired t-test gaps between power and interest

	Paired differences interest-power							
	Mean	Std. deviation	Std. error mean	95% confidence interval of the difference		t	df	Sig. (2-tailed)
				Lower	Upper			
Main contractors	0.130	1.373	0.032	0.067	0.193	4.028	1819	0.000
Developers	−0.027	1.087	0.047	−0.120	0.067	−0.562	524	0.574
Governments	−0.653	1.468	0.064	−0.779	−0.527	−10.199	524	0.000
Consultants	0.216	1.361	0.039	0.140	0.293	5.563	1224	0.000

6.5   Recommendations to improve project social responsibility

6.5.1   Project social responsibility calls for stakeholder collaboration

Based on the proximity of stakeholders relationships within projects, stakeholders can be divided into the direct-internal-contractual and the indirect-external-public groups (Aaltonen & Kujala, 2010; Zeng et al., 2015). From the stakeholder-SRT network analysis, it can be concluded that all stakeholders, including internal and external ones, have unique power and corresponding responsibilities in implementing project social responsibility tasks. Therefore, all the internal and external stakeholders that have abilities to influence should jointly participate in implementing social responsibility tasks. The previous research mainly focused on internal stakeholders, such as major contractor and developer companies, while underestimated the influence of external stakeholders (Huang & Lien, 2012; Jones et al. , 2006). By contrast, it was found in this study that the external stakeholders had their important roles in some social responsibility tasks. District councils have strong power over community issues, many of which are environment and human right issues. NGOs are main defenders in waste control, eco-friendly land use, and habitat protection. End users have a significant role in stakeholder platform development. Besides the legitimacy associated with their roles as customers, end users also have the potential to withhold purchase as the source of power. Because social responsibility tasks are mostly philanthropic and altruistic in nature, external stakeholders constitute important driving force. External pressures, such as public voices and mass media reports, are demonstrated as indispensable in facilitating project social responsibility, since companies may not voluntarily invest resources if it shows no profitability (Bovaird, 2005; Steurer, 2010). Recent literature also begins to show the scholarly and political attention on the collaboration between public and private sectors in co-creation of social responsibility values (Bendell et al. , 2010; Bryson et al. , 2006; McDonald & Young, 2012). Compared with intensive attention on internal project stakeholders, the power and influences of external stakeholders require more attention especially on the social issues (Aaltonen & Kujala, 2010; Aaltonen & Sivonen, 2009).

6.5.2   Create motivations of the right stakeholders

(1) Core three stakeholders

There is a common misunderstanding in general perceptions that only internal stakeholders have strong power to influence project objectives. It is not the case of social issues because this research found that the most powerful stakeholders on social responsibility include both internal and external stakeholders. They are governments, main contractors, and developers. As external stakeholders, governments are the most powerful stakeholders to put forward legislations and bottom lines because they have the direct institutional legitimacy to enact policies to encourage good behaviors and penalize misconduct. Developers play a key role in initiating social responsibility standards in contracts because they possess the firsthand power to elicit requirements and negotiate on the additional costs. Main contractors have power to put the social responsibility tasks into practice since they are the coordinators of resources and activities in construction process. The power of the three core stakeholders not only generates from their unique resources, but also from their positional characteristics in network. Maignan et al. (2002) point out that the power of stakeholders on social responsibility is not only determined by resources, the ability of stakeholders to communicate with others to coordinate their advocacy is also vital. This result is in conformity with resource-dependence and structural power theories indicating that the sources of stakeholder power are from both critical resources and network positions (Emerson, 1962; Rowley, 1997).

The three core stakeholders' power is not consistently high in project life cycles, which conforms to the emergent and dynamic nature of construction projects (Aaltonen & Kujala, 2010; Missonier & Loufrani-Fedida, 2014). The results indicated that the governments and developers had the highest power at project initiating and planning stage. Their power decreased significantly at project execution stage. This result corroborates the conclusion of Shen et al. (2010) that governments and owners play significant roles at a project's inception and design stage. By contrast, main contractors had nearly no involvement at project planning stage, especially in traditional design-build projects. But they became the commanders at the construction stage because they control the operations on site, execute the project, and coordinate important resources. The specialty of contractors on health and safety issues in construction projects was also evidently observed from the results. This is because main contractors manage the most dangerous phase, the construction process; they have the vital role in protecting the employees, neighborhoods, the public from the health and safety risks emerging from construction activities. Consultants have knowledge and experiences on environmental design, sustainable materials, and advanced techniques, therefore having potential power to give advice from a professional perspective. Although consultants have a significant role in proposing advice in projects, they don't have adequate power to implement them in projects because they need to obey the decisions of their clients (Othman, 2009).

(2) Public benefit defenders: District councils and NGOs

Little research has shown attention to the role of district councils in social responsibility in construction projects. District councils are elected regional representatives for benefits of local communities in eighteen regions in Hong Kong. District councils are not completely governmental departments; they are consisted of community committees. Community power has been addressed in previous literature as an important part of external pressures for social responsibility (Boehm, 2002; Thornton & Leahy, 2011). District councils are obligated to defend the interests of local communities, so they have the legitimate power to supervise construction projects working in their regions. They act as the communication bridge between governments and local residents. The research findings show that district councils have considerate power to advocate social responsibility tasks in construction projects.

NGOs are regarded as one of the most important driving forces for social responsibility introduction and implementation (Doh & Guay, 2006; Jamali & Keshishian, 2009; Thijssens et al. , 2015). In Hong Kong, there is a number of NGOs for almost every social issue with different scales and influences. However, it was noted from the results that NGOs in Hong Kong have generally limited power on social responsibility tasks in construction projects. This may due to the fact that individual power of NGOs is small, but through lobbying governments and big corporations their claims can be strengthened (Frooman, 1999; Hendry, 2005). Another interesting point is the power of the district council decreases along project life cycle, while the power of NGOs increases in contrast. Unlike secondary stakeholders' power, which often decreases as project proceeds (Aaltonen & Kujala, 2010), district councils and NGOs have complementary power along project stages. District councils can raise the community and environmental concerns at project initiating and construction stages. NGOs can continuously monitor the project social and environmental influences after key stakeholders exit from projects.

(3) Inadequate end users' power

In social responsibility research in general business management, the roles of consumers are regarded as significant (Alberg Mosgaard et al. , 2016; Henriques & Sadorsky, 1999; Sharma & Henriques, 2005), because they create demands for social responsibility products by using abilities to withdraw money for unsatisfactory project outcomes (Henriques & Sadorsky, 1999). However, it was found from the results that end users were ranked bottom in power hierarchy in construction projects. It revealed that although in Hong Kong public participation was highly emphasized by the governments, public power was still inadequate to effectively express their requirements on social responsibility. Li et al. (2012) indicate that public in Eastern countries is less likely to engage in project decision making owing to the traditional culture of compliance. This calls for a development of communication channels or stakeholder platforms for project users to put forward their demands.

6.5.3 Notice of the power-interest gaps

The project stakeholders' diverse interest and power have been noticed by some scholars (Olander, 2007; Olander & Landin, 2005); however, their attention is mainly on giving priorities to stakeholders with high power and/or interest.

According to Olander (2007), companies can make responding strategies, such as managing closely with the stakeholders with high interest and power, keeping the stakeholders with high power and low interest satisfied, keeping the stakeholders with high interest but low power informed, and keeping monitoring the stakeholders without power and interest. This research used an innovative perspective to find out gaps between stakeholder interest and power.

The comparisons between stakeholders' average interest and power reveal that stakeholders' interests are generally higher than their power on social responsibility tasks, showing the demands for collaboration and joint efforts. On some social responsibility tasks, such as labor protection, fair operation, customer issues, and environmental issues, stakeholders have higher interest than power, which means stakeholders have already realized these challenges, but individual stakeholder's ability is not enough to successfully complete these issues. By contrast, on some other social responsibility tasks, including disclosure of project impacts, stakeholder regular meeting, the resettlement for employees after project closing, and environmental feasibility, it is found that stakeholders have less interest than power. It means that the project stakeholders are reluctant to implement these issues; therefore, the incentives to motivate stakeholders are especially needed.

The results of paired t-test analysis showed that contractors and consultants had higher interest than power. Although their commitments to implementing social responsibility are high, they do not have enough competence to implement these issues. Developers, by contrast, have enough power and considerate interest in social responsibility tasks, because no significant difference was found between their power and interest. However, as the most powerful stakeholder, governments were found with inadequate interest in social responsibility tasks. Hong Kong government should devote more legislation concerns to social responsibility tasks in construction projects.

6. 5. 4　Evaluate stakeholder engagement in project social responsibility

Stakeholder engagement in project social responsibility is the essential goal of this research. However, the key question to ask is how to decide the extent to which stakeholders should become engaged. A few studies have identified power as one of the dominant predictors of stakeholder's abilities to influence a project's objectives (Leung et al. , 2013; Prado-Lorenzo et al. , 2009). With sufficient power, stakeholders can "alter social and political forces, as well as their capacity to influence project objectives, obtain resources from the community, and maintain social relationships" (Leung et al. , 2013, p. 2).

However, it was found from the questionnaire analysis that stakeholders do not necessarily have the equivalent power and interest in the social responsibility tasks. Based on the literature, the engagement levels of stakeholders in implementing social responsibility should be attributed to their power, because power represents the capacity of stakeholders to raise the initiatives and influence others to follow. However, stakeholder interest, as intrinsic intention and attitude, is also an important determinant for efficient engagement. Interest stands for the probability that stakeholders would like to incorporate certain objectives into their operations (Bourne & Walker, 2005). It is mostly depended on organizational strategies, commitment to society, leadership styles, organizational cultures, backgrounds, management strategies, etc.

Since the results identified significant gaps between stakeholders' interest and power, it can be safe to assume that stakeholders' engagement levels cannot simply be determined by their power. Stakeholders who have motivations to carry out social responsibility may not have enough power to exert their wills, while the powerful stakeholders can be reluctant to fulfil their responsibilities. This difference between power and interest can be different from project to project. Therefore, stakeholder engagement levels in social responsibility tasks in construction projects should be evaluated by both stakeholder's power and interest in the issues.

6.6　Summary of the chapter

This chapter reported the analysis results of the questionnaire data. The findings and discussions in this chapter provided a better understanding of dynamic stakeholder power on the complicated social responsibility tasks. Normally, people see project social responsibility as an overall performance. However, in practice, it actually involves very diverse and dynamic requirements, which call for effective collaboration of multiple stakeholders. It is important to know in advance the different advantages of each stakeholder in terms of handling the emerging social responsibility issues. By a structurally designed survey, we cannot identify every single condition that stakeholders may face in a dynamic project environment. However, the general pattern of stakeholder power fluctuation across project stages and on different social responsibility dimensions can provide a useful reference for project managers to coordinate necessary resources. It also helped stakeholders to find their roles and positions in implementing project social responsibility instead of taking themselves as outsiders.

The research gap was also filled about no empirical findings have been obtained for evaluating the stakeholder dynamics in construction projects. The findings in this chapter can be a supplement to stakeholder dynamics and heterogeneity. Significant gaps were found between stakeholders' power and interest, which raised the demand to create motivations for powerful stakeholders to pursue their obliged responsibilities. The findings also showed the unique roles associated with the internal and external stakeholders in implementing social responsibility tasks. It informed the following study on how stakeholders with different power can exercise their influences on each other.

Chapter 7

Stakeholders' Influence Strategies

7.1 How stakeholders use their power also matters

After investigating the dynamic power of stakeholders, the next question to be answered is what behavioral strategies and tactics stakeholders use to influence others in social responsibility tasks. According to the literature review, current stakeholder influence research mostly concentrates on dyadic stakeholder relationships around a focal organization. In this chapter, the qualitative data collected from the interview survey described in section 5.2.2 was analyzed to reveal stakeholders' influence strategies in driving the implementation of PSR. This chapter reported the analysis results by the text mining software Leximancer. The concept map automatically generated by Leximancer was presented, in which the identified themes and concepts, as well as the relationships, were explained. By using this interactive concept map, the excerpts that relate to stakeholders' inter-influence were extracted and interpreted. The results of this chapter unfolded in three parts: 1) stakeholders' influencing strategies and tactics identified from the excerpts; 2) stakeholder influence map depicting all the internal and external stakeholders' inter-influence; 3) the potential determinants that cause stakeholders to choose aggressive and/or cooperative strategies.

7.2 The concept map by Leximancer

The concept map generated by Leximancer is shown in figure 7-1, in which 14 themes are automatically clustered based on the algorithm of the concepts' frequency and co-occurrence. The links and distances on the concept map stand for semantic connections between two concepts. The list of all themes and the included concepts that appear on the concept map are listed in table 7-1. The intensity of the themes means the observed frequency of the concepts in each theme in the corpus.

Table 7-1   Themes and concepts generated from the concept map

Theme	Concept	Intensity
Project	Project; environment; take; construction; issue; process	263 hits
Developer	Developer; building; people; manager; community; work; green	259 hits
Government	Government; responsibility; public; representative; CSR issue; social; issue, workers;	221 hits
Contractor	Contractor; main contractor; main	182 hits
Subcontractor	Subcontractors; materials; use; build; cost	166 hits
Consultant	Consultants; money; time; residents	164 hits
Investor	Investor; company; development; CSR; employees	97 hits
Supplier	Suppliers; GBCA; council	53 hits
NGO	TPB; NGO	40 hits
Tenants	Tenants	38 hits
Consumers	Consumers	18 hits

On the concept map, the theme of project is the top-frequent theme from the interviews, followed by government and main contractor, consultant, project, and the public. It shows that the government departments and main contractor

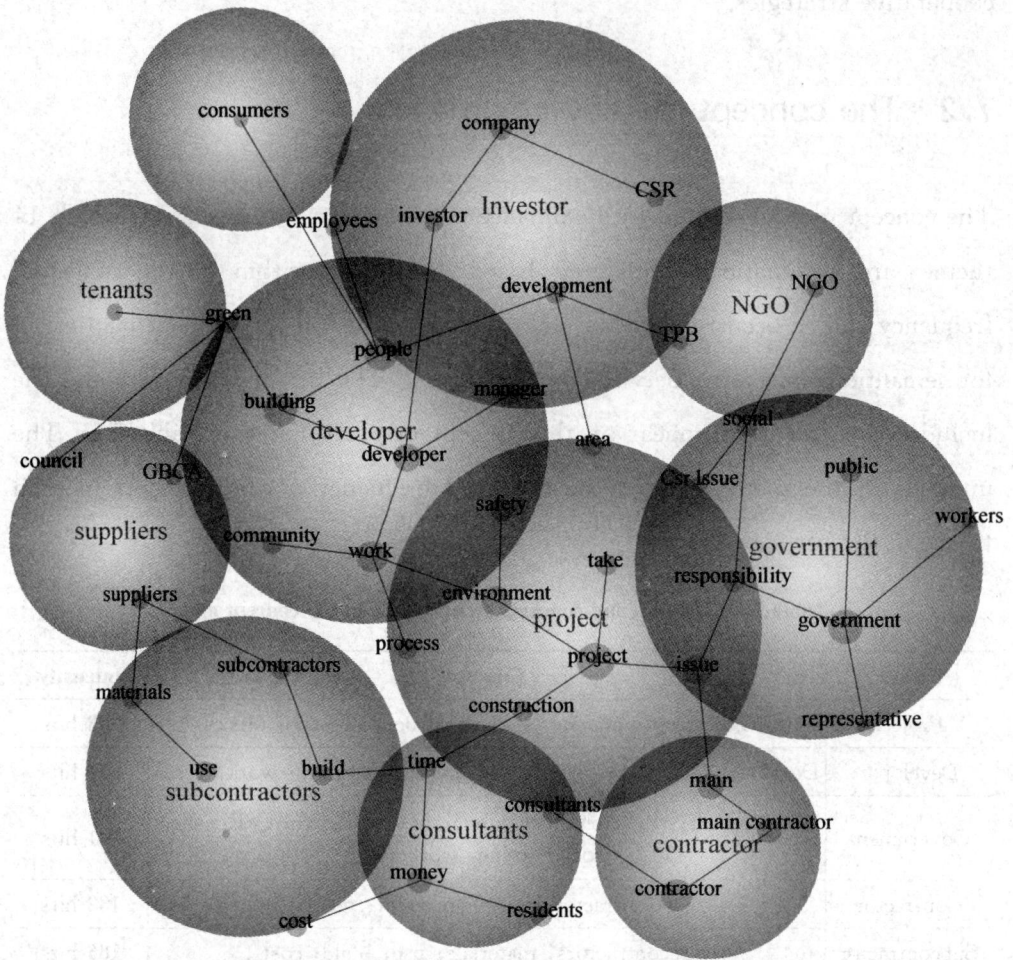

Figure 7-1   Concept map generated by Leximancer.

companies were the most frequently mentioned stakeholders when the topics were related to PSR. Some stakeholders were found with low frequency, for example, the tenants, residents, workers, and consumers. For obtaining a comprehensive map of stakeholder influences on PSR implementation, all stakeholders generated from the interviews were included for the analysis. From the locations of the themes, relationships between the themes can be found based on semantic structures embedded in the interview transcriptions. For example, the theme of developer is associated frequently with cost, investor, subcontractor and supplier. The government and main contractor themes are surrounded by the consultant, project, and the public. The theme of NGOs is close to community and resident. In the following section, the results of the analysis of the excerpts from the transcriptions will be illustrated with detailed strategies adopted by each stakeholder group.

7.3   Stakeholders' influences from the interviews

7.3.1   Communities and the public

From the interviews, the awareness of communities and the public on social responsibility tasks arises when their benefits are at risks, such as threatening their health and safety, pollutions, noises, and other risks. Communities or the representative organizations often organize multi-party meetings to discuss these concerned issues regarding the project's activities. Stakeholder collaborations can be achieved by gathering all parties in one room and putting the issues on the table for discussion. When the issues become urgent and the benefits of communities or the public are under major threats, communities and the public's legitimacy to raise their complaints also increases. In such occasions, the strategies that are applied to draw attentions from government or project leaders are more aggressive, for example, complaint, report, or protest.

7.3.2   NGOs

NGOs possess expert resources including their professional knowledge and experiences regarding the focused issues. However, they need the collaborations from the governments to put their visions in practice by enacting relevant laws and regulations. Besides, the interdependency of NGOs and companies becomes increasingly important. On the one hand, NGOs rely on companies' abundant resources; on the other hand NGOs can offer complimentary capacities, such as professional knowledge, experience, network, and community trust, which can be critical in coping with the emerging social responsibility tasks (Jonker & Nijhof, 2006). Therefore, under most conditions, NGOs adopt soft and cooperative strategies and for the share of scarce resources from governments or companies to realize their social objectives, such as lobbying, visit, emails.

Some initiatives launched by NGOs regarding their focused issues can inspire the industry to participate. The reason why companies are voluntarily involved is that they can network and share experiences on sustainability with other industrial leaders. Meanwhile the value that the organizations deliver in such initiatives can also inspire the companies to show their commitments to the society. Cooperative strategies were found, such as NGOs that voluntarily provide professional advise to developers, such as providing sustainable options and demonstrating the profitability of such options. They also provide training services in order to help developers to market their buildings with green features.

When the problems or consequences become severe and require urgent response, for example, severe environmental pollution and ecological harm, NGOs also choose aggressive strategy to force governments and contractors to take rectified actions. Because of the weak bargaining power in negotiation, forming coalitions with other powerful stakeholders is a common strategy adopted by NGOs (Frooman & Murrel, 2003). Frooman and Murrell (2005)'s model states that NGOs tend to pursue indirect strategies since the target organizations are often not dependent on NGOs' resources. Sometimes indirect influence may be more effective than direct strategy when the influencing targets have no dependency on the NGOs and the communication channel is absent (Frooman, 1999). Through allying with powerful stakeholders, NGOs can obtain the power to exert and aggressively propose their legitimate and urgent requests. The empirical evidence in this research shows that NGOs adopt direct coercive strategy to push when they hold legitimacy and urgency on their advocacy.

7.3.3   Governments

Government is the most powerful stakeholder in regulating the market and sanctioning irresponsible behaviors. The obligations to safeguard public wellness are embedded in the legitimacy of governmental departments through institutionalization. Therefore, governments have authorized right and power to use aggressive strategies, such as legalization and regulations to enforce necessary measures to meet at least the bottom lines, for example, mandatory environmental and social assessment and noise provision hours.

Besides legislation, another important influence of governments is to coordinate multiple stakeholders' interests and demands, and balance the conflicting benefits. Governments can adopt cooperative strategies with the public and communities to alleviate the conflicts. Compensations and intermediation are normally the ways that government departments use to pacify communities and local residents for disturbing their lives by the construction projects. Government departments hold public hearings and consult community representatives to ensure the efficient communications of each party's demands. But conflicts still happen in the whole life cycle of construction projects; governments need to respond to public complaints, investigate the situations, negotiate with different parties, intermediate and resolve the tensions.

Construction projects, especially in urban areas inevitably generate impacts on local lives, both positively and negatively. In the short run, the negative externalities can cause severe conflicts with local residents. However, in view of the long-term urbanization and development, construction projects may bring enormous economic and social benefits. One of the key roles of governments is to ensure the private companies to build the projects in a way that creates shared values instead of maximization of capital returns.

7. 3. 4   End users

Purchase of end users of construction projects is an important part of influencing PSR. End users can raise the motivation of both developers and main contractors to incorporate socially responsible features into their products. Their demands will become the motivations for developers to incorporate the social responsibility into project design, and transfer to contractor and subcontractors in construction supply chain. For example, in the interview, a client of a famous bank required the builder to construct their headquarter building that adhered to a certain green-building standard. Also, a tenant asked the real estate company to provide the green-building stars certificate when they decided to rent their houses.

Sometimes if the companies' irresponsible behaviors are severe, aggressive strategies like protests and boycott will be adopted by consumers. In construction projects, if the projects cause serious pollutions and have bad reputations, end users can exert the influence by refusing to buy or rent the building.

7. 3. 5   Developers and investors

Developers and investors possess the most significant resources; they have the power advantage to manipulate the behaviors of contractors and subcontractors to follow their socially responsible initiatives. By using financial power, they can easily drive contractors to implement environmental design or waste controls in projects by listing the issues in investment criteria or showing interests in related issues. For getting the contracts or building good relationships with upper echelons, the contractors are very likely to put developers' SR visions into their priority. When confronting urgent issues, for example, contractors conduct misconduct or cause consequences that may harm the socially responsible image of the developers, developers and investors can use the aggressive strategy of withholding the payment to force their contractors and subcontractors to change the unsatisfied situations.

7.3.6   Main contractors

Main contractors dominate the implementation of most of the social responsibility tasks in the construction execution process because they are at the position to control the overall construction process. One strategy to influence other companies is through sourcing and procurement in the supply chain. Subcontractors who can incorporate social responsibility criteria into their products, in return can gain the competitiveness in main contractors' selecting pool. In this way the social responsibility commitments are diffused in the supply chain echelons in the industry.

Because of the increasingly networked society, partnerships become an important consideration of corporations. Subcontractors and suppliers are keen on maintaining good relationships with main contractors, so they would like to follow their social responsibility practices and visions. This is also one of the strategies that contractor companies use to influence their lower echelons to follow their initiative. It is a rational choice because both parties, including the buyers and sellers, can gain benefit from the relationships in the long run.

Main contractors have power to coordinate different parties in construction execution process. For example, when they receive a request from the society, they can call for support from all the other stakeholders by using their superior mobilization ability in projects. For example, one contractor company received a letter from a foundation for supporting poor families with kidney disease. They called for a fund-raising and gathered the money required in a very short time. Big companies like main contractors usually receive many requests from NGOs and the public, so they know well about the social needs. By using their influences, they can easily appeal support and coordinate a collaboration of multiple stakeholders.

Construction projects have inevitable disturbances on local environment, sometimes internal stakeholders also need the understanding and cooperation from the community. Constructors need to get "license to build" from the local residents. Developers are the ones that should obtain such legitimacy, but contractors are often the ones that face pressures of project delay or cost overrun. Therefore, many contractors use cooperative strategies, such as site exhibition and community engagement activities to communicate and get along with local people. By organizing these activities, contractors deliver the information on project objectives and potential benefits that the projects will bring to the local environment and economy, and the measures they are undertaking to guarantee safety, health and environmental protection for local people. For example, a contractor collaborated with local kindergarten on organizing an activity to let the children draw on the fencing walls around the construction sites.

Also, main contractors sometimes confront some complaints about their workers' abusive behaviors and damages to environment during their off-hours. For example, one contractor company received complaint calls and letters about the workers breaking public facilities and harassing local residents. Contractors immediately adopted an aggressive way to stop such harassment by calling help from the police station.

7.3.7 Consultants

Consultants possess professional knowledge and management experiences to help companies to carry out their SR visions. In order to persuade their clients, cooperative tactics, such as professional advice and demonstrating the potential financial returns and cost benefits, are often adopted by consultants to promote innovative social responsibility techniques and measures.

Sometimes consultants serve in projects as developers or government agents, so they are vested with the legitimacy to ensure other project participants follow the social responsibility standards. Strategies like providing written instructions and monitoring the project progress were used to accomplish this mission.

7.3.8   Subcontractors and employees

Subcontractors and suppliers have rarely focused on their social responsibility in the past. However, in recent years, governments and the public began to realize that they are the sources of the main carbon footprints. The social responsibility performance of cement and steel companies became more and more relevant in public views. Especially when main contractor expresses their attention on environmental and social issues, the subcontractors and suppliers are likely to follow.

Employees are also a very special population in PSR. They are both the implementor and object of companies' social responsibility visions and strategies. It was found from the interviews that employees' organizational commitments can be increased by involving in their companies' social responsibility programs. Their attitudes can be influenced by the organizational culture and leadership's preference. Employees show more loyalty to the company by following the social responsibility initiatives if companies establish a culture to give back to society.

7.4   Summary of the interview findings

7.4.1   Stakeholder influencing strategies and tactics

From the findings of interview data analysis, governments, developers, and main contractors were the three most powerful stakeholders on social responsibility tasks, while other stakeholders including district councils (representative of communities and the public), consultants, NGOs, and end users, were relatively powerless. However, power only determines the capacity to influence, whilst the behavioral strategies and tactics that stakeholders take to influence are critical to the success of the implementation of PSR. This chapter adopted Co and Barro (2009)'s classification to summarize stakeholders' influencing strategies and tactics: 1) aggressive strategies in coercive manner to change targets' behaviors by threatening to decrease benefits or increase cost; 2) cooperative strategies in reciprocal manner to change targets' behaviors by committing to bring benefits or decrease cost.

The strategies and tactics adopted by the internal and external stakeholders were organized in terms of stakeholder groups: 1) external stakeholders including communities and the public, NGOs, and governments; 2) internal stakeholders including end users, developers and investors, main contractors, consultants, and subcontractors and employees. Table 7-2 shows a summary of all the identified influence strategies and tactics on PSR.

Table 7-2 also shows the targets of each stakeholder's influences, reflecting the influence relationships between stakeholders that drive PSR implementation. As it was found in the questionnaire, the most powerful one among the external stakeholders is governments. Governments have power to set the social responsibility standards in projects to influence the behaviors of developers and contractors; meanwhile they also mediate and negotiate with communities and the public. Influences of communities and the public (district councils) are often targeted on the three core stakeholders, which are governments, contractors, and developers. Besides, NGOs' influences on the one hand point to the three core stakeholders, on the other hand point to communities and the public. To summarize, the external influences mostly directed to the three core stakeholders: governments, developers, and contractors. Among the internal stakeholders, the influence flows mostly occur downward the construction supply chain. End users use purchase to drive developers and investors to implement social responsibility. Developers use contracts and tendering documents to influence main contractors and consultants. How these complex internal and external influence flows form a holistic network structure will be further discussed in the next section.

Table 7-2   Stakeholder influencing strategies and tactics induced from the interviews

	Stakeholder	Target	Aggressive	Cooperative
External stakeholders	Communities and the public	Governments Developers and investors Main contractors	Hotline, complain	Multi-party meeting
	NGOs	Governments Developers and investors Main contractors Communities and the public	Protest, pressure, ally	Lobby, letter, email, visit, training, advice, industry initiatives, forum
	Governments	Developers and investors Main contractors Communities and the public	Legalize, regulate	Stakeholder platform, mediation, negotiation, compensation, balancing conflicting interests
Internal stakeholders	Developers and investors	Main contractors Consultants	Payment withholding	Selecting criteria, tendering requirements
	Main contractors	Subcontractors and workers	Contract conditions, external force	Green procurement, partnering, cultural influence, community engagement, donation raise
	Consultants	Main contractors Developers and investors	Providing written instructions, monitor	Technical advice, financial evaluation
	End users	Developers and investors	Refusing to buy or rent	Demands

7. 4. 2   Network structure of stakeholder inter-influence

Figure 7-2 shows the holistic network structures of the stakeholder interinfluences identified from the interviews. Based on the unique influences, the stakeholders were further categorized into eight groups, including the claimant, the promoter, the regulator, the motivator, the initiator, the advisor, the operator, and the follower. Unlike the traditional stakeholder classifications, this stakeholder map provides the clarified roles and responsibilities of stakeholders specifically in implementing PSR. It shows a holistic view of the diffusion of social responsibility values among internal and external stakeholders.

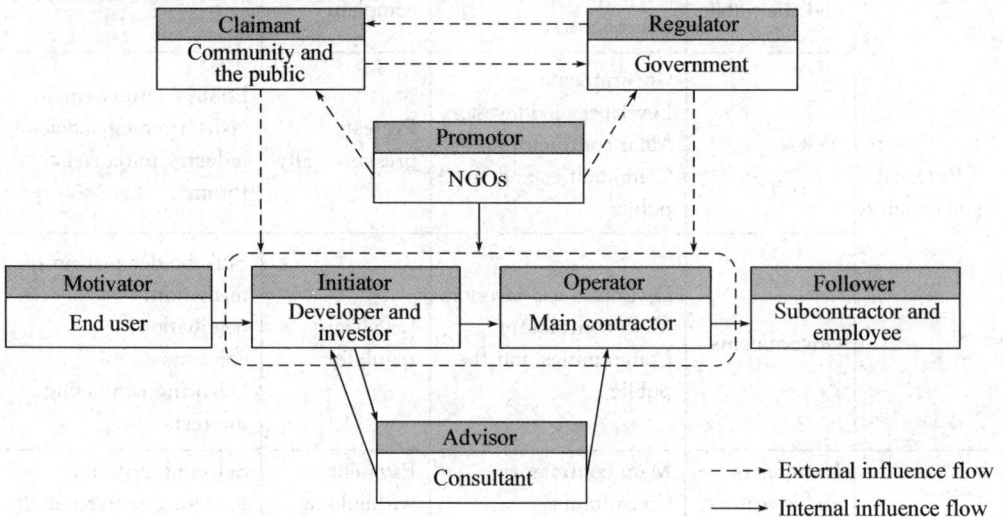

Figure 7-2   Stakeholder influence map in implementing PSR.

Firstly, among the external stakeholders, communities and the public are the claimants in PSR implementation. They can be the effected groups and also have legitimacy to raise demands to governments and project leaders about their concerned social or environmental issues. The role that NGOs play is the promotor. It is corroborated by Deegan and Blomquist (2006) that NGOs are one of the important sources of pressure to promote environmental and social practices. On legitimate and urgent issues, NGOs can use aggressive strategies, such as protests or coalition, to put pressures on the related stakeholders to respond to the problems caused by projects. It is also supported by Hendry

(2005) that protests and complaints are direct strategies that NGOs commonly used to draw immediate attention. The experiment of Frooman and Murrel (2003) also adds evidence that environmental organizations are more inclined to use ally as indirect influence strategy due to the lack of efficient resources. When NGOs intend to raise their initiatives that need other stakeholders to provide resources, cooperative tactics like lobby, letter, email, visits are often adopted. Hendry (2005) indicates that NGOs often pursue lobby with all other non-lobbying tactics because it is a non-specific and soft strategy to influence the targets. The expertise and specialized skills held by NGOs are critical to developers especially when these resources are costly, inefficient, and time-consuming from external sources (Peloza & Falkenberg, 2009). NGOs also launch industry initiatives and value transmission programs regularly to encourage proactive engagement in social responsibility tasks. Deegan and Blomquist (2006) also conclude that initiatives launched by NGOs can drive the industry to revise codes of conduct as well as influence their sustainable reporting behaviors. In addition, NGOs can organize forums or education programs to transmit social responsibility knowledge and value to community and the public to motivate them to defend the environment and society. Governments are the regulators to legalize the practicable proposals, enact regulations, and set benchmarks. Governments also have the authorized power to provide incentive policies, such as tax reduction and green labels, to drive project leaders to consider social responsibility tasks. Actually in most times, governments act as conflict resolvers instead of initiating social responsibility tasks (Olander, 2007). Governments need to coordinate with communities and the public to facilitate stakeholder communication, mediate conflicting interests, compensate and pacify the affected residents.

The influences among internal stakeholders flow along the construction supply chain. First, end user is the motivator. The demands of end users are the original driving force of PSR implementation. End customers' demands of the information on sustainability, green certificate, and report for social responsibility practices can directly attract companies' reactions (Henriques & Sharma, 2005). When come across urgent issues, end users can also coerce developers to change their misconduct by refusing to buy or rent the buildings. Investors and developers play the role of the initiator. In order to gain competitiveness, developers will incorporate social responsibility features into project planning, and diffuse commitments to contractors and subcontractors. The general tactic they often adopt is putting their requirements in selecting criteria or tendering documents. When contractors fail to fulfil these requirements, developers have the legitimacy to withhold payments or give sanctions based on consented contract conditions. Boyd et al. (2007) also document such tactics that buyers use to influence their suppliers, including requesting green labels or environmental standards. In the influence between developers and main contractors, consultants act as the advisor to propose social responsibility plans to their clients and supervise main contractors to implement them. Consultants have professional experiences and knowledge on issues like green materials and sustainable technics. They can influence by convincing developers and investors to peruse such innovative approaches by demonstrating the technical feasibility, the benefits to society and environment, and the estimated returns and cost savings. Othman (2009) also highlights the responsibility of consultants to provide successful cases to convince their clients that social responsibility programs can be achieved within their cost planning. Consultants are authorized with legitimacy to monitor the implementation of social responsibility tasks in projects. Main contractors, as the operators of social responsibility collaboration, can coordinate resources for implementing the social responsibility tasks. Main contractors use procurement strategies and partnerships to motivate subcontractors to provide social responsibility materials or services. Social responsibility in procurement behaviors means not only the environmental features of the production, but also other social goals, such as human right, labor protection, community issues, should also be addressed (Maignan et al., 2002). In addition, contractors can also organize voluntary social services and build culture to give back to society, in order to let employees participate in PSR implementation.

7. 4. 3　Potential determinants of stakeholder influencing strategies

The existing research states that the factor that can determine the choice of coercive or soft influence strategies is the degree of power imbalance (Frooman, 1999; Somech & Drach-Zahavy, 2002). It was found in the interviews that all stakeholders, no matter powerful or not, adopted both aggressive and cooperative strategies in different occasions to influence in terms of their concerned PSR issues. For example, governments were identified as the most powerful stakeholders from the questionnaire. According to Frooman (1999), powerful stakeholders tend to adopt coercive strategies and use their power to force others. However, it was found in the interviews that cooperative strategies were employed most frequently, such as incentive policies, stakeholder communications, and mediations between community and project leaders. The reason may be that social responsibility had the intrinsic nature of voluntariness and altruism. When stakeholders want to influence others to follow their good will, they imply the inter-dependence, trust, and sharing of the understanding that collaboration will bring benefits to all. As found in this research, end users and NGOs were the most powerless stakeholders, while aggressive strategies were also used from time to time, especially when their benefits were at risks or major threats. It leads to the question that if power is not the only determinant, then what else can be the factor that leads stakeholders to choose aggressive rather than cooperative strategies?

Tsai et al. (2005) find that institutional legitimacy is also an important determinant that decides their influence strategies. They point out that when firms' actions have high legitimacy that meets social norms and expectations, most stakeholders tend to adopt compromise or conformity instead of coercive strategies. In addition, it is found in the interviews that the degree of urgency of the issues concerned by stakeholders is also an important attribute. Aggressive strategies are often adopted by stakeholders when the issues are perceived as urgent (Co & Barro, 2009). In Mitchell's salience model, urgency is reflected on two dimensions: 1) whether the issue is time sensitive; 2) whether the issue is considered critical by the stakeholder.

It is plausible to assume that power can only imply the ability of stakeholders to influence. Nevertheless, legitimacy and urgency perceived by stakeholders related to the targeted issues are significant attributes that determine what strategies stakeholders may use to exert influences. This conclusion can be supported by (Co & Barro, 2009) that stakeholders tend to choose aggressive strategies, with the sense of urgency on the issues, difficulty in conveying legitimacy, and lack of faith that all stakeholders will do their share. By contrast, stakeholders can choose cooperative strategies when they are mutually dependent, share the urgency to collaborate and understand that the collaboration will bring benefits to all. According to Mitchell et al. (1997), the three attributes, power, legitimacy, and urgency, are interrelated and collectively form the salience of stakeholders. Stakeholder legitimacy can be gained by seizing stakeholder power perceived by the target organization, as well as putting forward urgent and critical issues. When considering whether or not a stakeholder may take aggressive strategy in construction projects to influence on PSR issues, rather than power, legitimacy and urgency are two important factors to evaluate.

7.5   Summary of the chapter

This chapter summarized multiple stakeholders' influence strategies in driving the implementation of PSR based on the analysis of interview data. The summary table provided a glimpse of how stakeholders use their power to influence each other in terms of social and environmental concerns. A holistic map depicting how the influence flows among internal and external stakeholders also enriched the knowledge on how SR values diffuse in construction projects and what specific roles different stakeholders play. The findings in this chapter provided a reference for both scholars and practitioners to better understand the mechanism of PSR implementation in a complex stakeholder environment. In a networked society, we often say that no single organization or individual could take all of the responsibilities. Only through effective collaborations with a well-informed skeleton, the socially responsible efforts could bring favorable outcomes. For different groups of interests, this chapter can provide some practical examples for practitioners to exert their legitimate wills. More importantly, project managers who want to prevent potential aggressiveness of stakeholders can use this finding to evaluate multiple stakeholders' demands and design strategies to respond.

Chapter 8
Management Framework for
PSR Implementation

8.1 Need for developing a PSR management framework

The previous chapters introduced stakeholders' capacity, willingness, and approaches in PSR implementation. However, those findings had a general basis. Like project management, PSR implementation is also a unique mission. There are different SRTs and diverse stakeholder capacities for each particular project. How can project managers make decisions and design management procedures based on a clear understanding of their project stakeholders? How can government agencies coordinate multiple sectors and resources to realize PSR performance? These are the questions that cannot be answered by survey data.

Design science is to develop solutions to management problems by employing knowledge or empirical evidence in real situations. This chapter develops a management framework to collect project information about SRTs and stakeholder in projects, and then analyzes the information for providing decision support for project managers and coordinators in PSR implementation. The knowledge generated from the investigation was used to craft the key evaluations in the management framework. One consideration is who should engage in implementing the SRTs. The analysis of interest and power shows that the engagement of stakeholders is determined by both stakeholder's capacity to resolve the issue and its willingness to do it. Therefore, the framework needs to evaluate stakeholders' power and interests in different SRTs. The other consideration is to help project managers or governors to identify potential aggressive strategies that stakeholders may take to influence, and therefore, they can prepare in advance, reach out for communication, and allocate resources to resolve the concerns or problems. According to the interview survey, this part needs to evaluate stakeholders' urgency and legitimacy towards the related issues. In this chapter, a management framework will be developed with detailed procedures of how managers could incorporate these two considerations and make better decisions.

8.2   Stakeholder power index

For designing an operational way to determine stakeholders' engagement levels, the stakeholder power-interest index (SPI) is designed as a quantifiable attribute. According to the findings in chapter 6, stakeholder engagement levels in PSR implementation are determined by both stakeholder's power and interest in the issues. Here I adopt the risk evaluation formula to express this compound effect of power and interest. In risk management, risks are assessed by the product of potential impacts and probabilities. In this study, power is a stakeholder's capability and resources to carry out a social responsibility task, while stakeholder interest is the willingness of stakeholders to engage. Therefore, this study designed an index that combined power and interest to determine stakeholders' levels of engagement in PSR. Designing stakeholder power index to evaluate their capability to influence has been employed in previous research. Bourne and Walker (2005) propose a vested interest impacts index to evaluate stakeholders' potential influences on projects. Olander (2007) also calculates the product of stakeholders' interest and power to assess stakeholders' impact levels. This study proposed Stakeholder Power Index (SPI), which is the geometric mean of power and interest minus the geometric mean of stakeholders' average power and interest in the target project. This standard version of power index could support a cross-project and cross-stage comparison. The formula of SPI is as follows:

$$SPI_{ij} = \sqrt{\frac{(pwr)_{ij} \times (int)_{ij}}{5 \times 5}} - \sqrt{\frac{\sum_{i=1}^{n} (pwr)_{ij}}{n} \times \frac{\sum_{i=1}^{n} (int)_{ij}}{n}}$$

SPI_{ij} stands for the SPI of the stakeholder i over the SRT j; $(pwr)_{ij}$ is the power of the stakeholder i has over the SRT j; and $(int)_{ij}$ is the extent of stakeholder i's interest of the stakeholder i has on the SRT j. n is the total number of the related stakeholders.

If $SPI_{ij} > 0$, it means that stakeholder i has high power index, therefore having relatively high interest and power on the SRT j.

If $SPI_{ij} = 0$, it shows that the stakeholder i has the average power index with moderate power and interest on the SRT j;

If $SPI_{ij} < 0$, it means that the stakeholder i has low power index, therefore having limited interest and power on the SRT j.

According to the range of the SPI, stakeholders engagement levels can be located on a continuum from proactive engagement to reactive engagement (see figure 8-1), adapting from Clarkson (1995)'s scale of proactive-reactive engagement in social responsibility. Stakeholders having a high SPI means that the stakeholder has both high probabilities and capacities to implement the SRT. Therefore, they locate at the right end of the continuum as proactive engagement. The proactive engagement informs that stakeholders have active attitudes and leading responsibilities on the social responsibility tasks. Actions are suggested including putting forward initiatives, taking a leadership role, organizing stakeholder meetings, making implementation plans, gathering necessary resources, supervising the implementation process, and examining the outcomes. Stakeholders' low SPIs mean that the stakeholder has lower willingness and abilities to carry out the task. These stakeholders fall into the other end of the continuum as reactive engagement. Actions are suggested, such as responding to others' SR appeals, following instructions, collaborating with other companies, providing necessary support, keeping open communications, maintaining stakeholder relationships, and giving feedback. However, even when a stakeholder is labeled as reactive engagement, it does not mean that these stakeholders have no value to motivate. Sometimes, it also reflects that the motivations for these stakeholders are not sufficient to raise their willingness to be involved in PSR implementation. Therefore the decision support needs to consider realistic situations.

SPI$<$0   SPI$>$0

Reactive engagement	Proactive engagement
Respond to the appeals	Raise the initiatives
Follow the arrangement	Take the leadership
Prepare to cooperate	Organize stakeholder meetings
Provide necessary resources	Seek support
Keep communications	Make systematic plans
Maintain relationships	Gather necessary resources
Give feedbacks	Supervise the process
...	Examine the outcomes
	...

Figure 8-1   The continuum of reactive-proactive stakeholder engagement.

8.3   Stakeholder influence index

By evaluating stakeholders' SPI, we can provide solutions to how stakeholders

can be engaged. However, aggressive strategies of stakeholders is an important
risk threatening the continuity of project process. Therefore, there exists a need
to evaluate the probability of a stakeholder choosing to use an aggressive strategy
to exert influences. According to the main results in chapter 7, a stakeholder's
choice of either cooperative or aggressive strategy pertaining to their concerns
depends mostly on the urgency of the issue, as well as the legitimacy that
stakeholders hold to influence. Therefore, in the management framework, I
designed a stakeholder influence index (SII) as a combination of stakeholders'
perceived urgency and legitimacy over the issues, for evaluating the potentiality
of stakeholders to choose aggressive rather than cooperative influence strategies.

Similarly, SII was developed by integrating stakeholders' perceived legitimacy and
urgency on the identified SRTs. As it was discussed previously, the existing
research mostly uses power as the only determinant, while neglecting other
important factors. In institutional theory, legitimacy means the extent to which
the behaviors are accepted or expected by conventional social norms (Tsai et al. ,
2005). In this book, stakeholder legitimacy means the rationality that
stakeholders have to raise, initiate, or implement the PSR. Urgency stands for
the time-sensitivity and criticality of the problems perceived by the stakeholders
(Mitchell et al. , 1997). Therefore, the value of SII is evaluated based on: 1) the
degree of legitimacy held by the stakeholder to drive the implementation of the
SRT; 2) the level of time-sensitivity and criticality perceived by the stakeholder.
The higher SII value shows higher possibility that stakeholders choose to adopt
an aggressive strategy.

The formula for the SII is presented as following:

$$SII_{ij} = \sqrt{\frac{(lgt)_{ij} \times (urg)_{ij}}{5 \times 5}} - \sqrt{\frac{\sum_{i=1}^{n}(lgt)_{ij}}{n} \times \frac{\sum_{i=1}^{n}(urg)_{ij}}{n}}{5 \times 5}}$$

SII_{ij} stands for the SII of the stakeholder i on the SRT j; $(lgt)_{ij}$ is the legitimacy of the stakeholder i has on the SRT j; and $(urg)_{ij}$ is the value of urgency of stakeholder i on the SRT j. n is the total number of the related stakeholders.

If $SII_{ij} > 0$, it means that stakeholder i has high influence index, therefore having relatively high legitimacy and urgency to implement the SRT j.

If $SII_{ij} = 0$, it shows that the stakeholder i has the average influence index with moderate legitimacy and urgency to implement the SRT j.

If $SII_{ij} < 0$, it represents that the stakeholder i has low influence index, therefore having under-average legitimacy and urgency on the SRT j.

According to the findings of the interviews, all stakeholders including the external and internal stakeholders can choose to use aggressive strategy and/or cooperative strategy. Aggressive strategy means to force targets in coercive manner to change their behaviors by threats, while cooperative strategy means to alter targets' behaviors in reciprocal manner by committing to bring benefits or decrease cost.

The value of SII helps to predict a stakeholder's influence strategy on the continuum from cooperative to aggressive strategies (see figure 8-2). A high SII value means that the stakeholders have more possibilities to adopt an aggressive strategy to force the target to respond to their concerns. A low SII value stands for stakeholders that would be more inclined to a cooperative and soft strategy to seek collaborations on realizing their SR visions. It is noteworthy that there are two characteristics of the stakeholder influencing strategy according to the interview findings: 1) most stakeholders tend to choose mixed strategies instead of any single kind (aggressive or cooperative), so SII determines the inclination of either aggressive or cooperative strategy; 2) cooperative strategy is practiced in more conditions compared to aggressiveness because SR means voluntary and discretional. Considering the findings of the interviews, in the management framework, only when SII is higher than a dangerous level, we say that the stakeholders may tend to adopt an aggressive strategy.

SII<0   SII>0

Cooperative strategy	Aggressive strategy
Stakeholder meetings; lobbying; letters or emails; advice; initiatives; value penetration; forum and trainings; incentive policy; mediation; compensation; negotiation; green procurement; partnering; donation raise	Complaining; protest; pressures; ally; legalization; regulation; money withholding; contract conditions; external force; providing written instructions; monitoring; refusing to buy or rent

Figure 8-2   The continuum of cooperative-aggressive influence strategy.

Aggressive strategy is not totally a negative thing that should be prevented. It is also one of the important driving forces in PSR implementation. When collusions that may cause serious harm to community or public wellness occur, an aggressive influence is essential to change project implementation back to the right track. On the one hand, the SII can be an alert system for project leaders to avoid potential aggressiveness. On the other hand, they should also take precautions and respond to stakeholders' urgent and legitimate claims. Therefore, when a high SII is identified, managers should not only take actions to cope with the risks, but also try to improve communication, enhance supervision, and ensure that projects are conducted in a socially responsible way. When a low SII is found, we say that stakeholders tend to adopt "soft" strategy, such as lobbying and meetings to exert their influences. Suggestions could be provided for managers to keep in good relationships with these stakeholders and provide necessary information.

8.4   Procedures of the management framework

Linking theoretical knowledge and professional practices in reality is essential to extending implications of theories (Montaño, 2012). In this study, the development of SPI and SII is based on the theoretical foundations found in empirical investigations. A management framework was then developed using SPI and SII as two quantifications to provide decision support for PSR implementation. As it has been discussed so far, the obstacles to PSR implementation are the complex stakeholders and unclarified roles and responsibilities. The management framework developed in this chapter aimed at providing a managerial solution. Managers or governors could make action plans based on the evaluation outcomes of SPI and SII.

All management, operations, and decision making in construction projects are conducted at two levels: the organizational and project levels. The management framework also provides separate modules for each level: 1) the organizational level, which evaluates SPI and SII of all involved stakeholders for the identified SRTs and provide action plans; 2) the project level, which depicts the overall collaborative structure among multiple stakeholders.

A design science approach was adopted for developing a generally applicable solution to problems under different conditions and individual backgrounds, based on problem-directed theories or experiences. Unlike the typical positivistic empirical methodology, design science strategy follows the "paradigms of practices" as the problem-solving roadmap. According to Van Strien (1997)'s regulative cycle for design science research, the management framework was developed containing five steps (see figure 8-3): 1) identification of problems, 2) diagnosis of the situation, 3) plan of actions, 4) intervention, 5) evaluation of new situations. Detailed instructions of each step are illustrated

The stakeholder collaboration framework on implementing social responsibility issues in construction projects

| STEP 1 Identification of problems | STEP 2 Diagnosis of the situation | STEP 3 Plan of actions | STEP 4 Implementations | STEP 5 Evaluations of new situations |

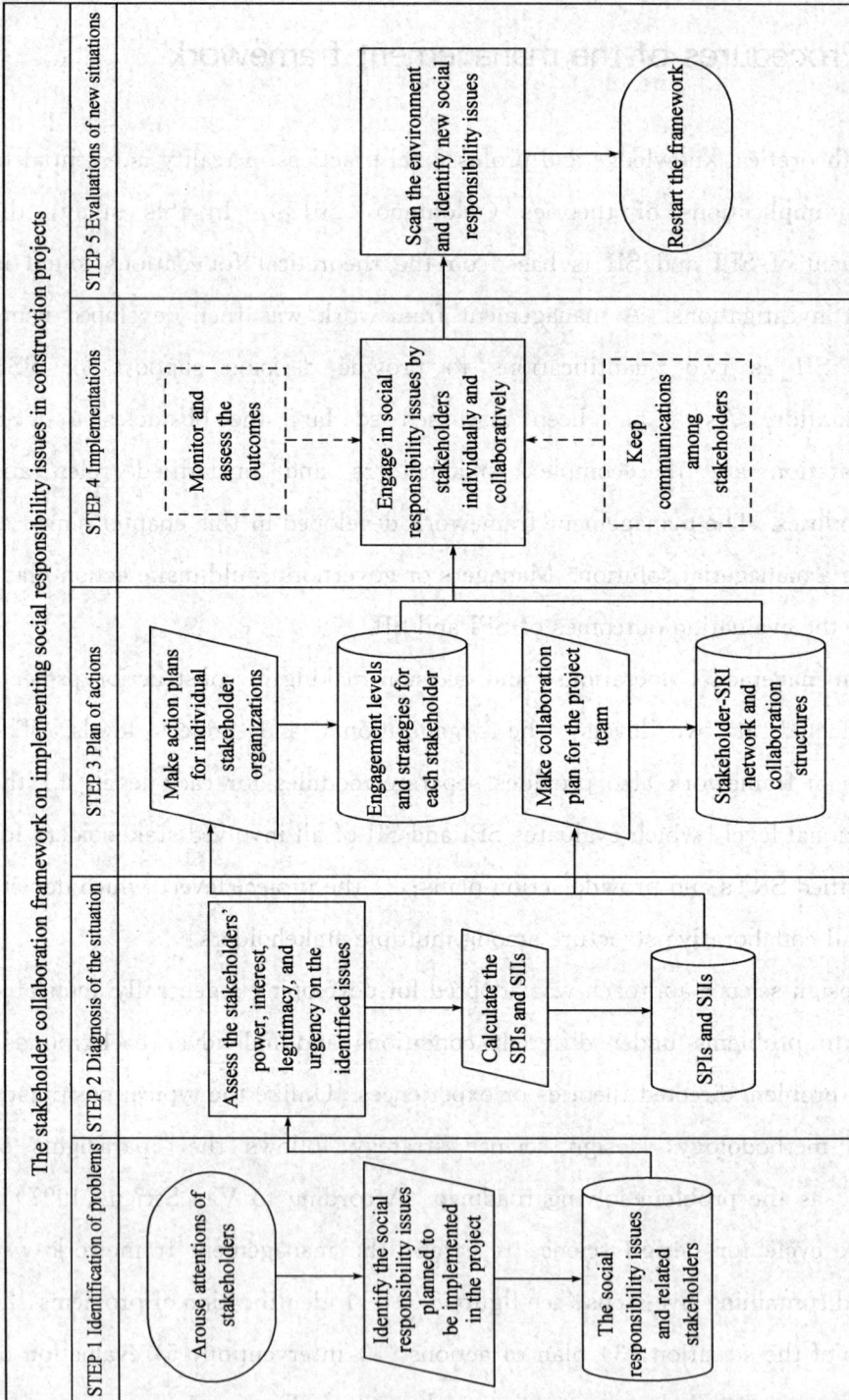

Figure 8-3 The stakeholder collaboration framework on social responsibility tasks.

in the following sections.

Step 1: Identification of problems

The first step is finding out the SRTs that are planned to be implemented in given projects. Two procedures are involved in this step:

  1) Arouse attention of related stakeholders.

  2) Identify the SRTs planned to be implemented in the project.

In this step, all project stakeholders especially the effected ones must be involved in collecting their demands and expectations about PSR. Social responsibility tasks are responding to the benefits of those "salient" stakeholders, such as the public, community, and employees. They usually are the ones whose benefits may be at risks of being overlooked or compromised in project decision making. Identification of the SRTs planned to be implemented is an important prequisite of following evaluations.

This procedure can be carried out during usual gatherings, such as project briefing, stakeholder meetings, management workshops, and public hearings. Therefore, this step can be embedded in the events when external and internal stakeholders are both involved. Conflicting interests among multiple stakeholders is the main difficulty. Achieving a balance of interests is the main purpose of this dialogue. Also, it is not easy for stakeholders to agree on the share of responsibilities and cost in PSR implementation. At this stage, we only encourage stakeholders to raise their concerns and requirements freely. Then according to the evaluation of stakeholders' multiple attributes, responsibilities can be then distributed by suggesting different actions or strategies.

Step 2: Diagnosis of the situations

This step is to estimate the stakeholders' attributes on the identified social responsibility tasks:

1) Assess the stakeholders' power, interest, legitimacy, and urgency over the SRTs.

2) Calculate stakeholders' SPIs and SIIs.

The assessment can be made through objective evaluations conducted by a third party, or through subjective reflections of the stakeholders themselves. In the management framework, the former option is suggested because some attributes like interest and power can have indispensable bias if evaluated by self-reports. However, if an objective third party is not easy to find, managers can also design and distribute questionnaire with a list of identified SRTs to all related stakeholder representatives. The stakeholder representatives can evaluate their perceived interest, power, legitimacy, and urgency on the listed social responsibility tasks (sample of the questionnaire see Appendix E).

It is noteworthy that the genuineness and accuracy of assessment results are essential. Some stakeholders with reluctant attitudes may provide inaccurate answers; therefore, measures should be taken to ensure the data validity. First, before filling the questionnaire, it should be explained to the stakeholders that the information is only for internal managerial and administrative purposes, no compulsory works will be forced. It should also be addressed that the aim of the framework is to improve overall social performance of the project, which will benefit all stakeholders and ensure the success of project objectives in the long run. Nevertheless, some powerful stakeholders can be reluctant because they are clear that many of the SRTs should be carried on their shoulders. In this way, it is important to motivate them by showing that the framework is an effective way to cope with potential risks and conflicts that may have serious impacts on project goals. In this step, managers fostering a mutual trust and beneficial environment can help stakeholders provide more genuine information.

The wording in assessments should avoid using confusing academic terminologies; by contrast, the use of daily language is preferred to enhance the intelligibility. To ask stakeholders' power, the question is "do you think your organization can influence the following issues?" Power is sometimes associated with aggressive and negative connotations, so we should be very cautious about using it. To assess stakeholders' interest, we can directly ask "to what extent do you think your organization is interested in implementing the social responsibility issue?" As for legitimacy and urgency, the questions can be "do you think your organization should raise the issue?" and "to what extent do you think the issue is urgent?"

Also, during the assessment, increasing the number of respondents in each stakeholder organization can also increase the data reliability. Respondents are those who can be representative in the organizations or those who are familiar with related practices or policies. For construction organizations, participants can be project managers, site supervisors, managers in HSE, sustainability, public relations, etc. As for public institutions, participants can be community committee members, NGO directors, government officials, etc. After assessment, the SPIs and SIIs on the identified SRTs will be calculated using the formula proposed in Section 8. 2 and 8. 3.

Step 3: Plan of actions

Next stage is to design action plans for stakeholders to be engaged in PSR according to their SPIs and SIIs.

1) Make action plans for individual stakeholders.

2) Make collaboration plan for the project team.

For each stakeholder, an action plan for how to engage in each social responsibility task will be provided. The action plan can help the leaders to find priorities and directions in driving PSR performance, as well as allocate limited resources in an optimal way. The action plans involve which SRTs stakeholder should put most of the resources on to bring best effect, and which SRTs should be addressed in an urgent schedule.

At the project level, a network depicting how stakeholders should be engaged in each SRT is provided at this stage. Many social network software and plug-in programs can assist the visualization of the network. The network nodes are the identified SRTs and related stakeholders. The links are weighted lines of stakeholders' SPIs toward the SRTs. The network structures provide a holistic map for project managers to understand stakeholder collaborative groups for different SRTs. The centralities of nodes provide information on stakeholders' leading or following roles in collaboration groups. Managers could use the map to make a collaboration plan for each SRT according to the cluster of stakeholders linked to it and stakeholders' different roles (leading or following). Also, the colors of the links provide a map of potentiality of an aggressive influence from the linked stakeholder over the linked issue. Managers could use this information to find priorities and different collaborative strategies to implement the identified SRTs and improve PSR performance.

Step 4: Implementation of SRTs

The action plans will be sent to each stakeholder and manager to carry out the identified SRTs at both organizational and project levels.

For each stakeholder, he or she can easily find out which SRT should be put in priority. Stakeholders can allocate resources in a strategic way. The abstract concept of PSR is transcribed into concrete actions and practices. From this view, the framework can support the decision making on what they should do in project SR implementation. For project managers, the action plan provides a visualized map of complex stakeholder relationships and the SRTs planned to be carried out. It can be used as a map to coordinate stakeholders to build up small collaborative team for effective communication and implementation. Stakeholders in a collaborative team would be encouraged to communicate closely and support complementary resources to collectively implement the SRTs. The network also suggests the role of each stakeholder in the small collaborative team.

Continuous monitoring and communication are necessary at the implementation stage. Effects of the framework depend on how well the PSR action plans are communicated to the related stakeholders and how well these actions are actually carried out. For each involved stakeholder, communications about the progress and obstacles are as important as the implementation. Companies should be encouraged to use public media, periodical reports, Internet, and exhibitions to publicize their efforts and outcomes on the assigned SRTs. The public sector stakeholders need to be actively involved in monitoring and feedback. Corporate social responsibility behaviors can be reinforced by public recognition and feedback. In addition, positive outcomes of stakeholders' joint efforts can enhance future communications. Instead of interventions, this framework is more of a mutual support process among stakeholders. From the framework, stakeholders can identify the real demands of the local community or broader society and then seek to develop an optimal plan to create shared values. Stakeholders can work together to maintain effective communications, resource exchanges, and continuing feedback.

Step 5: Evaluations of new situations

PSR is a continuous task and has emerging tasks at project stage. Therefore, the last stages of the framework is to continuously scan for new SRTs over the project life cycle.

Given the dynamic project environment and changing stakeholder structures, evaluation of the new situations should be carried out during the projects to identify emerging issues and tasks that demand response. Sustaining attention on PSR can effectively improve social performance of the project. Thus, instead of only focusing on planning and design stage, the framework should be implemented in a spiral throughout the entire project life cycle.

8.5 Characteristics of the management framework

The management framework addressed the obstacles to stakeholder collaboration in PSR implementation identified in section 2. 3. The first obstacle is that stakeholders have conflicting interests; it is difficult for them to share critical resources to implement PSR. The framework provides a mechanism for collective responsibility, in which PSR is no longer taken by any single organization. The action plans clarify stakeholders' roles and responsibilities. Since PSR is a term with discretion and vagueness, which brings space for reluctance and buck-passing, the management framework brings a clearer map of what should be practiced and how. It also reminds stakeholders of putting limited resources in the tasks that they hold both power and interests. In this way, stakeholders understand well about their roles and responsibilities. The conflicting interests can be balanced if stakeholders could build up trust and common goals through the framework procedures. Even though self-efficient stakeholders wouldn't voluntarily engage themselves, the framework also has the purpose to reinforce the awareness of the effected stakeholders to use their power to put pressures.

The second obstacle identified to implementing PSR is the complicated power structures and interactions of stakeholders. The collaboration plans and stakeholder-SRT network provide a holistic visualization and guidance for managers to coordinate complex relationships. Social network is a graph theory that is usually used to visualize and analyze complex relational structures. By using a two-mode network visualization and centrality measures, complicated stakeholder power structures towards SRTs can be integrated and depicted on one map, providing coordination plans for stakeholder collaboration.

One primary problem identified in the literature is the ignorance of the imbalanced power and responsibility, as well as the lack of managerial tools to direct stakeholder interactions. The management framework developed in this chapter addresses precisely this gap, by providing a solution to coordinate stakeholder interactions to collaboratively implement PSR. By assessing stakeholders' power/interest/urgency/legitimacy, the framework could generate suggestions for each stakeholder to use different influence and take actions to realize the balance of power and responsibility. The framework provides a multi-level collaborative management tool to facilitate stakeholder collaboration in complicated and dynamic power structures.

8.6   Comparisons with other stakeholder tools

8.6.1   Mitchell's salience model

The three-attribute stakeholder salience model of Mitchell et al. (1997) was introduced in details in literature review. As described in figure 4-1, stakeholders can be categorized into seven groups using three attributes: power, urgency, and legitimacy. Mitchell's model has been broadly adopted by researchers and practitioners. It provides an effective tool to build strategies to maximize satisfactions of stakeholders. The three-attribute model has its theoretical significance for the construction of stakeholder salience concept. However, there exist some deficiencies. First, the analysis perspective is from the organizational perspective to craft responsive strategies instead of focusing on stakeholder-stakeholder interactions. The management framework developed in this chapter aims not only at responding to stakeholders for their satisfactions, but also at clarifying structures of stakeholder interactions to joint PSR implementation. Second, the use of attributes in Mitchell's model is binary, either has or does not have power, legitimacy or urgency, giving no distinction between one with a lot of salience and the other with little salience (Mainardes et al. , 2012). To overcome this shortfall, the framework develops two quantifiable measures, which are SPI and SII. Third, the analysis of stakeholders' attributes is based on general evaluations in Mitchell's model, ignoring stakeholder dynamics. In the framework, stakeholders' attributes are assessed based on the specific contexts of a certain SRT. Therefore, the management framework extends traditional general stakeholder management to an issue-focused stakeholder management arena.

8. 6. 2　Power/interest matrix

Power/interest matrix is a graphic visualization tool for categorizing stakeholders based on two attributes, power and interest, which is broadly adopted by managers in practical stakeholder management. Mendelow (1981) develops a matrix model with two dimensions: stakeholders' dynamism and power. Stakeholders fall into four quadrants that require different coping strategies, from continuous scanning, irregular scanning, periodic scanning, to no scanning. Savage et al. (1991) use stakeholders' potential to threaten or cooperate with organizations as two axes to design a matrix model that categorizes stakeholders into four types: collaborate, supportive, non-supportive, and marginal. The most widely used matrix tool for stakeholder management is the power/interest matrix proposed by Scholes and Johnson (2002). Olander and Landin (2005) introduce the power/interest matrix to project management for project managers making corresponding stakeholder management strategies. As it is shown in figure 8-4, stakeholders can be grouped into four categories based on their power and interest. The major flaw of this model is that by this simple classification, the effected stakeholders, such as communities, the public, and NGOs, will be gradually marginalized by project management because they have less power but high interest in the projects. In this matrix, these stakeholders are suggested to project managers to keep them informed rather than pay attention to their demands. The original purpose of this model is improving companies' management against risks caused by stakeholders. By using this matrix, the concerns of powerless stakeholders will not be addressed because they are labelled as less threatening to the project objectives. The framework developed in this study focuses on PSR; therefore I want to provide a non-purely-managerial tool, which also allows powerless stakeholders to involve in the decision making, and empowers them with certain influence strategies. Another defect is that in the matrix model, the evaluations of stakeholders' attributes are based on absolute value rather than relative value. Absolute value is simpler for calculation, but it is insufficient in cross-case comparisons because the ranges of power/interest value vary in different cases. The SPI and SII formula developed in this book use standardized value, so it creates a platform for cross-project comparisons.

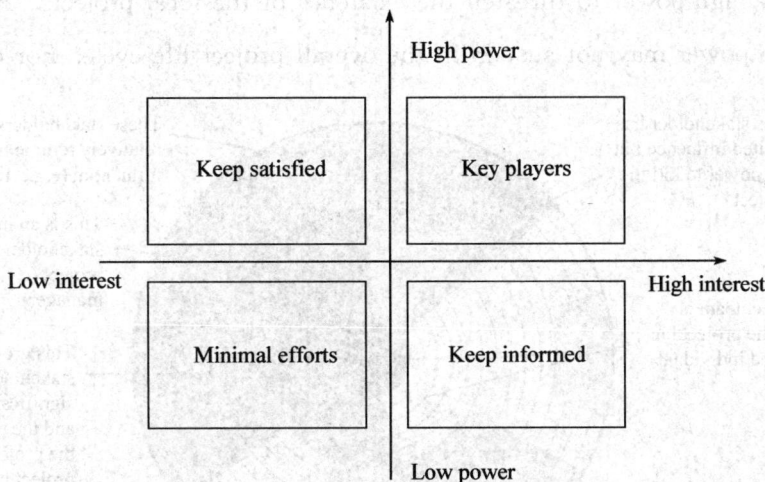

Figure 8-4   The stakeholder power/interest matrix

(Source: Olander & Landin, 2005, 322)

8.6.3   Stakeholder circle

Bourne and Walker (2005) develop the stakeholder circle to visualize stakeholders' influences on project success or failure through five steps: identify, prioritize, visualize, engage, and monitor. The stakeholder circle was registered as a patent and has been tested and refined based on several case studies and received positive feedback (Bourne & Walker, 2006, 2008). This model employs three stakeholder attributes to evaluate stakeholder influences, including urgency, power, and proximity of stakeholder-project relationships. A radial circle depicting all stakeholder influences on the project shows the stakeholders' scope of influences, degree of influences, and the distance of influences (see figure 8-5 for the sample of stakeholder circle). Unlike other models, stakeholder circle has its specialty in using an integrative graph to depict the proximity, strength, and scale of stakeholders' influences on the projects. The same problem of this model is that the attributes of stakeholders are general evaluations instead of focusing on specific issues. For example, a stakeholder has extremely high power to threaten the existence of the focal projects. However, such high power may not sustain in the overall project life cycle. For example,

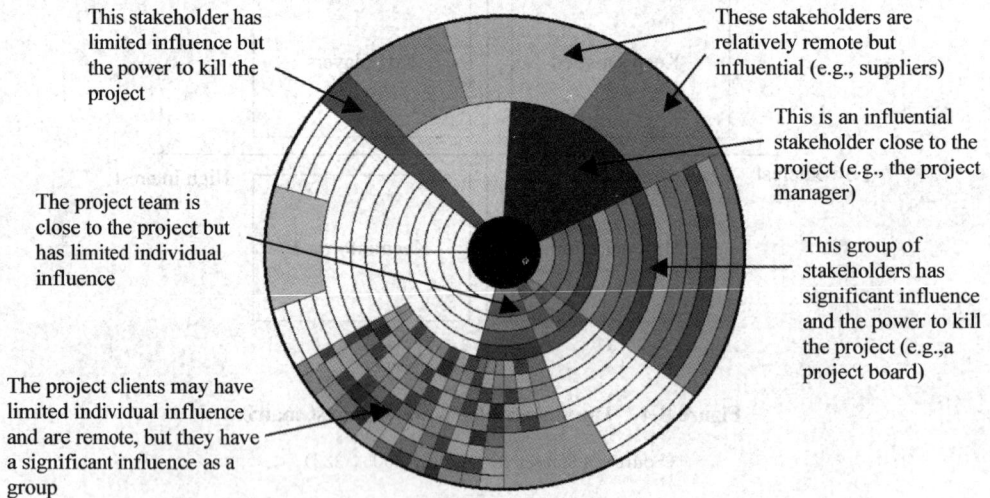

Figure 8-5   The sample of stakeholder circle

(Source: Bourne & Walker, 2005, 656)

the planning departments can put down a project in approval phase but become less relevant after construction begins. The framework developed in this study evaluates stakeholders' attributes based on specific SRTs instead of evaluating their general importance.

8. 6. 4   Rowley's network

Rowley (1997) introduces a network stakeholder model to provide strategies for organizations in different stakeholder network structures. He integrates social network concepts to analyze complicated stakeholder interactions rather than focuses on single organization. The network measures he employs are density and centrality. The constraint ability of a stakeholder increases when the network density grows. The defending ability of a focal organization to cope with stakeholders' pressures increases with its node centrality. Table 8-1 shows organizations' strategies under conditions of different network densities and centralities. Rowley's work transforms the research focus from stakeholders as independent agencies to interactive network relationships among multiple stakeholders. The focal organizations are not at the central point in a hub-spoke model anymore; instead, they are one of the nodes that interact with other nodes in networks. Referring to Rowley's network model, the framework developed in this book also employs a network perspective to create managerial insights on stakeholder collaborative structures. Rowley's network focuses on network measures of stakeholder interactions using one-mode network analysis, while my framework addresses the stakeholder-issue relationships by using a two-mode network analysis. Furthermore, my framework considers stakeholders' heterogeneity and dynamics, presenting a dynamic approach to visualize not only stakeholder interactions, but also how stakeholders are involved in diverse SRTs.

Table 8-1   The organization strategies in Rowley's network model

		Centrality of the focal organization	
		High	Low
Density of the stakeholder network	High	Compromiser	Subordinate
	Low	Commander	Solitarian

(Source: Rowley, 1997, 901)

8.7   Summary of the chapter

This chapter developed a management framework to provide decision support to managers and governors for engaging and coordinating multiple stakeholders in PSR implementation. It provided a solution to the obstacles to PSR caused by complex and dynamic stakeholder environment in construction arena. The development and logics of the two quantifiable indexes, SPI and SII, were illustrated. The two standardized indexes are to assess stakeholders' engagement levels and potential aggressiveness towards the identified SRTs. The step-by-step procedures and instructions were reported in this chapter. The detailed and easy-to-follow framework and procedures provided an alternative tool for project managers to improve stakeholder management, especially in terms of practicing social responsibility and building reputational images. Compared with several existing stakeholder management tools like power/interest matrix and stakeholder circle, the management framework developed in this study supplemented deficiencies of the existing tools and provided an approach to evaluate stakeholders based on specific contexts. For practitioners to choose from multiple existing tools, the framework built in this chapter has the following characteristics: 1) attention on the balance of power and responsibilities rather than simply satisfying stakeholders; 2) consider stakeholders as equal organizations rather than focus on one focal organization; 3) develop quantifiable indexes to replace the binary attribute; 4) address stakeholder dynamics by evaluating stakeholders based on the SRTs; 5) the indexes enable cross-project and pre-post comparisons.

Chapter 9
A Practical Case of the
Management Framework

9.1 Background information of the case project

9.1.1 The Hong Kong-Zhuhai-Macao Bridge [1]

The best way to test whether a management framework is applicable or effective
now is practicing it in a real construction project case. In this book, I present a
case study of performing the management framework in a subproject in the
famous Hong Kong-Zhuhai-Macao Bridge (HZMB) project, hereinafter referred
to as the HKZB project or the project. The overall project is a mega sea-crossing
transportation infrastructure linking the Hong Kong Special Administrative
Region (Lantau Island, Tung Chung, and the Hong Kong International
Airport), Zhuhai of Guangdong Province, and Macao Special Administrative
Region. The project was planned since 2007, and the construction commenced in
December 2009. The entire length of the crossing was about 35.6 km. The main
bridge in Guangdong was 29.6 km long including the sea-crossing dual 3 lane

---

1   The information in this section is from http://www.hzmb.hk/eng/about.html, and http://www.
hzmb.org/en/default.asp, as well as the archival data from the case study.

bridge, two artificial islands, and a 6. 7 km under-sea tunnel. After around ten years of construction, the overall project was completed on February 6, 2018, and was opened to the public on October 24 in the same year. The HZMB is the world's longest sea-crossing highway at the time when this book is published, and it was commended as one of the seven wonders in the modern world, which will be recorded as a marvel in human history. The project dramatically reduced the travel time between Hong Kong and Macao from five hours to around forty-five minutes. The project will accelerate The integration and co-development of the three regions by combining the competitiveness and shortening distances. The main bridge cost about 38. 1 billion yuan. Part of the money was jointly invested by the three governments, and the rest was independently financed by the HZMB authority. The HZMB project is mega-sized, far-reaching, and very complex in construction and management.

9. 1. 2   Why is the project selected?

The project was selected as the case for two main reasons: 1) the project team faced demands and challenges in implementing social responsibility; 2) the project involved complex stakeholder interactions and had difficulties in collaborating multiple parties.

In the HZMB project, SR issues emerged continuously ever since the planning of the project. A matter that received wide concern was the damage to the natural habitat of an endangered species, Chinese White Dolphin. The potential noises and pollution from construction activities inevitably disturbed the heritages of local marine lives. Another issue that gained great public attention was air pollution caused by the construction. A protest from local residents in Tung Chung was one of the issues. There was a tension between the project and the local communities. According to the China News [1], a resident in Tung Chung asserted that the project caused serious health threats to local residents and challenged the administrative admission for the project. This crisis caused serious delay and cost overrun of the project. Considering the public tensions and various impacts on local environments, the project is a very typical case to test whether our framework could improve SR management in such a complex situation.

In addition, the project involved complicated and dynamic stakeholder interactions. A large number of stakeholders were engaged in the projects, which brought enormous conflicts and risks. The official developer of the project is the HZMB authority, co-organized by governments of three regions, to control and supervise the construction, commissioning, maintenance, governance, and management of the project. The main contract was undertaken by a joint venture led by the China Communications Construction Company Limited (CCCC). The supervision, initial design, engineering, quality management, and surveying and design service are delivered to numerous subcontractors and joint ventures. There were a large number of companies and professional institutions involved in different periods of the project. Also, there were many governmental departments, public institutions, and civil organizations involved in the project. It is almost impossible for a project manager to rationally untangle the complicated relationships of stakeholders.

9.2   Data collection process

The detailed case study plan used in this study was presented in Appendix D. The data collection was conducted in three steps.

The first step was identifying the SRTs that need to be implemented in the

---

1   http://www.chinanews.com/ga/2011/09-29/3361633.shtml

project and the related stakeholders. Four in-depth semi-structured interviews and one focused group interview with five departmental representatives were conducted for collecting the SRTs that were most focused currently in the project, and the involved stakeholders for each SRT. The interviews were conducted through on-line chat, telephone calls, and face-to-face conversations. All interviews lasted more than one hour. The focus group was conducted in the office at project base, lasting about 30 minutes. The individual and focus group interviews identified the list of SRTs planned to be implemented and the related stakeholders.

The second step is evaluating stakeholders' attributes on the identified SRTs. A sample of the questionnaire used for this purpose was attached in Appendix E. The questionnaires were distributed to the representatives invited from the identified stakeholders. They were asked to evaluate power, interest, legitimacy, and urgency on each SRT using five-point scale. The questionnaire distribution and collection were conducted face-to-face and through email.

The third step is collecting the feedback for framework validations. After data analysis, a report containing the action plans for implementing the SRTs in the project was sent back to the respondents for feedback evaluations. The report included three sections: 1) the introduction of all the identified SRTs; 2) suggested engagement levels and priorities; 3) the stakeholder-SRT network, with suggestions for collaborations. Along with the reports, a feedback form was also delivered to them to collect their comments on the framework. All feedback were collected after communicating with the participants by emails and telephones.

The activities in data collection processes were summarized in table 9-1.

Table 9-1   The data collection process of the case study

Step	Process	Activity	Participants
Step 1	Identify the social responsibility tasks and related stakeholders	1st interview	Project manager from the main contractor joint venture
		2nd interview	Senior engineer of the main contract
		3rd interview	Representative of the developer
		4th interview	Representative of the community
		The focused group	5 representatives from HSE department, sustainability department, green building department, project management team, and public relation team
Step 2	Evaluate the stakeholders and make action plans	Questionnaire distribution and collection	22 representatives from the developers, contractors, consultants, NGOs, maritime authority, white dolphin protection authority, national planning and research institute
Step 3	Evaluate the outcomes of the framework	Feedback collection	All participants from the last two steps were filling the feedback form for validating the framework

9.3   Identified social responsibility tasks

SRT 1   Disclosure of project impacts on China White Dolphins (CWDs)

Because the project crossed the Pearl River Estuary waters, which is the habitat of the endangered species CWD. According to project disclosure[1], great efforts have been paid on protecting the CWDs, including regular trainings, setting dolphin observer, using new construction techniques to reduce underwater vibration. After the project commenced in 2011, only one report in 2014 disclosed that there was a decrease of twenty-seven in number compared with that

---

1   http://www.hzmb.org/cn/default.asp

of 2012. [1] No data has been publicized since then. The monitors on CWD habitat are carried out regularly; however, the data disclosure is only occasional. Many organizations require the project to publicize the assessment reports periodically, letting the public know about the actual impacts on the species of CWD.

SRT 2　Reserve ecological diversity

The project has an influence on local marine ecology. During the environmental assessment, the Hong Kong government proposed to build a 10,000 m³ marine park at the borders of north Lantau Island. Fish will be released in the artificial reef for the reservation of marine habitat, as the compensation of the marine fishery resources in the water body. Media and the public are demanding the project to take a similar measure in Zhuhai to reserve local marine ecology.

SRT 3　Control offshore construction waste and sewage

Since most of the construction activities are carried out at the offshore construction platforms, the waste, slop, and sewage generated from the construction process if discharged not properly may cause irreversible damages to the marine environment and ecology. Due to the tight project schedule, waste management was not prioritized by project participants. The public required that all construction waste discharged into sea should be treated and tested. It must be guaranteed that the treated waste will cause minimum impacts on the marine environment and ecology.

SRT 4　Environmental data monitoring and disclosure

To meet the requirements of the Environmental Monitoring and Audit (EM & A) by the Hong Kong Government, the updated data on environmental monitoring

---

1　http://www.hzmb.org/cn/bencandy.asp? id=2415

including air quality, landfill gas, noise, water quality, and ecology were continuously disclosed and reported by the environmental project office. [1] While the environmental assessment was also conducted in Zhuhai project, however, no accurate data was disclosed on public website. Local residents asked for environmental monitoring data to be disclosed, so they know the potential influence on their health.

SRT 5   Health care for the workers

Working at the poor working environment offshore, isolated and often under severe weather, the construction workers were at the risks of physical and psychological health hazards. The project participants should take measures for the care of the health of the construction workers working on site, for example, regular health examinations, on-site doctors, cooling measures, improvement of working conditions, and entertainment activities from time to time.

SRT 6   Safety training for extreme maritime weather

Extreme maritime weather occurred occasionally, such as typhoons, thunderstorms, and intense heat. The workers and staff on the offshore platform faced the health and safety risks under extreme weather conditions. The project should improve contingency management under extreme weather to organize trainings and drills, make emergency plans, prepare necessary safety equipment to ensure the safety of the workers and staff in emergency.

SRT 7   Public and community relationships

Although most of the construction activities were offshore and away from local residents, the public relations were intense because of the broad influences of the

---

1   http://www.hzmbenpo.com/

project. The case in Tung Chung was one of the examples. In order to reduce the conflicts, project participants should take measures to develop good community relationships, for example, raising community development funding, supporting local public infrastructures or facilities, organizing open day.

SRT 8   Public participation workshops

The project lasted for a long period of time and encountered emerging social issues, which needed participants to make decisions collectively, for example the potential delayed completion time, and the dilemma of social and economic performance. In order to ensure good communication and improve project social performance, public participation workshops should be held periodically. The workshops can provide a platform for disclosing updated information and receiving public comments on related social issues. The workshops also provide a platform for joint decision making of multiple project participants.

SRT 9   Social philanthropy or volunteer activities

The project is a super infrastructure, which has responsibilities to focus on social issues, generate shared values, and make a good example to be followed by other projects. Activities such as philanthropy, fund-raising, and encouraging staff to participate in volunteer activities are all important to building up project image. These activities not only can improve the reputation of the project, but also can produce far-reaching influences on the construction industry and foster a socially responsible culture.

SRT 10   Energy saving and emission reduction plans

Considering the enormous energy consumption of the construction and operations, the project participants should consider adopting more energy saving and emission reduction techniques, plans, materials, and management. Reducing carbon emission and saving energy is an important social responsibility of a mega project like the HZMB project.

9.4 Stakeholders related to the SRTs

Nine stakeholders were identified as related with the implementation of the social responsibility tasks, as shown in table 9-2.

Table 9-2 List of related stakeholders for PSR implementation

No.	Stakeholder	Abbreviation	Role in the project
1	Hong Kong-Zhuhai-Macao Bridge Authority	HZMB authority	The developer
2	Hong Kong-Zhuhai-Macao committee	HZM committee	The government department
3	China Communication Construction Co., Ltd.	CCCC	The main contractor
4	Island & tunnel project department	I & T project department	The main contractor
5	China Railway Survey and Design Co., Ltd.	CRSD	The consultant
6	Zhuhai Lin Kee Recycling Co., Ltd.	ZLKR	The subcontractor
7	Maritime authority	MA	The government department
8	China white dolphin protection authority	CWD authority	The public institution
9	Sea planning and environmental research institute	SPER institute	The public institution

As the vital player, HZMB authority was the developer and the major manager of the project. The HZM committee represented the governments of Hong Kong SAR, Guangdong Province, and Macao SAR, to perform the administrative duty in the project; therefore, it had important responsibilities to control the quality, environment, and health and safety. CCCC was the organizer of the main contractor joint venture. The main construction work was undertaken by CCCC joint venture, including the main bridge projects and island and tunnel projects. The I & T project department was the headquarter for directing the design and construction of the artificial islands and the subsea tunnel, which was also one of the most complex parts of the project. The I & T project department was affiliated to the main contractor company CCCC, but independently took charge of the island and tunnel project management. It had relationships with multiple important stakeholders including the developers, consultants, subcontractors and suppliers, therefore having superior power to coordinate sufficient resources. CRSD provided surveying and supervision services for the main bridge construction. It had the responsibilities for monitoring and reducing the project's environmental impacts. ZLKR was a subcontractor for waste and material recycling in the project. It was a small waste treatment company. The reason why it was identified as related was that this company had important roles in waste control of offshore platforms. MA was a governmental department that was in charge of the safety and environment management of sea transportations in Guangdong Province. The safety and environmental performance of the project was governed by MA. CWD protection authority was the governmental institute aiming at protecting CWD habitat. SPER was also a governmental institute that was in charge of the marine geology survey, environment monitor, and marine environment research.

9.5   Results and findings of the case study

According to the data analysis, suggestions for action plans were provided based on the evaluation of the stakeholders' attributes. The results were displayed and explained in the following sections. The charts show the SPIs and SIIs of the SRTs. The first column enlists the identified SRTs; the second column contains the values of the SPI for each SRT, showing the engagement levels of the stakeholder group on each issue. The higher value of SPI indicates that the stakeholder should put it in higher priorities, invest more resources, and take active plans. The third column contains the values of the SIIs, which represent the urgency level of each SRT perceived by the stakeholders collectively. A high SII means that the stakeholder deemed it as critical and urgent, indicating the inclination for an aggressive strategy. Therefore, SRTs with higher SIIs are the ones that project managers should pay attention to and take precautionary action against so as to avoid potential aggressiveness.

9.5.1   Hong Kong-Zhuhai-Macao Bridge authority

Table 9-3 shows the SPIs and SIIs for HZMB authority. The framework suggested that priorities should be put on building marine parks and philanthropic and volunteer activities. A lower priority could be community relationships, public participation workshops, energy saving and emission reduction plans, and waste management issues. Also, the project manager should be warned that HZMB authority tends to adopt an aggressive strategy to enforce philanthropic and volunteer activities in the project.

Table 9-3   The action plans for the HZMB authority

	Engagement level	Influence strategy
Information disclosure on CWD	0.03	0.10
Marine parks	0.29	0.14
Waste management	0.17	0.19
Environment monitor stations	0.10	0.11
Health care for workers	0.22	0.15
Safety management in extreme weather	0.11	0.17
Community relationships	0.24	0.14
Public participation	0.21	0.13
Philanthropic & volunteer activities	0.28	0.25
Energy saving & emission reduction plans	0.22	0.19

9.5.2   Hong Kong-Zhuhai-Macao committee

Table 9-4 shows the assessment results of HZM committee. HZM committee was suggested to put priorities on energy saving and emission reduction. HZM committee was suggested that they had power to enable regulation to force the safety management in extreme weather. It should also proactively promote philanthropic and volunteer activities. For government authorities, safety accidents are the most dangerous risk that should be avoided and put great efforts, especially when severe weather like strong typhoons and storms happen frequently. The manager should notice that HZM was most likely to adopt an aggressive strategy in regulating the safety measures for emergencies.

Table 9-4   The action plans for the HZM committee

	Engagement level	Influence strategy
Information disclosure on CWD	0.00	−0.07
Marine parks	−0.16	−0.22
Waste management	−0.04	0.02
Environment monitor stations	0.05	−0.05
Health care for workers	0.01	0.02
Safety management in extreme weather	0.06	0.03
Community relationships	−0.14	−0.30
Public participation	−0.07	−0.26
Philanthropic & volunteer activities	0.06	−0.08
Energy saving & emission reduction plans	0.08	−0.05

9.5.3   China Communication Construction Co., Ltd.

CCCC was the key promoter of social responsibility tasks in the project. The priority should be the workers' health care. Regarding to this, the company should start to plan workers' health care programs, such as health checks and medical services on site, since such measures should and ought to be taken by a contractor to protect its workers. The secondary priorities of CCCC were organizing public participation workshops, disclosing CWD information, and waste management. Overall, CCCC has the potential to adopt aggressive strategy to drive other stakeholders to collaborate or support, for example, ask for reports on environmental monitoring or CWD information (except for building marine parks, which might bring large amount of extra costs and was usually considered as the responsibility of governments).

Table 9-5   The action plans for the CCCC

	Engagement level	Influence strategy
Information disclosure on CWD	0. 16	0. 16
Marine parks	−0. 16	−0. 28
Waste management	0. 15	0. 09
Environment monitor stations	0. 09	0. 20
Health care for workers	0. 20	0. 05
Safety management in extreme weather	0. 14	0. 07
Community relationships	0. 15	0. 09
Public participation	0. 18	0. 06
Philanthropic & volunteer activities	0. 16	0. 13
Energy saving & emission reduction plans	0. 16	0. 11

9.5.4   Islands & tunnel project department

The suggested priority for I & T project team was to promote public participation. The engagement level is high and aggressive index is intense. From the interviews, it was acknowledged that due to the complicated engineering conditions, I & T project has major controversy and misunderstandings of the public. Many of the advanced techniques and measures that were taken to alleviate projects' environmental impacts were not acknowledged by the public. Therefore they are eager to organize events to inform the public and communities about their efforts and performance, in order to avoid any potential public opposition.

Table 9-6   The action plans for the I & T project department

	Engagement level	Influence strategy
Information disclosure on CWD	0. 22	0. 16
Marine parks	0. 04	0. 01
Waste management	0. 15	0. 15
Environment monitor stations	0. 01	-0. 06
Health care for workers	0. 22	0. 13
Safety management in extreme weather	0. 16	0. 17
Community relationships	0. 31	0. 28
Public participation	0. 38	0. 30
Philanthropic & volunteer activities	0. 28	0. 25
Energy saving & emission reduction plans	0. 16	0. 13

9.5.5   China Railway Survey and Design Co.,Ltd.

CRSD was suggested with proactive engagements in promoting building marine park to preserve ecological diversity. CRSD was the main consulting company that had the firsthand data about the marine environment and the potential impacts on ecological diversity. It had sufficient knowledge and legitimacy to persuade the authorities by raising the criticality of the marine environment. The second priority should be given to the health care for construction workers offshore. It could provide protocols and supervisions for the health and safety measures taken by the contractors and subcontractors. CRSD was found with intense concern for the marine part and workers' health care, the managers should keep close communication with CRSD about their concerns and find potential solutions.

Table 9-7   The action plans for the CRSD

	Engagement level	Influence strategy
Information disclosure on CWD	0. 06	−0. 11
Marine parks	0. 24	0. 15
Waste management	0. 07	−0. 04
Environment monitor stations	0. 13	0. 04
Health care for workers	0. 22	0. 15
Safety management in extreme weather	0. 16	−0. 05
Community relationships	−0. 05	−0. 06
Public participation	0. 06	−0. 02
Philanthropic & volunteer activities	0. 07	−0. 05
Energy saving & emission reduction plans	0. 02	−0. 01

9. 5. 6   Zhuhai Lin Kee Recycling Co., Ltd.

According to the data, ZLKR was suggested to take reactive engagements in all of the social responsibility tasks, mostly because it has very limited power as a small subcontractor in a huge project. Generally speaking, ZLKR's role in

Table 9-8   The action plans for the ZLKR

	Engagement level	Influence strategy
Information disclosure on CWD	−0. 52	−0. 31
Marine parks	−0. 36	−0. 45
Waste management	−0. 03	−0. 24
Environment monitor stations	−0. 36	−0. 46
Health care for workers	−0. 38	−0. 45
Safety management in extreme weather	−0. 49	−0. 38
Community relationships	−0. 45	−0. 38
Public participation	−0. 34	−0. 34
Philanthropic & volunteer activities	−0. 27	−0. 37
Energy saving & emission reduction plans	−0. 58	−0. 53

implementing these tasks was a subordinator. However, it has professionalism in waste control and treatment. It should provide necessary support and even persuade the authorities and contractors to adopt advanced measures for their waste control offshore. It should play a role of solution providers for the waste management plan in the project.

9.5.7　Maritime authority

According to the results, MA should take a proactive engagement primarily in public participation workshops and the information disclosure on CWD. If the developer and contractor hesitated about the extra costs or works, maritime authority should engage and support. For example, to provide incentives or professional services for promoting the implementation of these plans. It was also found that MA thought the public participation events were in an urgent need, especially under the pressure that public media was spreading information about the endangered CWD species. The manager should pay attention to these worries of MA and get involved in possible ways to alleviate them.

Table 9-9　The action plans for the maritime authority

	Engagement level	Influence strategy
Information disclosure on CWD	0.06	−0.20
Marine parks	−0.36	−0.20
Waste management	−0.03	−0.01
Environment monitor stations	−0.45	−0.29
Health care for workers	−0.33	−0.22
Safety management in extreme weather	−0.06	−0.05
Community relationships	−0.05	−0.06
Public participation	0.15	0.18
Philanthropic & volunteer activities	−0.13	−0.08
Energy saving & emission reduction plans	−0.09	−0.01

9.5.8 White dolphin protection authority

According to the table 9-10, CWD protection authority was suggested to put the priority on the disclosure of information on CWD. It has most authoritative and updated data on the species of CWD in the influenced waterbody. They should be the main leader and implementer in the disclosure of such information to the public. However, it might come across some reluctance or obstacles, strategies such as allying with public media or governmental power could be used. Related to the CWD protection, the secondary priorities should be given to building marine parks and disclosing environment monitor data for reserving and monitoring marine habitat. Actions like organizing CWD protection initiatives and providing trainings and professional data were suggested.

Table 9-10 The action plans for the CWD protection authority

	Engagement level	Influence strategy
Information disclosure on CWD	0. 18	0. 20
Marine parks	0. 07	−0. 02
Waste management	−0. 05	−0. 18
Environment monitor stations	0. 13	0. 04
Health care for workers	−0. 38	−0. 40
Safety management in extreme weather	−0. 14	−0. 23
Community relationships	−0. 05	−0. 06
Public participation	−0. 26	−0. 13
Philanthropic & volunteer activities	−0. 33	−0. 37
Energy saving & emission reduction plans	−0. 18	−0. 32

9.5.9 Sea planning and environmental research institute

The priority of SPER should be given to building marine parks to reserve ecological diversity. To some extent, this activity was difficult to be undertaken voluntarily because of the cost and work burden, so the project participants would not be willing to do it unless it was required by authorities. SPER was suggested to raise a demand for preservation of marine ecology. They could also use allying strategies to put pressures on key stakeholders. Also, SPER could lobby the governments to provide incentives or compensations for the cost of building marine parks. The secondary priority should be given to environmental disclosure, waste management, and health care for workers.

Table 9-11   The action plans for the SPER institute

	Engagement level	Influence strategy
Information disclosure on CWD	−0. 23	−0. 20
Marine parks	0. 33	0. 24
Waste management	0. 17	0. 19
Environment monitor stations	0. 25	−0. 05
Health care for workers	0. 22	0. 15
Safety management in extreme weather	0. 16	0. 07
Community relationships	−0. 02	−0. 03
Public participation	−0. 34	−0. 28
Philanthropic &. volunteer activities	−0. 02	−0. 05
Energy saving &. emission reduction plans	0. 22	0. 19

9. 5. 10   Stakeholder collaborative clusters

As it was introduced in the case study plan, a stakeholder-SRT network was visualized and shown in figure 9-1. It was developed by using the stakeholders and the social responsibility tasks as nodes and the value of SPIs as the weighted links (only links with above-average values were visible). The square nodes were the stakeholders while the round nodes were the social responsibility tasks that were planned to be implemented. The node sizes represented the degree centralities. The larger size of the node, the higher level of engagement should

be taken by the stakeholder, for example, as a leader or coordinator. The sizes of
the round nodes showed the extent to which the social responsibility tasks
demand multiple stakeholders' engagements.

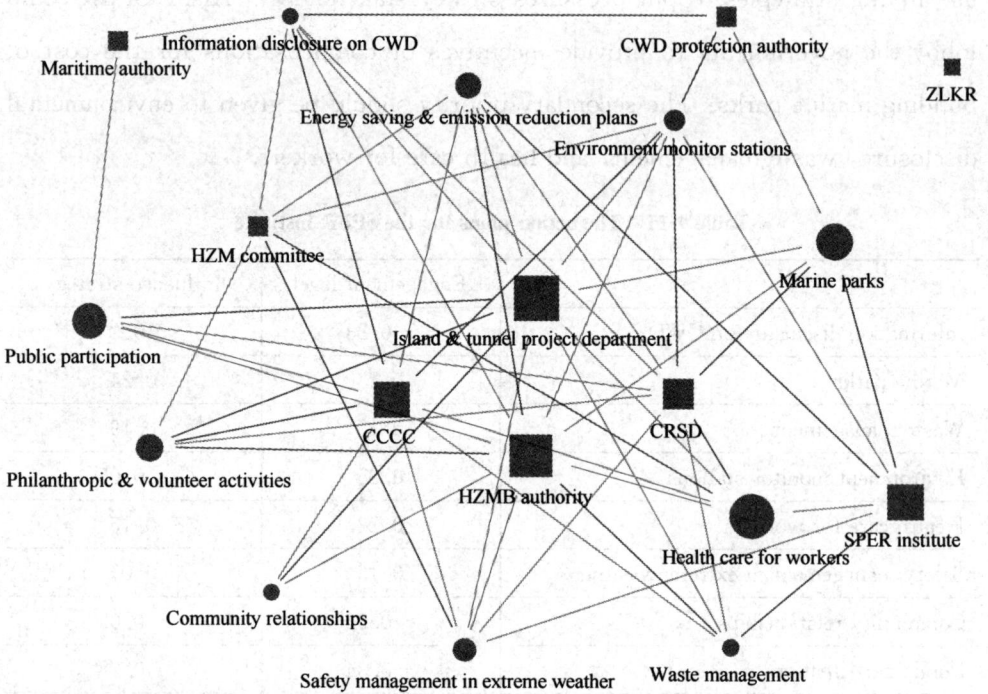

Figure 9-1   The stakeholder collaboration network in the case project

(Generated by Netminer based on my data analysis)

In the middle of the stakeholder-SRT network, the HZMB authority, I & T
project department, CCCC, and CRSD form the headquarter team for implementing
PSR. Their commitments to social responsibility implementation in the project
were significant to the engagement of other stakeholders. They should build a
close cluster and take the leadership for PSR implementation.

From the network, the SRTs that were most in need of stakeholder
collaborative engagement were workers' health care plans, marine parks, public
participation events, and philanthropic and volunteer activities. Among these

issues, building marine parks and public participation require the most diverse resources and multiple stakeholders' commitments.

The stakeholder-SRT network also showed complicated power structures and interactions. The four key stakeholders in the middle should unite as the PSR headquarter. They should interact frequently to share information, exchange resources, and supervise PSR implementation performance. Other stakeholders were also important to collaborating on some specific tasks according to their expertise and special needs. For example, maritime authority was suggested to lead in CWD protection initiatives and public participation events.

Information can be obtained from the stakeholder-SRT network for stakeholder collaborations at the project level. For each task, the responsible stakeholders can be easily identified by tracing the links. For example, community relationships required collaborative engagement of CCCC, I & T project team, and HZMB authority. Many stakeholders including maritime authority, CWD protection authority, HZM committee, HZMB authority, CCCC, and the I & T project department should all be actively involved in the information disclosure on CWD. The colors of links (black and gray) also showed the probability of an aggressive strategy taken by the associated stakeholder regarding the linked SRT. Project management should put primary focuses on these stakeholders' concerns marked by "black lines", for reducing the potential conflicts and aggressiveness.

9.6   Participants' feedback

After communicating the action plans to the participants, they were asked to fill in a feedback form and return for the evaluation of the framework. In the feedback form, the participants were asked to assess the applicability and the effectiveness of the framework. A sample of the feedback form is attached in Appendix F.

According to the feedback, the framework received positive comments (agree or strongly agree) on its effectiveness in facilitating PSR implementation. 82% of the participants agreed that the framework can improve social responsibility implementation in construction projects. 73% of the participants thought that through implementing the framework, the project social performance can be improved. 68% of the participants reported that the framework procedures help multiple stakeholders to exchange information. The effectiveness in facilitating stakeholder collaboration was supported by 73% of the participants. 86% of the respondents agreed that this framework can assist their organizations in implementing social responsibility by ranking the priorities of SRTs and clarifying who should be collaborated with. The average score of the five validation questions for framework effectiveness was 4. 3. The result showed that the framework has great potential in PSR implementation.

With regard to the applicability of framework, there were 36% disagreements on the statement that the framework can be easily applied to construction project management. This may due to the concerns about the time consuming of the procedures, difficulties in gathering data from all stakeholders, reluctant stakeholder participation, and potential resistance for avoiding extra work and costs for PSR implementation. The respondents reported a positive attitude towards the procedures. About 72% of the participants thought the framework steps were clear and easy to follow, and 68% considered the results from the framework were easy to comprehend and instructive. 77% thought that their organizations would like to participate in this framework for implementing PSR. Although there were some concerns about changes and institutionalization process of a new management approach, most held positive attitudes and had willingness to participate in PSR implementation.

In the open-ended questions on the feedback form, some valuable comments were provided. Some addressed that the framework was well-organized and very useful in construction practices because PSR was underestimated by most construction organizations. One suggestion was that the framework should involve more stakeholders from public and civil society instead of focusing only on several internal stakeholders. Another one mentioned that the actions suggested by the framework were in conflict with their tight construction schedule. The project progress had already been delayed due to the technical difficulties. All stakeholders aimed at chasing up the schedule, so inevitably, some SRTs had to give way. One claimed that powerful stakeholders may be reluctant to participate because they can expect great responsibilities on these identified issues. Thus they would avoid such risks and be reluctant to participate. Many comments emphasized that the results generated from the framework were reasonable, but whether those responsible stakeholders would take the assigned actions was invisible and hard to supervise.

The framework implementation in future should take note to the above problems. For example, the identification of SRTs should not only limit to the environmental or safety issues, according to the different situations, some project difficulties like project delay should also be included in the list for collaborative considerations. Project delay will become the first priority of some capable stakeholders to figure out a balance of social and economic performance. This framework is for reducing stakeholder conflicts by providing priorities for stakeholders with their most capable and urgent issues to first deal with. About the reluctance, future cases should involve more external stakeholders, such as civil organizations, public institutions, and press. They can put pressures and monitor the actions that should be taken by key stakeholders.

9.7   Summary of the chapter

The theoretical foundation established in this book argued that PSR can be facilitated by clarifying multiple stakeholders' power and influence on diverse issues. Based on this statement, a management framework was developed, attempting to evaluate stakeholders' preferences and abilities, and make corresponding decision support for PSR implementation. In order to find out whether the management framework has values in facilitating PSR implementation, it was conducted in a real project with complex environment, the HZMB project. Following the designed procedures, action plans were provided for participants who were working in the project. Based on their feedback, we found that the framework has its value in the effectiveness to promote PSR implementation, help multiple stakeholders to identify their priorities, and help managers to coordinate and avoid potential aggressiveness. The framework provided an easy-to-follow procedure to practitioners, especially from government or developer side, to plan and organize the implementation of social responsibility. Also, the feedback pointed out some drawbacks that needed to be improved. In the following research of the author, more case studies on different types and scales of projects will be carried out to test and improve the framework.

Chapter 10
Conclusion

10.1 Research is in need for PSR

Unsatisfactory social performance becomes an obstacle to the sustainability and development of public projects. To improve social responsibility performance, project stakeholders need to collaboratively share resources and respond to the emerging social issues over the project life cycle. At present, only a little academic literature was found focusing on social responsibility in construction sector, most of which was conceptual research. The existing research in this particular area is limited and fragmented. This book addressed this gap and provided an in-depth study to generate both descriptive and prescriptive knowledge on what project social responsibility is like, why it is different from corporate social responsibility, and how multiple stakeholders can implement project social responsibility in the temporary organization and turbulent environment as in public projects.

10.2 Main conclusion

From the reviews of the existing literature, stakeholder power and influence were the key focuses for solving the problems in social responsibility collaboration. In previous studies, some factors like trust, partnership, culture, and regulations are reported having relations with stakeholder collaboration. Power and influence are overlooked in SR studies. However, in a project environment, the exercise of power and influence is an important prerequisite to achieve common objectives. A central assumption here is that PSR requires effective engagement and collaborations of powerful stakeholders. By identifying critical stakeholder power and influence, the flows of resources scattered at different sources can be gathered to collectively respond to contemporary PSR issues.

10. 2. 1   Stakeholder dynamic power

The current literature review revealed that the ignorance of the imbalanced power among stakeholders is the primary problem and obstacle to stakeholder collaboration (Hardy & Phillips, 1998; Loosemore, 1999). Because stakeholders' power distributions are dynamic and complicated, it is extremely difficult for stakeholders with conflicting interests and limited resources to jointly devote to a common goal. Powerful stakeholders are supposed to take more responsibility because they are more capable of accessing scarce resources and obtaining support from other stakeholders. The right usage of power can pass PSR commitments along the upper and lower echelons in the construction supply chain, and facilitate stakeholders' collaboration on implementing common tasks (Jones et al. , 2006). To add value to this problem, this book provided empirical evidence of the stakeholders' diverse power over a series of SRTs, which was presented in Chapter 6. The main conclusions were summarized as follows.

Through the two-mode social network analysis of the data obtained from a questionnaire in Hong Kong, the underlying stakeholder power on the thirty-five social responsibility tasks over the construction project life cycle were revealed. Both internal and external stakeholders have irreplaceable roles and responsibilities in promoting social responsibility in construction projects.

The three core stakeholders for PSR implementation are governments, main contractors, and developers. They have superior power over almost all social responsibility tasks. However, their power fluctuates remarkably along the project life cycle due to the dynamic environment. The findings showed that both governments and developers have the highest power at project initiating and planning stage. However, their power decreases dramatically after construction commences. By contrast, main contractors dominate at the construction stage, while they have relatively low power at the pre- and post- construction stages. Some may argue that stakeholders' roles and responsibilities may vary significantly in different types of contracts. This study addressed that stakeholders' power on social responsibility tasks not only depends on their resources, but also on the abilities to communicate their advocacy and call for support from others in stakeholder network. Moreover, it is also found that stakeholders have different domains on social responsibility in construction projects. For example, governments show exclusive power over human right issues, such as equal opportunity for minorities and discrimination. Contractors have great power compared with others on the labor protection issues. Compared with the three core stakeholders, consultants have very limited power on social responsibility tasks. Although they possess abundant knowledge and experiences to promote social responsibility initiatives, they are not the ones who take charges because their plans can be easily turned down by their clients (Othman, 2009).

District councils and NGOs are found as the main defenders of community and public benefits. Before this study, limited research has been conducted on the roles of district councils in social responsibility implementation in construction projects. Considering scope of authorities, district councils are mainly responsible for the community related issues. They have strong power, only lower than that of the three core stakeholders, to monitor and influence the project activities for safeguarding the benefits of local communities. By contrast, the overall power of NGOs is rather weak. Despite their vital and active roles in solving environmental and social problems, NGOs have inadequate controls over social responsibility in construction projects. The power of NGOs keeps increasing as project proceeds, although the overall power is limited. Therefore, NGOs can continuously monitor the social and environmental impacts during project operations, demolitions, and even rehabilitations.

End users have the least power among all stakeholders. This result does not conform to the common situation in general management that consumers are the most significant source of pressure for social responsibility implementation (Alberg Mosgaard et al., 2016; Henriques & Sadorsky, 1999; Sharma & Henriques, 2005). This result reveals that although public participation is highly emphasized by governments, project end users still lack effective channels to put forward their requirements and participate in the project decisions.

It is noteworthy that stakeholders with great power do not have same level of interest in the social responsibility tasks. Comparison results show significant gaps between the stakeholders' power and their interest. It means that although powerful stakeholders have the abilities to implement social responsibility, generally they do not have intrinsic intentions to do it. Through discussions on stakeholder power and interests, one proposition obtained is that stakeholder engagement levels in implementing social responsibility tasks are determined by both stakeholder power and interest.

10. 2. 2   Stakeholder influence strategies

In this book, it is argued that stakeholders' awareness of their power does not definitely lead to collaboration, and the exercise of external and internal influences is equally essential. Stakeholder power only reflects that one has capacity to influence, while there can be no effects on the targets if necessary stakeholder influence does not exist. Stakeholders have different strategies to drive their targets to respond to their demands or initiatives (Frooman, 1999). If stakeholders adopt proper strategies, the targets may react and even proactively engage themselves towards the desired directions (Sharma & Henriques, 2005). However, inappropriate influencing strategies may not necessarily lead to compliance and even damage stakeholder relationships (Boyd et al., 2007). Therefore, the diverse influence strategies and tactics of each project stakeholder in driving PSR implementation were identified in Chapter 7. The main conclusions were as follows.

The strategies and tactics of stakeholder inter-influences on social responsibility in construction projects were identified based on a small-scale interview survey. Strategies that each stakeholder usually used regarding a PSR issue were asked and recorded. Apart from this, the analysis also put an emphasis on the determinants of stakeholders' aggressive influence. In previous research, stakeholders with relatively high leverages in negotiations tended to adopt hard strategies to force the targets, while stakeholders without power chose rational or soft strategies (Somech & Drach-Zahavy, 2002). However, the results suggested that all stakeholders including those with or without power exercised both aggressive and cooperative strategies. This book argued that the determinants of adopting an aggressive influence in terms of a PSR issue are not simply the power held by a stakeholder. Based on the discussions, the perceived legitimacy and urgency over the issue perceived by stakeholders could be more important in predicting an aggressive attitude. It means that if stakeholders think the initiative is legitimate, and the situations are urgent, they would rather take an aggressive strategy. However, it is also worth noting from the findings that for SR issues, cooperative strategies are frequently used by stakeholders in most of the times.

Instead of only focusing on dyadic relationships, this study developed a holistic network view to look into the influence flows among complex external and internal stakeholders. A map depicting the diffusion of influences within and out of the construction supply chain was provided using the data from the investigation. Based on different influencing strategies and targets, project stakeholders on the map were categorized into eight roles: the claimant (communities and the public), the promoter (NGOs), the regulator (governments), the motivator (end users), the initiator (developers and investors), the advisor (consultants), the operator (main contractors), and the follower (subcontractors and employees). It was shown from the map that all stakeholders have irreplaceable roles in implementing PSR.

Among the external stakeholders, governments act as the regulator. They set the bottom lines by legislations and regulations. Besides, governments can offer the incentive policies, labels, or tax reductions for promoting construction organizations to take PSR in their plans. Another important role of governments is to bridge the communication between the public and construction companies for resolving conflicts, mediating disputes, and compensating affected groups. It is learnt that community power is also vital. In construction projects, communities and the public are the claimants that raise their concerns and requests to related authorities. Although NGOs have no adequate power on social responsibility tasks, they have various influence strategies to gain power through coalition and lobbying. NGOs can ally with governments or district councils to put joint pressures on project leaders. Mostly, NGOs tend to build cooperative relationships with construction companies, in order to ask investment and support in their initiatives.

The influence flows among the internal stakeholders run downstream the supply chain echelons. End users are the motivator for developer companies to think about implementing social responsibility. Despite their powerlessness, the demands of end users regarding social issues in projects are the original driving force of PSR. Developers and investors, as the initiators, would react to end users' demands, and incorporate their initiatives into project visions. Holding the financial power, developers can effectively guarantee their PSR standards and requirements are met by their contractors. Social responsibility commitments are then transmitted downwards to contractors and subcontractors. For building good business partnership, rational contractors would choose to voluntarily respond to and engage in developers' PSR plan. Consultants work as the advisor between developers and contractors. Because consultants have weak decision-making power, they mostly perform the orders of developers, or persuade their clients by demonstrating technical feasibilities, benefits to society and environment, and estimated returns and cost saving. As one of the three most powerful stakeholders, contractors act as the operator to perform the detailed tasks during construction executions. In order to maintain the partnering relationships with contractors, subcontractors and suppliers would voluntarily engage in these tasks organized by contractors, such as volunteer social service or charity donations.

Social responsibility collaboration on construction projects is like a sophisticated machine in which the stakeholders form the critical components with irreplaceable functions to ensure the successful operations and output of productions. Vacancy of any stakeholder's endeavor can lead to the failure of a common task. The findings of the stakeholder influence network provide a guidance for stakeholders to better understand their roles and positions in PSR implementation.

10.2.3   Management framework to facilitate PSR implementation

In practice, stakeholder collaboration on social responsibility faces the challenges of an emergent and dynamic environment. A management framework was developed in this book, offering an alternative solution. According to Reed

(2008), the best practices for stakeholder collaboration include the clarified common objectives, systematic analysis of relevant stakeholders, the empowerment and equity, the involvement throughout the life cycle, and the definition of participation and appropriate level of engagement. The framework developed in this study highlighted these practices and focused on the improvement of stakeholder collaboration in SRTs.

Based on the prior findings in stakeholder power and influence, two indexes were developed, the stakeholder power index (SPI) and stakeholder influence index (SII), as quantifiable variables for evaluating stakeholders' engagement in the social responsibility tasks. The framework generates action plans from two levels: the organizational and project levels. For each related stakeholder, it suggests appropriate engagement levels and priority rankings of the related social responsibility tasks. For project managers, a stakeholder-SRT network can be provided to guide the coordination of stakeholder collaboration. Following the prescribed suggestions, project stakeholders can strategically deal with the social responsibility tasks individually, and collaborate with other stakeholders. The mechanism behind the framework is that stakeholder collaboration can be facilitated when stakeholders concentrate on their capable issues and use power and influences for obtaining necessary resources. The framework can be used as a solution for guiding stakeholders' engagement and interactions in social responsibility tasks, turning unstructured stakeholder interactions into well-organized and traceable collaborations.

From the feedback in a case study, the framework showed positive effects on assisting stakeholder collaboration, facilitating social responsibility implementation, and improving overall project social performance. Compared with the conventional stakeholder models, the framework developed in this study has the following characteristics:

First, the stakeholder analysis perspective is based on inter-stakeholder relationships rather than dyadic organization-stakeholder relations. More insights can be obtained from removing the central position of a focal organization and taking all stakeholders as equal actors to influence each other.

Second, in conventional stakeholder models, powerful stakeholders are associated with high risks that require additional attention, while powerless stakeholders are often neglected. However, in this framework stakeholder power is linked with the corresponding responsibilities, and even powerless stakeholders are attached importance to in driving social responsibility implementation.

Third, stakeholders are evaluated based on scales, giving distinctions to stakeholders with a lot of salience and with little salience, instead of using binary black-or-white assessment. In addition, the evaluation tool is designed in relative value rather than absolute value, and therefore it is applicable to cross-project comparisons.

Fourth, evaluations of stakeholders are based on different social responsibility tasks instead of general perceptions. Stakeholders' dynamic nature is addressed by conducting stakeholder analysis in issue arenas.

Fifth, instead of using subjective external evaluations, this framework reduces single-party bias by adopting multi-stakeholders' self-perception in the identification and assessment of stakeholders.

Along with the rapid development of society, the social responsibility tasks in construction project keep changing dramatically. This framework is applicable to the changing social environment. It addresses the dynamic project environment and helps stakeholders quickly find their positions and respond to the new challenges.

APPENDICES

Appendix A: Sample of preliminary questionnaire in the Delphi Method

Q1. Which type is your experience in the construction field? (Please check the most relevant option)

☐Work experiences in the industry

☐Research experiences in academia

☐Both

Q2. How long have you been working or researching in the construction field altogether? (Please check the most relevant option)

☐1 to 5 years

☐6 to 10 years

☐11 to 15 years

☐Above 16 years

Q3. Which SR issues do you think are NOT important or IRRELEVANT in construction projects and which STRs on the list should be eliminated?

Notice: Please check as many as possible the SRTs that you consider should be eliminated.

Project Inception Stage (15 items):

□1. Disclosure of policies, decisions and activities related to new projects about likely impacts on society and the environment

□2. Establishing channels for stakeholders to freely communicate their views and interests in new projects

□3. Discussing human rights policies and procedures in place to improve human rights performance during project planning

□4. Identifying future health and safety risks to employees and proposing protection measures during project planning

□5. Making land use selection decisions for project site and considering adverse impacts on ecosystem, agricultural land, biodiversity and habitats

□6. Evaluating project feasibility and considering the potential air pollution, water pollution, noise pollution, and waste generation

□7. Assessing and setting objectives and policies to minimize future greenhouse gas emission of the project life cycle

□8. Assessing and setting objectives and policies to minimize resource consumptions in project life cycle

□9. Making procedures and policies to prevent anti-competitive behaviors in project bidding and procurements

□10. Calling upon agreements on transparent environment and establishing common codes of ethics for new projects

□11. Identifying and proposing measures to prevent any future health and safety risk to project users

□12. Ensuring the harmonious resettlement of local residents for land acquisition for new projects

□13. Providing a platform for the public and local community to acknowledge, participate and complain in new project planning

☐14. Identifying and proposing measures to minimize negative impacts on local inhabitants, cultural heritage, and local environment

☐15. Incorporating benefits to local community into the project planning, including improvement of local infrastructure, economy and employment

Project Design Stage (12 items):

☐16. Developing effective communication mechanism to ensure all stakeholders' requirements are incorporated into the design process

☐17. Incorporating all environmental considerations for the whole project life cycle into project designing (e. g. , GHG emissions, resource exploitation, and environmental pollution)

☐18. Considering improvement opportunities of energy performance in the design of new projects

☐19. Choosing eco-materials or eco-friendly materials for material selection in project design

☐20. Encouraging innovation and R&D for improving environmental performance in project design

☐21. Ensuring the durability of buildings in project design

☐22. Ensuring the aesthetical and visual effects of project design and taking economic efficiency into consideration

☐23. Considering all health and safety risks, such as fire, earthquake, flood, radiation, and eco-environmental accidents in designing process

☐24. Adoption of international ratings, standards, and methods for assessing project design, e. g. , Leadership in Energy and Environmental Design (LEED), Design Quality Indicator (DQI)

☐25. Protection of property rights of project design

☐26. Enhancing end-users' satisfaction through listening to their demands in the design process

☐27. Educating project end users to enhance their understanding of the project and awareness of socially responsible consumption

Project Construction Stage (33 items):

☐28. Disclosure of sustainable performance in the project construction process using international reporting standards (e. g. , Global Reporting Initiatives G3 and G4 for sustainability disclosure)

☐29. Promoting cooperation and collaboration culture among stakeholders in projects

☐30. Regular meetings and conferences among stakeholders to discuss the conflicts and interests in socially responsible issues in construction process

☐31. Avoiding discrimination and providing equal treatments and equal opportunities for different genders, minorities and the disabled

☐32. No engagement in forced labor and child labor

☐33. Providing education to avoid harassment in projects

☐34. Protection and care for migrant labors, including legal contracts, medical insurance, occupational health and safety, "left-behind" children, and avoiding defaulting wages

☐35. Providing protection measures, training programs and on-site supervisions to prevent employees from health and safety risks in the construction process

☐36. Ensuring the working conditions comply with national laws and regulations (e. g. , work hours, environments, welfare)

☐37. Providing medical insurance and regular medical checks for employees

☐38. Education and activities for effective emergency management procedures during construction (e. g. , injuries, accidents and occupational diseases)

☐39. On-site and off-site facilities for labors (e. g. , staff areas, drinking water, and food)

☐40. Promoting occupational health and safety culture in projects

☐41. Programs or trainings to improve the capability and employability of employees

☐42. Utilizing land effectively, reducing earthwork and excavation, and taking measures to avoid land pollution

☐43. Protection of living environment for both human beings and animals in construction process

☐44. Reducing and controlling generation and emission of dust, harmful gas or substances (e. g. , CO, SO_2, SO, NO_2 and ozone depleting substances) during construction

☐45. Reducing noise and vibration from project construction and avoiding disturbance for local residents

☐46. Treatment and control of sewage on site

☐47. Supporting the purchase of eco-friendly and energy efficient materials, plants and services

☐48. Reducing the generation of construction waste and implementing proper classification, pile, treatment, and dispose of construction waste

☐49. Taking measures to reduce greenhouse gas emission, e. g. , saving energy and resource consumption, arrangement of material and plant transportation, reuse of building components or materials, using off-site fabrication in construction process

☐50. Investment in implementing environmental management, including labor, plant, material, and finance

☐51. Application of environmental management system in construction process, e. g. , ISO 14000, ISO26000

☐52. Adoption of environmental management consultancy, environmental management facilities, energy saving technology, pollution reduction technology, and waste reduction technology

☐53. Implementing programs, procedures and policies to prevent bribe and corruption during construction

☐54. Legal actions for anti-competitive behavior, trust and monopoly practices in construction process

☐55. Incorporating social, ethical, environmental criteria into purchasing and distributing

☐56. Ensuring no misleading marketing and information is delivered to project users

☐57. Ensuring the in-door environment will not be harmful to project users' health

☐58. Considering local suppliers for purchasing labors, materials, plants and services

☐59. Facilities and measures to reduce the impacts on normal transportation, work and life in local community

☐60. Provision of warning boards and signals, safety facilities to avoid health and safety risks of local residents

Project Operation Stage (10 items):

☐61. Continuously monitoring and recording the generation of pollution, energy and resource consumption (e. g. , electricity, water, and fossil) during the operation of project

☐62. Providing workshops and training programs for instructions of application of green facilities in project

☐63. Application of building environmental performance assessment methods or certificates, e. g. , Hong Kong Building Environmental Assessment Method (HKBEAM), Greenstar, Green Home Evaluation Manual (GHEM), Building Research Establishment Environmental Assessment Methodology

(BREEAM)

☐64. Programs or activities to promote the culture of environmental protection and resource saving during the operation of projects

☐65. Providing follow-up services and maintenance of project

☐66. Providing education to enhance project users' understanding of the project and awareness of social responsibility issues

☐67. Reviewing project users' complaints and taking actions to prevent recurrence

☐68. Resolving disputes and enhancing project users' satisfaction

☐69. Reducing the adverse impacts on local community during the operation of project

☐70. Provision of spaces and facilities beneficial to the development of local community

Project Demolition Stage (10 items):

☐71. Measures to avoid safety risks during project demolition from explosion, dismantling, toxic materials, and radioactive materials

☐72. Compensation and resettlement for the involuntarily dismissed employees because of end of project

☐73. Adequate demolition plan to reduce or recycle the hazardous materials and waste

☐74. Supervision and control of the demolition activities to protect the environment

☐75. Adoption of technologies to alleviate the disturbance on eco-environment systems and neighborhoods

☐76. Classification of demolition waste for enabling effective treatment and disposal

☐77. Special treatment given to toxic materials, heavy metals, radioactive chemicals released from demolition

☐78. Recycling and reclaiming of useful materials, such as steel, brick, glass, timber, and some equipments

☐79. Rehabilitation for the damaged environment for the local residential facilities, land, water, and ecosystem for local community

☐80. Ensure the public awareness of the project demolition, ensure the safety of around residents and avoid harmful impacts on local environment

Q4. Do you recommend any additional important SRT that is not included on this list? Please indicate in the following text box any recommendation or comment.

Appendix B: Sample of stakeholder power questionnaire

Section A: Background Information

Q1. Please indicate the name of your organization. (Optional)

_____

Q2. Please indicate the nature of your organization.

☐Private company

☐Public listed company

☐Government department

☐Public institution

☐Others (please indicate): _____

Q3. Please indicate the usual role of your organization in construction projects.

☐Main contractor

☐Developer

☐End user

☐Government

☐Financial institution

☐Sub-contractor (including supplier)

☐Consultant (including architect/engineer, project management and supervision)

☐Non-government organization

☐District council

☐Town planning board

□Others (please indicate): _____

Q4. Please indicate how long you have been working in your organization.

□Less than 5 years

□6 to 10 years

□11 to 15 years

□Above 16 years

Q5. Please indicate how long you have been working in construction industry.

□Less than 5 years

□6 to 10 years

□11 to 15 years

□Above 16 years

Q6. Please indicate your level in your organization.

□Senior management level

□Project management level

□Site supervisory level

□Junior level or workforce

□Others (please indicate): _____

Section B: Stakeholder Power on Social Responsibility Tasks (SRTs)

Instructions: In this section, please rate the SRTs based on your organization's interest levels, and evaluate stakeholders' power on the implementation of these SRTs in construction projects.

Q7. For each SRT, please answer the following two questions.

1) **Level of concern:** In the grey column, please indicate to what extent your

organization is interested in or concerned with this SRT using the following scale.

　　5= *extremely concerned*; 4 = *very concerned*; 3 = *moderately concerned*; 2 = *slightly concerned*; 1 = *not at all concerned*.

　　2) **Stakeholder power**: In each blank in the matrix, please fill with numbers indicating stakeholder's power to implement each SRT using the following scale.

　　5 = *extremely powerful*; 4 = *very powerful*; 3 = *moderately powerful*; 2 = *slightly powerful*; *leave it blank* = *not at all powerful*.

Project stage	Social responsibility task	1) Level of concern	2) Stakeholder power						
			Main contractor	Developer	End user	Government	Consultant	NGO	District council
Initiating and planning stage	Disclosing social and environmental impacts of new project	□1 □2 □3 □4 □5							
	Establishing stakeholder (including the public) engagement platform	□1 □2 □3 □4 □5							
	Discussing human rights policies during project planning	□1 □2 □3 □4 □5							
	Identifying H&S[1] risks for employees during planning	□1 □2 □3 □4 □5							
	Minimizing adverse impacts of land use plan on ecosystems	□1 □2 □3 □4 □5							
	Evaluating project feasibility considering environmental impacts	□1 □2 □3 □4 □5							
	Prioritizing life cycle environmental performance in design	□1 □2 □3 □4 □5							
	Preventing anti-competitive behaviors in bidding and procurements	□1 □2 □3 □4 □5							
	Establishing codes of ethics for new projects	□1 □2 □3 □4 □5							

1 Health and safety

Project stage	Social responsibility task	1) Level of concern	2) Stakeholder power						
			Main contractor	Developer	End user	Government	Consultant	NGO	District council
	Identifying H&S risks to project users during design	□1 □2 □3 □4 □5							
	Compensating and resettling relocated household	□1 □2 □3 □4 □5							
	Making development plan for local community	□1 □2 □3 □4 □5							
	Meeting stakeholders regularly to discuss conflicts during construction	□1 □2 □3 □4 □5							
	Protecting the rights of migrant labors	□1 □2 □3 □4 □5							
	Protecting employees from H&S risks	□1 □2 □3 □4 □5							
Execution stage	Promoting H&S culture in project	□1 □2 □3 □4 □5							
	Protecting living habitat for both human beings and animals	□1 □2 □3 □4 □5							
	Controlling construction dust, gas, sewage, waste and noise	□1 □2 □3 □4 □5							
	Using green materials, plants, technologies and services	□1 □2 □3 □4 □5							

(Continued)

Project stage	Social responsibility task	1) Level of concern	2) Stakeholder power						
			Main contractor	Developer	End user	Government	Consultant	NGO	District council
	Implementing environmental management system 1	□1 □2 □3 □4 □5							
	Implementing transparency management and promoting trust climate	□1 □2 □3 □4 □5							
	Ensuring healthy in-door environment	□1 □2 □3 □4 □5							
	Considering local suppliers for procurements	□1 □2 □3 □4 □5							
	Reducing adverse impacts on local transportation, work and life	□1 □2 □3 □4 □5							
	Protecting global residents from H&S risks during construction	□1 □2 □3 □4 □5							
Controlling and closing stage	Monitoring and reporting project sustainable performance	□1 □2 □3 □4 □5							
	Avoiding discrimination and providing equal opportunities during operation	□1 □2 □3 □4 □5							
	Protecting employees from risks of demolition	□1 □2 □3 □4 □5							

1 For example, ISO14000 environmental management systems and ISO26000 guidance on social responsibility.

(Continued)

Project stage	Social responsibility task	1) Level of concern	2) Stakeholder power						
			Main contractor	Developer	End user	Government	Consultant	NGO	District council
	Resettling involuntarily dismissed employees because of the end of project	☐1 ☐2 ☐3 ☐4 ☐5							
	Providing training programs of green facilities	☐1 ☐2 ☐3 ☐4 ☐5							
	Promoting environmental protection and energy saving culture	☐1 ☐2 ☐3 ☐4 ☐5							
	Alleviating disturbance on eco-system and neighborhoods by demolition	☐1 ☐2 ☐3 ☐4 ☐5							
	Avoiding bribe and corruptions during operation	☐1 ☐2 ☐3 ☐4 ☐5							
	Reviewing project users' complaints and making responses	☐1 ☐2 ☐3 ☐4 ☐5							
	Rehabilitating damaged local environment	☐1 ☐2 ☐3 ☐4 ☐5							

Apart from the above issues, are there any other SRT that your organization intends to implement in construction projects? Please indicate

Please insert your email for follow-up and update: _____

利益相关者对建设项目中企业社会责任实施的影响调查问卷

第一部分：背景资料

问题1：贵工作单位的名称（选填）

_____

问题2：贵工作单位的性质

□私有企业

□国有企业

□政府

□公共机构

□其他，请指出：_____

问题3：贵工作单位在项目中常担任的角色（多选）

□总承包商

□业主或开发商

□项目使用者

□政府机构

□投资机构

□分包商（包括专业分包、供应商等）

□咨询公司（包括设计、勘测、规划、监理公司等）

□非政府组织

□居民委员会

□其他，请指出：_____

问题 4:您在贵单位的工龄

□少于 5 年

□6—10 年

□11—15 年

□16 年以上

问题 5:您在建设行业中的工龄

□少于 5 年

□6—10 年

□11—15 年

□16 年以上

问题 6:请指出您在机构中所处的位置

□高级管理层

□项目管理层

□现场管理层

□助理或初级人员

□其他,请指出:＿＿＿＿＿＿＿＿＿＿＿＿

第二部分:企业社会责任事项及利益相关者影响

说明:此部分请回答贵单位在建设项目中对实施下列企业社会责任事项的意向和兴趣,并评估项目各参与方对这些事项的影响力。

名词解释:

企业社会责任事项是指建设项目中各参与方除了以营利为目的外,还应参与实施的与环境、社会、生态的可持续发展相关的社会事项。

针对表格中每个企业社会责任事项,请进行如下操作:

(1) 实施意向:首先在灰色列中,请指出贵单位对此企业社会责任事项实施的

兴趣或意向,在符合的数字前打钩:

1=无实施意向,2=有较小意向,3=有一般意向,4=有较大意向,5=非常有意向。

(2) 利益相关者影响:请在余下的空格内填写对应数字,表明该利益相关者对此企业社会责任事项实施的影响的程度:

1=无影响,2=有较小影响,3=有一般影响,4=有较大影响,5=非常有影响。

项目阶段	企业社会责任事项	(1) 实施意向	(2) 利益相关者影响						
			总承包商	开发商	项目使用者	政府机构	咨询公司	非政府组织	居民委员会
建设前阶段	公开报告新项目可能造成的社会及环境影响	□1 □2 □3 □4 □5							
	建立利益相关者沟通平台（包括公众参与）	□1 □2 □3 □4 □5							
	在项目计划期讨论项目中的人权问题及对策	□1 □2 □3 □4 □5							
	在项目计划期识别员工的健康安全风险	□1 □2 □3 □4 □5							
	减少项目用地对当地生态环境的影响	□1 □2 □3 □4 □5							
	项目可行性评估时优先考虑环境影响	□1 □2 □3 □4 □5							
	在设计中优先考虑项目全生命周期的环境绩效	□1 □2 □3 □4 □5							
	防止项目招标及采购中的不正当竞争行为	□1 □2 □3 □4 □5							
	为新项目制定道德守则	□1 □2 □3 □4 □5							
	在设计中识别项目使用者的健康安全风险	□1 □2 □3 □4 □5							
	对征地拆迁的当地居民给予合理赔偿安置	□1 □2 □3 □4 □5							
	制定发展当地社区的计划	□1 □2 □3 □4 □5							
	组织利益相关者定期会议讨论冲突及解决方案	□1 □2 □3 □4 □5							
建设阶段	保护农民工权益	□1 □2 □3 □4 □5							
	提供保护措施，降低员工的健康安全风险	□1 □2 □3 □4 □5							
	促进项目中的健康安全文化	□1 □2 □3 □4 □5							
	保护动物栖息地及附近居住环境	□1 □2 □3 □4 □5							
	控制建筑粉尘、有害气体及化学物质的排放	□1 □2 □3 □4 □5							
	使用绿色材料、设备、技术及服务	□1 □2 □3 □4 □5							

（续表）

项目阶段	企业社会责任事项	(1) 实施意向	(2) 利益相关者影响						
			总承包商	开发商	项目使用者	政府机构	咨询公司	非政府组织	居民委员会
建设阶段	实施环境管理系统 1	□1 □2 □3 □4 □5							
	实施反腐倡廉管理，营造信任文化	□1 □2 □3 □4 □5							
	确保健康的室内人居环境	□1 □2 □3 □4 □5							
	优先考虑本地供应商	□1 □2 □3 □4 □5							
	减少对当地居民的出行、工作和生活的影响	□1 □2 □3 □4 □5							
	设置安全设施，降低当地居民的健康安全风险	□1 □2 □3 □4 □5							
	持续监测并记录建设项目的可持续绩效	□1 □2 □3 □4 □5							
	在运营过程中提供公平等机会，避免歧视	□1 □2 □3 □4 □5							
	在拆除过程中保护员工健康安全	□1 □2 □3 □4 □5							
	对由于项目结束非自愿遣散的员工进行补偿安置	□1 □2 □3 □4 □5							
建设后阶段	提供绿色设施的使用培训	□1 □2 □3 □4 □5							
	促进环境保护和资源节约文化	□1 □2 □3 □4 □5							
	减少拆除对生态系统及周边的影响	□1 □2 □3 □4 □5							
	防止运营过程中的贪污腐败	□1 □2 □3 □4 □5							
	及时处理项目使用者的投诉，并采取相应措施	□1 □2 □3 □4 □5							
	复原项目拆除损坏的当地环境	□1 □2 □3 □4 □5							

除上述事项外，贵单位是否还有实施其他企业社会责任的计划？请指出
_____
请留下您的电子邮箱以便进行反馈和更新：_____ 再次非常感谢您的参与！

1：例如 ISO14000 环境管理系统和 ISO26000 社会责任指南

Appendix C: Sample of interview protocol

INTERVIEW PROTOCOL

A. Background

1. What is your position in this company?

2. How long have you been 1) in your present position? 2) at this company?

3. Can you tell me about your company's policies on SR? What SR issues are mainly included?

   Probes: OHS, environment, community impacts, philanthropy

4. How is your work related to SR? How do you define SR?

5. To what extent do legislative regulations, i. e. , EIS or SIS, fulfil SR? Is the term SR being replaced?

B. Stakeholder influence on SR

6. Who do you think are included in the internal stakeholders in the construction projects?

   Probes: builders, suppliers, subcontractors, consultants, advisors, developers, property management, end users, facility management companies

7. How do you communicate your SR values to these internal stakeholders?

   Probes: documents, emails, meetings

8. What strategies do you use to influence or motivate them to implement SR? Or how has your company been influenced by these stakeholders?

9. Have you ever collaborated on any SR issue with these stakeholders?

10. Has your organization been blamed for the misconduct or weaknesses of these stakeholders?

    Probes: low quality materials, unskilled labors, environmentally unfriendly design

11. What are the aspects that mainly hinder you from integrating SR with these stakeholders?

     Probes: communication, collaboration, disputes, financial issues

12. Who do you think are included in the external stakeholders in the construction projects?

     Probes: governments, NGOs, communities, the public, unions, etc.

13. Can you tell me how does your company communicate your SR values to the external stakeholders?

     Probes: advertisements, publications, reports, labels, public media

14. In what ways do the external stakeholders influence your company to implement SR? Or in what ways does your company respond to them?

15. Is there any SR program that shows the collaboration of your company and the external stakeholders?

16. Has your organization been blamed for their misconduct or weaknesses?

17. What are the aspects that mainly hinder you from integrating SR with the external stakeholders?

     Thank you very much again for participating in the interview. Your contribution to this research is sincerely appreciated and valued. And this research on extending the SR management to the whole construction supply chain instead of doing it in individual organization is of significance in both industrial practices and academia. For further information, I am pleased to send you the feedback upon your request.

End of the interview

Your participation is appreciated

Preparations for the interview:

    Institution: _____

Interviewee (title and name): _____

Interviewer: _____

Date and venue: _____

Background information about the institution:_____

_____

_____

Post-interview comments and observations:

Other topics discussed: _____

_____

Documents obtained: _____

_____

_____

Post-interview comments:

_____

Appendix D: The case study plan

建设项目中利益相关者协同实施社会责任事项的案例研究

整个案例研究包含以下几步：

- 第一步是识别项目中需要实施的社会责任事项及相关方。可采用焦点小组或访谈调查（用时约 5 分钟），调查对象可为企业员工、居民代表、业主、承包商、监理、设计等利益相关方。

* SR 为社会责任的缩写

1. 项目中 SR 的实施

询问项目是否有实施 SR 事项的计划（未实施的），包括环境、人权、生态、社区服务、公众参与、劳动者保护、公益、教育等。

2. 有影响的利益相关方

询问在以上提到的 SR 事项中，有影响的利益相关方包括哪些（组织及个人），如政府部门、业主、施工单位、项目经理、监理、设计、社区、公众等。

- 第二步为问卷调查，根据第一步识别出的社会责任事项及相关方进行问卷设计（用时 10 分钟）。对象为项目主要参与方代表，包括但不限于开发商、总包、设计、监理、物业管理、项目使用者、分包、政府、当地居民代表、环保或其他非政府组织等。目的是衡量各利益相关者对项目社会责任事项实施的影响。

- 第三步为意见反馈，使用反馈意见表（用时 3 分钟），调查对象为前两步所有参与者。完成前面两步后，作者会根据收集到的数据做出一份报告给所有参与者，为项目经理以及各项目方提供社会责任事项实施的决策依据，并为项目各相关方如何协同实施提供借鉴，并请各参与者根据参与体验反馈意见。

Appendix E: Sample of the questionnaire used in case study

利益相关者对项目社会责任实施的影响

港珠澳大桥案例研究调查问卷

第一部分:背景资料

问题1:贵工作单位的名称 _____

问题2:贵工作单位在项目中担任的角色

☐总承包商　　☐业主/开发商/投资方

☐分包商(包括专业分包商、供应商等)

☐咨询公司(包括设计、勘测、规划、监理公司等)　　☐政府机构

☐项目使用者　　☐非政府组织/环保团体　　☐社区代表/居民委员会

☐其他,请指出:_____

问题3:您在贵单位的工龄_____

问题4:您在建设行业中的工龄_____

问题5:您在贵单位的职务_____

第二部分:社会责任事项及利益相关者影响

问题6:社会责任事项是指建设项目除了质量、成本、工期等目标,还应参与实施的与环境、社会、生态的可持续发展相关的社会事项。请您针对表格中与项目相关的社会责任事项,评估贵单位在影响下列事项实施上的意向、权利、合法性、紧迫程度,并在相应的数字前打钩。在评价前,请先浏览所有社会责任事项,如有重要但未被包含的,请在后续的补充表上添加。

序号	社会责任事项	(1) 意向 贵单位对该社会责任事项的实施意向 (1~5分) 1=无意向 5=非常有意向	(2) 权利 贵单位对该社会责任事项实施的影响力大小 (1~5分) 1=无影响 5=非常有影响	(3) 合法性 贵单位是否有充分的合理性去影响该社会责任事项的实施 (1~5分) 1=不合理 5=非常合理	(4) 紧迫性 贵单位是否认为在项目中实施该社会责任事项具有紧迫性(1~5分) 1=不紧迫 5=非常紧迫
1	披露项目对白海豚的影响情况	□1 □2 □3 □4 □5	□1 □2 □3 □4 □5	□1 □2 □3 □4 □5	□1 □2 □3 □4 □5
2	建立海岸公园保育生态	□1 □2 □3 □4 □5	□1 □2 □3 □4 □5	□1 □2 □3 □4 □5	□1 □2 □3 □4 □5
3	施工垃圾,废油,污水处理	□1 □2 □3 □4 □5	□1 □2 □3 □4 □5	□1 □2 □3 □4 □5	□1 □2 □3 □4 □5
4	建立环境监测站,公布空气、噪音、水质环境监控及审核数据	□1 □2 □3 □4 □5	□1 □2 □3 □4 □5	□1 □2 □3 □4 □5	□1 □2 □3 □4 □5
5	对施工工人健康的关怀	□1 □2 □3 □4 □5	□1 □2 □3 □4 □5	□1 □2 □3 □4 □5	□1 □2 □3 □4 □5
6	极端天气的安全管理	□1 □2 □3 □4 □5	□1 □2 □3 □4 □5	□1 □2 □3 □4 □5	□1 □2 □3 □4 □5
7	维护与周边居民的关系	□1 □2 □3 □4 □5	□1 □2 □3 □4 □5	□1 □2 □3 □4 □5	□1 □2 □3 □4 □5
8	社区协作:公众参与工作坊	□1 □2 □3 □4 □5	□1 □2 □3 □4 □5	□1 □2 □3 □4 □5	□1 □2 □3 □4 □5
9	社会公益活动	□1 □2 □3 □4 □5	□1 □2 □3 □4 □5	□1 □2 □3 □4 □5	□1 □2 □3 □4 □5
10	项目节能减排方案	□1 □2 □3 □4 □5	□1 □2 □3 □4 □5	□1 □2 □3 □4 □5	□1 □2 □3 □4 □5

补充表:请填写您认为重要的其他社会责任事项

问题7:有影响的利益相关者是指能够影响项目中上述社会责任事项实施的单位或个人,请勾出您所从属的利益相关者单位,如果您认为有重要但未被包含的利益相关者,请在补充表内填写。

序号	利益相关方名称	请打钩
1	业主方	□
2	三地联合委员会	□
3	岛隧总项目部	□
4	项目安全环保部门	□
5	安全质量监督站	□
6	监理	□
7	分包商	□
8	顾问专家团队	□
9	海洋与渔业局	□
10	海事局	□
11	白海豚保护区管理局	□
12	社区	□
13	边防部门	□

补充表：请填写您认为重要的其他利益相关者

序号	利益相关方名称

再次非常感谢您的参与！

如方便，请留下您的电子邮箱或手机号码，以便我给您发送您发送分析结果报告并进行反馈调查：

Appendix F: Sample of the feedback forms in case study

谢谢您对本次案例分析的支持。根据本次案例分析的过程及结果，请结合您的感受作答。

可操作性：

1. 本方法在项目管理实践中具有可实施性。	□非常同意	□同意	□中立	□不同意	□非常不同意
2. 本方法的操作步骤清晰明确。	□非常同意	□同意	□中立	□不同意	□非常不同意
3. 本方法得到的结果易于理解。	□非常同意	□同意	□中立	□不同意	□非常不同意
4. 贵单位愿意参与本方法来促进项目社会责任实施。	□非常同意	□同意	□中立	□不同意	□非常不同意

有效性：

1. 本方法能够促进项目中社会责任的实施。	□非常同意	□同意	□中立	□不同意	□非常不同意
2. 本方法能够有效提高项目社会绩效。	□非常同意	□同意	□中立	□不同意	□非常不同意
3. 本方法能促进各项目方的沟通。	□非常同意	□同意	□中立	□不同意	□非常不同意
4. 本方法能促进各项目方的协作。	□非常同意	□同意	□中立	□不同意	□非常不同意
5. 本方法能够帮助贵单位实施社会责任。	□非常同意	□同意	□中立	□不同意	□非常不同意

请您为本研究提出宝贵的意见，并指出本方法存在的缺点和不足：_____

REFERENCES

Aaltonen, K. (2011). Project stakeholder analysis as an environmental interpretation process. *International Journal of Project Management*, 29 (2), 165 – 183.

Aaltonen, K. , & Kujala, J. (2010). A project life cycle perspective on stakeholder influence strategies in global projects. *Scandinavian Journal of Management*, 26(4), 381 – 397. doi: 10. 1016/j. scaman. 2010. 09. 001

Aaltonen, K. , & Sivonen, R. (2009). Response strategies to stakeholder pressures in global projects. *International Journal of Project Management*, 27(2), 131 – 141. doi: 10. 1016/j. ijproman. 2008. 09. 007

Aas, C. , Ladkin, A. , & Fletcher, J. (2005). Stakeholder collaboration and heritage management. *Annals of Tourism Research*, 32(1), 28 – 48. doi: 10. 1016/j. annals. 2004. 04. 005

Abbott, W. F. , & Monsen, R. J. (1979). Measurement of social responsibility self-reported disclosures: As a method of measuring corporate social involvement. *Academy of Management Journal*, 22(3), 501 – 515. doi: 10. 2307/255740

Achterkamp, M. C. , & Vos, J. F. (2008). Investigating the use of the stakeholder notion in project management literature, a meta-analysis. *International Journal of Project Management*, 26(7), 749 – 757.

Akiyama, T. (2010). CSR and inter-organisational network management of corporate groups: Case study on environmental management of Sekisui House Corporation Group. *Asian Business & Management*, 9(2), 223 – 243. doi: 10. 1057/abm. 2010. 4

Alberg Mosgaard, M. , Kerndrup, S. , & Riisgaard, H. (2016). Stakeholder constellations in energy renovation of a Danish hotel. *Journal of Cleaner Production*, 135, 836 – 846. doi: 10. 1016/j. jclepro. 2016. 06. 180

Apostol, O. , & Näsi, S. (2013). Firm – employee relationships from a social responsibility perspective: Developments from Communist thinking to market ideology in Romania. A mass media story. *Journal of Business Ethics*. 119(3), 301 – 315. doi: 10. 1007/s10551 – 013 – 1642 – 1

Arnaboldi, M. , & Spiller, N. (2011). Actor-network theory and stakeholder collaboration: The case of Cultural Districts. *Tourism Management*, 32(3), 641 – 654. doi: 10. 1016/j. tourman. 2010. 05. 016

Arnstein, S. R. (1969). A ladder of citizen participation. *Journal of the American Institute of Planners*, 35(4), 216 – 224. doi: 10. 1080/ 01944366908977225

Arvidsson, S. (2010). Communication of corporate social responsibility: A study of the views of management teams in large companies. *Journal of Business Ethics*, 96(3), 339 – 354. doi: 10. 1007/s10551 – 010 – 0469 – 2

Atkin, B. , & Skitmore, M. (2008). Editorial: Stakeholder management in construction. *Construction Management & Economics*, 26(6), 549 – 552. doi: 10. 1080/01446190802142405

Aupperle, K. E. , Carroll, A. B. , & Hatfield, J. D. (1985). An empirical examination of the relationship between corporate social responsibility and profitability. *Academy of Management Journal*, 28(2), 446 – 463. doi: 10. 2307/256210

Aviv, R. , Erlich, Z. , Ravid, G. , & Geva, A. (2003). Network analysis of knowledge construction in asynchronous learning networks. *Journal of*

Asynchronous Learning Networks, 7(3), 1 – 23.

Azzam, T. (2010). Evaluator responsiveness to stakeholders. *American Journal of Evaluation*, 31(1), 45 – 65. doi: 10. 1177/1098214009354917

Bal, M., Bryde, D., Fearon, D., & Ochieng, E. (2013). Stakeholder engagement: Achieving sustainability in the construction sector. *Sustainability*, 5(2), 695 – 710. doi: 10. 3390/su5020695

Barnett, M. L. (2007). Stakeholder influence capacity and the variability of financial returns to corporate social responsibility. *Academy of Management Review*, 32(3), 794 – 816. doi: 10. 5465/amr. 2007. 25275520

Barthorpe, S. (2010). Implementing corporate social responsibility in the UK construction industry. *Property Management*, 28(1), 4 – 17. doi: 10. 1108/02637471011017145

Basu, K., & Palazzo, G. (2008). Corporate social responsibility: A process model of sensemaking. *Academy of Management Review*, 33(1), 122 – 136. doi: 10. 5465/AMR. 2008. 27745504

Bendell, J., Collins, E., & Roper, J. (2010). Beyond partnerism: Toward a more expansive research agenda on multi-stakeholder collaboration for responsible business. *Business Strategy and the Environment*, 19(6), 351 – 355. doi: 10. 1002/bse. 685

Bhatia, A. (2012). The corporate social responsibility report: The hybridization of a "confused" genre (2007 – 2011). *Ieee Transactions on Professional Communication*, 55(3), 221 – 238. doi: 10. 1109/tpc. 2012. 2205732

Blau, P. M. (1964). *Exchange and power in social life.* Transaction Publishers.

Boehm, A. (2002). Corporate social responsibility: A complementary perspective of community and corporate leaders. *Business and Society Review*, 107(2), 171 – 194. doi: 10. 1111/1467 – 8594. 00131

Boote, D. N., & Beile, P. (2005). Scholars before researchers: On the centrality of the dissertation literature review in research preparation. *Educational Researcher*, 34(6), 3 - 15. doi: 10. 3102/0013189x034006003

Booth, W. C. , Colomb, G. G. , & Williams, J. M. (2003). *The craft of research*. University of Chicago Press.

Borgatti, S. P. (2005). Centrality and network flow. *Social Networks*, 27(1), 55 - 71. doi: 10. 1016/j. socnet. 2004. 11. 008

Borgatti, S. P. , & Everett, M. G. (1997). Network analysis of 2-mode data. *Social Networks*, 19(3), 243 - 269. doi: 10. 1016/S0378 - 8733(96)00301 - 2

Bourne, L. , & Walker, D. H. (2005). Visualising and mapping stakeholder influence. *Management Decision*, 43(5), 649 - 660.

Bourne, L. , & Walker, D. H. (2006). Using a visualising tool to study stakeholder influence—two Australian examples. *Journal of Project Management*, 37(1), 5 - 21.

Bourne, L. , & Walker, D. H. (2008). Project relationship management and the Stakeholder Circle™. *International Journal of Managing Projects in Business*, 1(1), 125 - 130.

Boutilier, R. G. (2007). Social capital in firm-stakeholder networks: A corporate role in community development. *Journal of Corporate Citizenship*, 26, 121 - 134.

Bovaird, T. (2005). Public governance: Balancing stakeholder power in a network society. *International Review of Administrative Sciences*, 71(2), 217 - 228. doi: 10. 1177/0020852305053881

Bowen, H. R. (1953). *Social responsibilities of the businessman*. Harper.

Boyd, D. E. , Spekman, R. E. , Kamauff, J. W. , & Werhane, P. (2007). Corporate social responsibility in global supply chains: A procedural justice perspective. *Long Range Planning*, 40(3), 341 - 356.

Brass, D. J. , & Burkhardt, M. E. (1993). Potential power and power use: An investigation of structure and behavior. *Academy of Management Journal*,

36(3), 441 - 470.

Brown, J. , & Parry, T. (2009). Corporate responsibility reporting in UK construction. *Engineering Sustainability*, 162 (4), 193 - 205. doi: 10. 1680/ensu. 2009. 162

Brown, T. J. , & Dacin, P. A. (1997). The company and the product: Corporate associations and consumer product responses. *Journal of Marketing*, 61(1), 68 - 84. doi: 10. 2307/1252190

Brugha, R. , & Varvasovszky, Z. (2000). Stakeholder analysis: A review. *Health Policy and Planning*, 15(3), 239 - 246.

Bryde, D. J. , & Robinson, L. (2005). Client versus contractor perspectives on project success criteria. *International Journal of Project Management*, 23 (8), 622 - 629. doi: 10. 1016/j. ijproman. 2005. 05. 003

Bryson, J. M. , Crosby, B. C. , & Stone, M. M. (2006). The design and implementation of cross-sector collaborations: Propositions from the literature. *Public Administration Review*, 66(SUPPL. 1), 44 - 55. doi: 10. 1111/j. 1540 - 6210. 2006. 00665. x

Capriotti, P. , & Moreno, A. (2007). Corporate citizenship and public relations: The importance and interactivity of social responsibility tasks on corporate websites. *Public Relations Review*, 33(1), 84 - 91. doi: 10. 1016/j. pubrev. 2006. 11. 012

Carroll, A. B. (1979). A three-dimensional conceptual model of corporate performance. *Academy of Management Executive*, 4(4), 497 - 505.

Carroll, A. B. (1991). The pyramid of corporate social responsibility: Toward the moral management of organizational stakeholders. *Business Horizons*, 34(4), 39 - 48.

Carroll, A. B. (1994). Social issues in management research: Experts' views, analysis, and commentary. *Business & Society*, 33(1), 5 - 29.

Carroll, A. B. (1999). Corporate social responsibility: Evolution of a definitional construct. *Business & Society*, 38 (3), 268 – 295. doi: 10. 1177/ 000765039903800303

Carter, C. R. , & Jennings, M. M. (2002). Social responsibility and supply chain relationships. *Transportation Research Part E: Logistics and Transportation Review*, 38(1), 37 – 52. doi: 10. 1016/S1366 – 5545(01) 00008 – 4

Cheng, E. W. L. , Li, H. , Love, P. E. D. , & Irani, Z. (2001). Network communication in the construction industry. *Corporate Communications: An International Journal*, 6(2), 61 – 70. doi:10. 1108/13563280110390314

Cherryholmes, C. H. (1992). Notes on pragmatism and scientific realism. *Educational Researcher*, 21(6), 13 – 17.

Clarkson, M. B. E. (1995). A stakeholder framework for analyzing and evaluating corporate social performance. *The Academy of Management Review*, 20(1), 92 – 117. doi: 10. 2307/258888

Co, H. C. , & Barro, F. (2009). Stakeholder theory and dynamics in supply chain collaboration. *International Journal of Operations & Production Management*, 29(6), 591 – 611. doi: 10. 1108/01443570910957573

Cook, K. S. (1977). Exchange and power in networks of interorganizational relations. *The Sociological Quarterly*, 18(1), 62 – 82.

Cook, K. S. , Emerson, R. M. , Gillmore, M. R. , & Yamagishi, T. (1983). The distribution of power in exchange networks: Theory and experimental results. *American Journal of Sociology*, 89(2), 275 – 305. doi: 10. 1086/ 227866

Cottrill, M. T. (1990). Corporate social responsibility and the marketplace. *Journal of Business Ethics*, 9, 723 – 729. doi: 10. 1007/bf00386355

Crane, A. , Palazzo, G. , Spence, L. J. , & Matten, D. (2014). Contesting the value of "creating shared value". *California Management Review*, 56(2), 130 – 153.

Creswell, J. W. (2013). *Research design: Qualitative, quantitative, and mixed methods approaches*. Sage.

Cruz, J. M. (2009). The impact of corporate social responsibility in supply chain management: Multicriteria decision-making approach. *Decision Support Systems*, 48(1), 224 - 236. doi: 10. 1016/j. dss. 2009. 07. 013

Cuppen, E. , Bosch-Rekveldt, M. G. C. , Pikaar, E. , & Mehos, D. C. (2016). Stakeholder engagement in large-scale energy infrastructure projects: Revealing perspectives using Q methodology. *International Journal of Project Management*, 34(7), 1347 - 1359. doi: 10. 1016/j. ijproman. 2016. 01. 003

Dahl, R. A. (1957). The concept of power. *Behavioral Science*, 2(3), 201 - 215.

Dahlsrud, A. (2008). How corporate social responsibility is defined: An analysis of 37 definitions. *Corporate Social Responsibility and Environmental Management*, 15(1), 1 - 13. doi: 10. 1002/csr. 132

Dainty, A. R. J. , Bryman, A. , & Price, A. D. F. (2002). Empowerment within the UK construction sector. *Leadership & Organization Development Journal*, 23(6), 333 - 342. doi: 10. 1108/01437730210441292

Davidson, W. N. , III, & Worrell, D. L. (1990). A comparison and test of the use of accounting and stock market data in relating corporate social responsibility and financial performance. *Akron Business and Economic Review*, 21(3), 7.

Davis, K. (1960). Can business afford to ignore social responsibilities? *California Management Review*, 2(3), 70 - 76.

Davis, K. (1967). Understanding the social responsibility puzzle. *Business Horizons*, 10(4), 45 - 50.

Davis, K. (1973). The case for and against business assumption of social responsibilities. *Academy of Management Journal*, 16(2), 312 - 322. doi:

10. 2307/255331

Davis, K. (2014). Different stakeholder groups and their perceptions of project success. *International Journal of Project Management*, 32(2), 189 – 201. doi: 10. 1016/j. ijproman. 2013. 02. 006

De Vaus, D. A. (2001). *Research Design in Social Research*. Sage.

Dean, C. (1996). *Empowerment Skills for Family Workers: A Worker Handbook*. Cornell Media Services.

Deegan, C. , & Blomquist, C. (2006). Stakeholder influence on corporate reporting: An exploration of the interaction between WWF-Australia and the Australian minerals industry. *Accounting, Organizations and Society*, 31(4 – 5), 343 – 372. doi: 10. 1016/j. aos. 2005. 04. 001

Deng, T. J. , & Zhou, X. Y. (2009). Developing a model for risk correlation analysis based on stakeholder theory for China's construction projects. Paper presented at the Proceedings of the Third International Conference on Management Science and Engineering Management, Liverpool, UK. ⟨Go to ISI⟩://WOS:000273340200032

Doane, D. (2005). Beyond corporate social responsibility: Minnows, mammoths and markets. *Futures*, 37(2 – 3), 215 – 229. doi: 10. 1016/j. futures. 2004. 03. 028

Doh, J. P. , & Guay, T. R. (2006). Corporate social responsibility, public policy, and NGO activism in Europe and the United States: An institutional-stakeholder perspective. *Journal of Management Studies*, 43(1), 47 – 73.

Donaldson, T. , & Dunfee, T. W. (1994). Toward a unified conception of business ethics: Integrative social contracts theory. *Academy of Management Review*, 19(2), 252 – 284.

Donaldson, T. , & Preston, L. E. (1995). The stakeholder theory of the corporation: Concepts, evidence, and implications. *Academy of Management Review*, 20(1), 65 – 91. doi: 10. 2307/258887

Eesley, C. , & Lenox, M. J. (2006). Firm responses to secondary stakeholder action. *Strategic Management Journal*, 27(8), 765 – 781. doi: 10. 1002/ smj. 536

Eisenhardt, K. M. (1989). Building theories from case study research. *Academy of Management Review*, 14(4), 532 – 550.

Elijido-Ten, E. , Kloot, L. , & Clarkson, P. (2010). Extending the application of stakeholder influence strategies to environmental disclosures: An exploratory study from a developing country. *Accounting, Auditing & Accountability Journal*, 23(8), 1032 – 1059. doi: 10. 1108/09513571011092547

Elo, S. , & Kyngäs, H. (2008). The qualitative content analysis process. *Journal of Advanced Nursing*, 62(1), 107 – 115.

Emerson, R. M. (1962). Power-dependence relations. *American Sociological Review*, 27(1), 31 – 41.

Emerson, R. M. (1976). Social exchange theory. *Annual Review of Sociology*, 21(1), 335 – 362.

Enderle, G. (2006). Corporate responsibility in the CSR debate. *Unternehmensethik im spannungsfeld der kulturen und religionen*, 14, 108.

Epstein, E. M. (1987). The corporate social policy process beyond business ethics, corporate social responsibility, and corporate social responsiveness. *California Management Review*, 29(3), 99 – 114.

Etzioni, A. (1975). *Comparative analysis of complex organizations, Rev. Ed.* Simon and Schuster.

Farneti, F. , & Guthrie, J. (2009). Sustainability reporting by Australian public sector organisations: Why they report. *Accounting Forum*, 33(2), 89 – 98. doi: 10. 1016/j. accfor. 2009. 04. 002

Faust, K. (1997). Centrality in affiliation networks. *Social Networks*, 19(2), 157 – 191. doi: 10. 1016/S0378 – 8733(96)00300 – 0

Fernandes, P. , Monte, A. P. , Pimenta, R. , & Afonso, S. (2013).

Comparison of methodologies of CSR index-application to the PSI 20 companies. *Proceedings of the 12th European Conference on Research Methodology for Business and Management Studies*, 137 - 143.

Frankental, P. (2001). Corporate social responsibility—a PR invention? *Corporate Communication: An International Journal*, 6(1), 18 - 23.

Frederick, W. C. (1994). From CSR1 to CSR2: The maturing of business-and-society thought. *Business & Society*, 33(2), 150 - 164. doi: 10.1177/000765039403300202

Freeman, L. C. (1978). Centrality in social networks conceptual clarification. *Social Networks*, 1(3), 215 - 239.

Freeman, L. C., Borgatti, S. P., & White, D. R. (1991). Centrality in valued graphs: A measure of betweenness based on network flow. *Social Networks*, 13(2), 141 - 154. doi: 10.1016/0378 - 8733(91)90017 - N

Freeman, R. E. (1984). *Strategic management: A stakeholder approach.* Pitman.

Freeman, R. E., & Velamuri, S. R. (2008). A new approach to CSR: Company stakeholder responsibility. In A. Kakabadse & M. Morsing (Eds.), *Corporate social responsibility: Reconciling aspiration with application* (pp. 9 - 23). Palgrave Macmillan UK.

French J. R. P., Jr., & Raven, B. H. (1959). The bases of social power. In D. Cartwright (Ed.), *Studies in social power* (pp. 150 - 167). Institute for Social Research.

Friedman, M. (1970). The social responsibility of business is to increase its profits. *New York Times Magazine*, September 13, 32 - 33, 122 - 124.

Friedman, M. T., & Mason, D. S. (2004). A stakeholder approach to understanding economic development decision making: Public subsidies for professional sport facilities. *Economic Development Quarterly*, 18(3), 236 - 254. doi: 10.1177/0891242404265795

Frooman, J. (1999). Stakeholder influence strategies. *Academy of Management Review*, 24(2), 191 - 205.

Frooman, J. , & Murrel, A. J. (2003). A logic for stakeholder behavior: A test of stakeholder influence strategies. *Academy of Management Proceedings*, 2003(1), F1 - F6. doi: 10. 5465/ambpp. 2003. 13792281

Frooman, J. , & Murrell, A. J. (2005). Stakeholder influence strategies: The roles of structural and demographic determinants. *Business & Society*, 44 (1), 3 - 31. doi: 10. 1177/0007650304273434

Garriga, E. , & Melé, D. (2004). Corporate social responsibility theories: Mapping the territory. *Journal of Business Ethics*, 53(1/2), 51 - 71.

Gaski, J. F. (1984). The theory of power and conflict in channels of distribution. *Journal of Marketing*, 48(3), 9 - 29.

Gjolberg, M. (2009). Measuring the immeasurable? Constructing an index of CSR practices and CSR performance in 20 countries. *Scandinavian Journal of Management*, 25(1), 10 - 22. doi: 10. 1016/j. scaman. 2008. 10. 003

Glaser, B. G. , & Strauss, A. L. (2009). *The discovery of grounded theory: Strategies for qualitative research*. Transaction Publishers.

Godfrey, P. C. , & Hatch, N. W. (2007). Researching corporate social responsibility: An agenda for the 21st century. *Journal of Business Ethics*, 70(1), 87 - 98. doi: 10. 1007/s10551 - 006 - 9080 - y

Goodpaster, K. E. (1991). Business ethics and stakeholder analysis. *Business Ethics Quarterly*, 1(1), 53 - 73. doi: 10. 2307/3857592

Graafland, J. , van de Ven, B. , & Stoffele, N. (2003). Strategies and instruments for organising CSR by small and large businesses in the Netherlands. *Journal of Business Ethics*, 47(1), 45 - 60. doi: 10. 1023/a:1026240912016

Grafstrom, M. , & Windell, K. (2011). The role of infomediaries: CSR in the business press during 2000 - 2009. *Journal of Business Ethics*, 103(2), 221 - 237. doi: 10. 1007/s10551 - 011 - 0862 - 5

Granovetter, M. S. (1973). The strength of weak ties. *American Journal of Sociology*, 78(6), 1360 – 1380.

Gray, B. (1989). *Collaborating: Finding common ground for multiparty problems*. Jossey Bass Publishers.

Grunig, J. E. (1979). New measure of public opinions on corporate social responsibility. *Academy of Management Journal*, 22(4), 738 – 764. doi: 10. 2307/255812

Gustavsson, L. , Joelsson, A. , & Sathre, R. (2010). Life cycle primary energy use and carbon emission of an eight-storey wood-framed apartment building. *Energy and Buildings*, 42(2), 230 – 242. doi: 10. 1016/j. enbuild. 2009. 08. 018

Hamid, K. , Akash, R. S. I. , Asghar, M. , & Ahmad, S. (2011). Corporate social performance, financial performance and market value behavior: An information asymmetry perspective. *African Journal of Business Management*, 5(15), 6342 – 6349.

Hardy, C. , & Phillips, N. (1998). Strategies of engagement: Lessons from the critical examination of collaboration and conflict in an interorganizational domain. *Organization Science*, 9(2), 217 – 230. doi: 10. 1287/orsc. 9. 2. 217

Harrison, J. S. , & Freeman, R. E. (1999). Stakeholders, social responsibility, and performance: Empirical evidence and theoretical perspectives. *Academy of Management Journal*, 42(5), 479 – 485. doi: 10. 2307/256971

Hemingway, C. A. , & Maclagan, P. W. (2004). Managers' personal values as drivers of corporate social responsibility. *Journal of Business Ethics*, 50 (1), 33 – 44.

Hendry, J. R. (2005). Stakeholder influence strategies: An empirical exploration. *Journal of Business Ethics*, 61(1), 79 – 99. doi: 10. 1007/ s10551 – 005 – 8502 – 6

Henriques, I. , & Sadorsky, P. (1999). The relationship between environmental commitment and managerial perceptions of stakeholder importance. *Academy of Management Journal*, 42(1), 87 – 99. doi: 10. 2307/256876

Henriques, I. , & Sharma, S. (2005). Pathways of stakeholder influence in the Canadian forestry industry. *Business Strategy and the Environment*, 14(6), 384 – 398. doi: 10. 1002/bse. 456

Heravi, A. , Coffey, V. , & Trigunarsyah, B. (2015). Evaluating the level of stakeholder involvement during the project planning processes of building projects. *International Journal of Project Management*, 33(5), 985 – 997. doi: 10. 1016/j. ijproman. 2014. 12. 007

Hickson, D. J. , Hinings, C. R. , Lee, C. A. , Schneck, R. E. , & Pennings, J. M. (1971). Strategic contingencies theory of intraorganizational power. *Administrative Science Quarterly*, 16(2), 216 – 229. doi: 10. 2307/2391831

Ho, C. (2013). Communication makes a corporate code of ethics effective: Lessons from Hong Kong. *Journal of Construction Engineering and Management*, 139(2), 128 – 137. doi: 10. 1061/(ASCE)CO. 1943 – 7862. 0000568

Ho, C. M. F. (2010). A critique of corporate ethics codes in Hong Kong construction. *Building Research & Information*, 38(4), 411 – 427. doi: 10. 1080/09613211003665125

Ho, C. M. F. (2011). Ethics management for the construction industry. *Engineering, Construction and Architectural Management*, 18(5), 516 – 537. doi: 10. 1108/09699981111165194

Holmes, S. L. (1976). Executive perspective of corporate social responsibility. *Business Horizons*, 19(3), 34 – 40. doi: 10. 1016/0007 – 6813(76)90049 – 5

Hsieh, H. -F. , & Shannon, S. E. (2005). Three approaches to qualitative content analysis. *Qualitative Health Research*, 15(9), 1277 – 1288.

Hsu, H. , & Lachenbruch, P. A. (2007). Paired t-test, *Wiley encyclopedia of clinical trials*. John Wiley & Sons, Inc.

Huang, C.-F., & Lien, H.-C. (2012). An empirical analysis of the influences of corporate social responsibility on organizational performance of Taiwan's construction industry: Using corporate image as a mediator environment. *Construction Management & Economics*, 30(4), 263 – 275.

Husted, B. W., & Salazar, J. D. J. (2006). Taking Friedman seriously: Maximizing profits and social performance. *Journal of Management Studies*, 43(1), 75 – 91. doi: 10. 1111/j. 1467 – 6486. 2006. 00583. x.

Isa, S. M., & Reast, J. (2012). *Measuring corporate social responsibility (CSR) with multi-dimensional scales: A caution on the risks of conceptual misspecification*. Paper presented at the Proceedings of the 8th European Conference on Management Leadership and Governance, Pafos, Cyprus. 〈Go to ISI〉://WOS:000321614900039

Jamal, T. B., & Getz, D. (1995). Collaboration theory and community tourism planning. *Annals of Tourism Research*, 22(1), 186 – 204. doi: 10. 1016/ 0160 – 7383(94)00067 – 3

Jamali, D. (2007). A stakeholder approach to corporate social responsibility: A fresh perspective into theory and practice. *Journal of Business Ethics*, 82(1), 213 – 231. doi: 10. 1007/s10551 – 007 – 9572 – 4

Jamali, D., & Keshishian, T. (2009). Uneasy alliances: Lessons learned from partnerships between businesses and NGOs in the context of CSR. *Journal of Business Ethics*, 84(2), 277 – 295. doi: 10. 1007/s10551 – 008 – 9708 – 1

Jamali, D., & Mirshak, R. (2007). Corporate Social Responsibility (CSR): Theory and practice in a developing country context. *Journal of Business Ethics*, 72(3), 243 – 262. doi: 10. 1007/s10551 – 006 – 9168 – 4

Jamali, D., Safieddine, A. M., & Rabbath, M. (2008). Corporate governance and corporate social responsibility synergies and interrelationships. *Corporate Governance: An International Review*, 16(5), 443 – 459. doi: 10. 1111/j.

1467 – 8683. 2008. 00702. x

Jawahar, I. M., & McLaughlin, G. L. (2001). Toward a descriptive stakeholder theory: An organizational life cycle approach. *Academy of Management Review*, 26(3), 397 – 414. doi: 10. 2307/259184

Jensen, M. C. (2002). Value maximization, stakeholder theory, and the corporate objective function. *Business Ethics Quarterly*, 12(2), 235 – 256. doi: 10. 2307/3857812

Jing, L. , & Qin, X. (2011). Understanding the key risks in green building in China from the perspectives of life cycle and stakeholder. Paper presented at the Proceedings of the 16th International Symposium on Advancement of Construction Management and Real Estate, Kowloon, Hong Kong SAR, China. 〈Go to ISI〉://WOS:000304017000090

Johansson, R. , & Svane, Ö. (2002). Environmental management in large-scale building projects—learning from Hammarby Sjöstad. *Corporate Social Responsibility and Environmental Management*, 9(4), 206 – 214. doi: 10. 1002/csr. 21

Jones, P. , Comfort, D. , & Hillier, D. (2006). Corporate social responsibility and the UK construction industry. *Journal of Corporate Real Estate*, 8(3), 134 – 150. doi:10. 1108/14630010610711757

Jones, T. M. (1980). Corporate social responsibility revisited, redefined. *California Management Review*, 22(3), 59 – 67.

Jones, T. M. (1995). Instrumental stakeholder theory: A synthesis of ethics and economics. *Academy of Management Review*, 20(2), 404 – 437. doi: 10. 2307/258852

Jonker, J. , & Nijhof, A. (2006). Looking through the eyes of others: Assessing mutual expectations and experiences in order to shape dialogue and collaboration between business and NGOs with respect to CSR. *Corporate Governance: An International Review*, 14(5), 456 – 466. doi:

10. 1111/j. 1467 – 8683. 2006. 00518. x

Joyner, B. E. , & Payne, D. (2002). Evolution and implementation: A study of values, business ethics and corporate social responsibility. *Journal of Business Ethics* ,41 (4), 297 – 311. doi: 10. 1023/A:1021237420663.

Juscius, V. , & Jonikas, D. (2013). Integration of CSR into value creation chain: Conceptual framework. *Inzinerine Ekonomika-Engineering Economics* , 24 (1), 63 – 70.

Kamada, T. , & Kawai, S. (1989). An algorithm for drawing general undirected graphs. *Information Processing Letters* , 31(1), 7 – 15. doi: 10. 1016/0020 – 0190(89)90102 – 6

Karlsen,J. T. (2002). Project stakeholder management. *Engineering Management Journal* , 14(4), 19 – 24. doi: 10. 1080/10429247. 2002. 11415180

Karlsen,J. T. , Graee, K. , & Massaoud, M. J. (2008). The role of trust in project-stakeholder relationships: A study of a construction project. *International Journal of Project Organisation and Management* , 1(1), 105 – 118.

Katavic, I. , & Kovacevic, A. (2011). Integrating corporate social responsibility into business strategies and practice. Paper presented at the 5th International Scientific Conference Entrepreneurship and Macroeconomic Management: Reflections on the World in Turmoil, Vol 2, Pula, Croatia. ⟨Go to ISI⟩://WOS:000319952800022

Kim, S. -Y. , & Reber, B. H. (2008). Public relations' place in corporate social responsibility: Practitioners define their role. *Public Relations Review* , 34 (4), 337 – 342. doi: 10. 1016/j. pubrev. 2008. 07. 003

Klassen, R. D. , & McLaughlin, C. P. (1996). The impact of environmental management on firm performance. *Management Science* , 42 (8), 1199 – 1214. doi: 10. 1287/mnsc. 42. 8. 1199

Kolk, A. , & Pinkse, J. (2006). Stakeholder mismanagement and corporate social responsibility crises. *European Management Journal*, 24(1), 59 – 72. doi: 10. 1016/j. emj. 2005. 12. 008

Latapy, M. , Magnien, C. , & Vecchio, N. D. (2008). Basic notions for the analysis of large two-mode networks. *Social Networks*, 30(1), 31 – 48.

Lenski, G. E. (1966). *Power and privilege: A theory of social stratification.* The University of North Carolina Press.

Leung, M. Y. , Yu, J. Y. , & Liang, Q. (2013). Improving public engagement in construction development projects from a stakeholder's perspective. *Journal of Construction Engineering and Management*, 139(11), doi: 10. 1061/(asce)co. 1943 – 7862. 0000754

Levy, Y. , & Ellis, T. J. (2006). A systems approach to conduct an effective literature review in support of information systems research. *Informing Science: The International Journal of an Emerging Transdiscipline*, 9(1), 181 – 212.

Lewis, P. , & Saunders, M. (2012). *Doing research in business and management: An essential guide to planning your project.* Financial Times/Prentice Hall.

Li, H. Y. T. , Ng, S. T. , & Skitmore, M. (2012). Conflict or consensus: An investigation of stakeholder concerns during the participation process of major infrastructure and construction projects in Hong Kong. *Habitat International*, 36(2), 333 – 342. doi: 10. 1016/j. habitatint. 2011. 10. 012

Li, Y. H. , Zhang, J. , & Foo, C. T. (2013). Towards a theory of social responsibility reporting empirical analysis of 613 CSR reports by listed corporations in China. *Chinese Management Studies*, 7(4), 519 – 534. doi: 10. 1108/cms – 09 – 2013 – 0167

Lindgreen, A. , Swaen, V. , & Johnston, W. (2009). Corporate social responsibility: An empirical investigation of U. S. organizations. *Journal of Business Ethics*, 85(2), 303 – 323. doi: 10. 1007/s10551 – 008 – 9738 – 8

Lingard, H. , & Rowlinson, S. (1998). Behavior-based safety management in

Hong Kong's construction industry. *Journal of Safety Research*, 28(4), 243 – 256.

Littau, P. , Jujagiri, N. J. , & Adlbrecht, G. (2010). 25 years of stakeholder theory in project management literature (1984 – 2009). *Project Management Journal*, 41(4), 17 – 29. doi: 10. 1002/pmj. 20195

Liu, J. (2011). Research on the CSR evaluation system of Chinese real estate enterprises. Paper presented at the Proceedings of the 7th Euro-Asia Conference on Environment and CSR: Technological Innovation and Management Science Session, Pt.Ⅱ, Berlin, Germany. 〈Go to ISI〉;// WOS:000296486800003

Loosemore, M. (1999). Responsibility, power and construction conflict. *Construction Management & Economics*, 17(6), 699 – 709.

Lu, S. , Ming, G. , Wenqi, S. , & Jinxin, T. (2007). Poor images call for CSR: Cause related analysis of China's construction sector. Paper presented at the Proceedings of 2007 International Conference on Construction & Real Estate Management, Vols 1 and 2, Beijing, China. 〈Go to ISI〉;//WOS: 000249584700015

Luoma-aho, V. , & Vos, M. (2010). Towards a more dynamic stakeholder model: Acknowledging multiple issue arenas. *Corporate Communications: An International Journal*, 15(3), 315 – 331. doi: 10. 1108/13563281011068159

Ma, R. Z. , & Zhai, Y. K. (2006). Exploring the corporate social responsibility of the Chinese construction enterprise from "Min-Gong-Huang". Paper presented at the Proceedings of 2006 International Conference on Construction & Real Estate Management, Vols 1 and 2: Collaboration and Development in Construction and Real Estate, Beijing, China. 〈Go to ISI〉;//WOS:000241855100025

Maignan, I. , Hillebrand, B. , & McAlister, D. (2002). Managing socially responsible buying: How to integrate non-economic criteria into the purchasing process. *European Management Journal*, 20(6), 641 – 648. doi: 10. 1016/S0263 – 2373(02)00115 – 9

Mainardes, E. W. , Alves, H. , & Raposo, M. (2012). A model for stakeholder classification and stakeholder relationships. *Management Decision*, 50(10), 1861 – 1879. doi: 10. 1108/00251741211279648

Maloni, M. , & Brown, M. (2006). Corporate social responsibility in the supply chain: An application in the food industry. *Journal of Business Ethics*, 68 (1), 35 – 52. doi: 10. 1007/s10551 – 006 – 9038 – 0

Manheim, J. B. , & Pratt, C. B. (1986). Communicating corporate social responsibility. *Public Relations Review*, 12(2), 9 – 18. doi: 10. 1016/s0363 – 8111(86)80022 – 4

Martinuzzi, A. , Kudlak, R. , Faber, C. , & Wiman, A. (2011). CSR activities and impacts of the construction sector. Sector profile based on a literature review developed in the course of the FP7 Project IMPACT-Impact Measurement and Performance Analysis of CSR, Vienna University of Economics and Business, Austria.

Matten, D. , & Crane, A. (2005). Corporate citizenship: Toward an extended theoretical conceptualization. *Academy of Management Review*, 30(1), 166 – 179. doi: 10. 5465/amr. 2005. 15281448

Matten, D. , & Moon, J. (2008). "Implicit" and "explicit" CSR: A conceptual framework for a comparative understanding of corporate social responsibility. *Academy of Management Review*, 33(2), 404 – 424. doi: 10. 5465/AMR. 2008. 31193458

McCutcheon, D. M. , & Meredith, J. R. (1993). Conducting case study research in operations management. *Journal of Operations Management*, 11(3), 239 – 256. doi: 10. 1016/0272 – 6963(93)90002 – 7

McDonald, S. , & Young, S. (2012). Cross-sector collaboration shaping corporate social responsibility best practice within the mining industry.

Journal of Cleaner Production, 37, 54 – 67. doi: 10. 1016/j. jclepro. 2012. 06. 007

McGuire, J. B. , Sundgren, A. , & Schneeweis, T. (1988). Corporate social responsibility and firm financial performance. *Academy of Management Journal*, 31(4), 854 – 872. doi: 10. 2307/256342

McGuirk, P. M. (2001). Situating communicative planning theory: Context, power, and knowledge. *Environment and Planning A*, 33(2), 195 – 217. doi: 10. 1068/a3355

McWilliams, A. , & Siegel, D. (2001). Corporate social responsibility: A theory of the firm perspective. *The Academy of Management Review*, 26(1), 117 – 117. doi: 10. 2307/259398

Mendelow, A. L. (1981). Environmental scanning: The impact of the stakeholder concept. Paper presented at the ICIS.

Milne, M. J. (1996). On sustainability: The environment and management accounting. *Management Accounting Research*, 7(1), 135 – 161.

Missonier, S. , & Loufrani-Fedida, S. (2014). Stakeholder analysis and engagement in projects: From stakeholder relational perspective to stakeholder relational ontology. *International Journal of Project Management*, 32(7), 1108 – 1122. doi: 10. 1016/j. ijproman. 2014. 02. 010

Mitchell, R. K. , Agle, B. R. , & Wood, D. J. (1997). Toward a theory of stakeholder identification and salience: Defining the principle of who and what really counts. *Academy of Management Review*, 22(4), 853 – 886. doi: 10. 5465/AMR. 1997. 9711022105

Mok, K. Y. , Shen, G. Q. , & Yang, J. (2015). Stakeholder management studies in mega construction projects: A review and future directions. *International Journal of Project Management*, 33(2), 446 – 457. doi: 10. 1016/j. ijproman. 2014. 08. 007

Montaño, C. (2012). Social work theory-practice relationship: Challenges to overcoming positivist and postmodern fragmentation. *International Social Work*, 55(3), 306 – 319.

Moodley, K. , Smith, N. , & Preece, C. N. (2008). Stakeholder matrix for ethical relationships in the construction industry. *Construction Management and Economics*, 26(6), 625 – 632. doi: 10. 1080/01446190801965368

Munilla, L. S. , & Miles, M. P. (2005). The corporate social responsibility continuum as a component of stakeholder theory. *Business and Society Review*, 110(4), 371 – 387. doi: 10. 1111/j. 0045 – 3609. 2005. 00021. x

Myers, D. (2005). A review of construction companies' attitudes to sustainability. *Construction Management and Economics*, 23 (8), 781 – 785. doi: 10. 1080/01446190500184360

Nasi, J. , Nasi, S. , Phillips, N. , & Zyglidopoulos, S. (1997). The evolution of corporate social responsiveness: An exploratory study of Finnish and Canadian forestry companies. *Business & Society*, 36(3), 296 – 321. doi: 10. 1177/000765039703600305

Newman, M. E. (2001). The structure of scientific collaboration networks. *Proceedings of the National Academy of Sciences of the United States of America*, 98(2), 404 – 409. doi: 10. 1073/pnas. 021544898

Oladinrin, T. O. , & Ho, C. M. F. (2014). Strategies for improving codes of ethics implementation in construction organizations. *Project Management Journal*, 45(5), 15 – 26. doi: 10. 1002/pmj. 21444

Oladinrin, T. O. , & Ho, C. M. F. (2015). Barriers to effective implementation of ethical codes in construction organizations: An empirical investigation. *International Journal of Construction Management*, 15(2), 117 – 125. doi: 10. 1080/15623599. 2015. 1033816

Olander, S. (2007). Stakeholder impact analysis in construction project management. *Construction Management and Economics*, 25(3), 277 – 287. doi: 10. 1080/01446190600879125

Olander, S. , & Landin, A. (2005). Evaluation of stakeholder influence in the implementation of construction projects. *International Journal of Project Management* , 23(4), 321 – 328. doi: 10. 1016/j. ijproman. 2005. 02. 002

Oliver, C. (1990). Determinants of interorganizational relationships: Integration and future directions. *Academy of Management Review* , 15(2), 241 – 265.

Onkila, T. (2011). Multiple forms of stakeholder interaction in environmental management: Business arguments regarding differences in stakeholder relationships. *Business Strategy and the Environment* , 20(6), 379 – 393. doi: 10. 1002/bse. 693

Opsahl, T. , Agneessens, F. , & Skvoretz, J. (2010). Node centrality in weighted networks: Generalizing degree and shortest paths. *Social Networks* , 32(3), 245 – 251. doi: 10. 1016/j. socnet. 2010. 03. 006

Ostlund, L. E. (1977). Attitudes of managers toward corporate social responsibility. *California Management Review* , 19(4), 35 – 49.

Othman, A. A. E. (2009). Corporate social responsibility of architectural design firms towards a sustainable built environment in South Africa. *Architectural Engineering and Design Management* , 5(1), 36 – 45. doi: 10. 3763/aedm. 2009. 0904

Packendorff, J. (1995). Inquiring into the temporary organization: New directions for project management research. *Scandinavian Journal of Management* , 11(4), 319 – 333. doi: 10. 1016/0956 – 5221(95)00018 – Q

Parent, M. M. , & Deephouse, D. L. (2007). A case study of stakeholder identification and prioritization by managers. *Journal of Business Ethics* , 75(1), 1 – 23. doi: 10. 1007/s10551 – 007 – 9533 – y

Peffers, K. , Tuunanen, T. , Rothenberger, M. A. , & Chatterjee, S. (2007). A design science research methodology for information systems research. *Journal of Management Information Systems* , 24(3), 45 – 77. doi: 10. 2753/MIS0742 – 1222240302

Peirce, C. S. (1905). What pragmatism is. *The Monist*, 15(2), 161 – 181. doi:
    10. 5840/monist190515230

Peloza, J. , & Falkenberg, L. (2009). The role of collaboration in achieving
    corporate social responsibility objectives. *California Management Review*,
    51(3), 95 – 113.

Petrovic-Lazarevic, S. (2008). The development of corporate social responsibility in
    the Australian construction industry. *Construction Management and Economics*,
    26(2), 93 – 101. doi: 10. 1080/01446190701819079

Pfeffer, J. (1992). Understanding power in organizations. *California
    Management Review*, 34(2), 29 – 50. doi:10. 2307/41166692

Pfeffer, J. , & Fong, C. T. (2005). Building organization theory from first
    principles: The self-enhancement motive and understanding power and
    influence. *Organization Science*, 16 (4), 372 – 388. doi: 10. 1287/orsc.
    1050. 0132

Phillips, R. , Freeman, R. E. , & Wicks, A. C. (2003). What stakeholder
    theory is not. *Business Ethics Quarterly*, 13(4), 479 – 502.

Polonsky, M. J. , & Scott, D. (2005). An empirical examination of the stakeholder
    strategy matrix. *European Journal of Marketing*, 39(9/10), 1199 – 1215.

Porter, M. E. , & Kramer, M. R. (2006). Strategy and society: The link
    between competitive advantage and corporate social responsibility. *Harvard
    Business Review*, 84(12), 78 – 92, 163.

Porter, M. E. , & Kramer, M. R. (2011). Creating shared value. *Harvard
    Business Review*, 89(1/2), 62 – 77.

Prado-Lorenzo, J. -M. , Gallego-Alvarez, I. , & Garcia-Sanchez, I. M. (2009).
    Stakeholder engagement and corporate social responsibility reporting: The
    ownership structure effect. *Corporate Social Responsibility and
    Environmental Management*, 16(2), 94 – 107. doi: 10. 1002/csr. 189

Prell, C. (2011). *Social network analysis: History, theory and methodology.*

Sage.

Preston, L. E., & Sapienza, H. J. (1990). Stakeholder management and corporate performance. *Journal of Behavioral Economics*, 19(4), 361 – 375. doi: 10. 1016/0090 – 5720(90)90023 – Z

Ramesh, T., Prakash, R., & Shukla, K. K. (2010). Life cycle energy analysis of buildings: An overview. *Energy and Buildings*, 42(10), 1592 – 1600. doi: 10. 1016/j. enbuild. 2010. 05. 007

Rattray, J., & Jones, M. C. (2007). Essential elements of questionnaire design and development. *Journal of Clinical Nursing*, 16(2), 234 – 243.

Reed, M. S. (2008). Stakeholder participation for environmental management: A literature review. *Biological Conservation*, 141(10), 2417 – 2431. doi: 10. 1016/j. biocon. 2008. 07. 014

Ringen, K., Seegal, J., & England, A. (1995). Safety and health in the construction industry. *Annual Review of Public Health*, 16(1), 165 – 188.

Roberts, N. C., & Bradley, R. T. (1991). Stakeholder collaboration and innovation: A study of public policy initiation at the state level. *The Journal of Applied Behavioral Science*, 27 (2), 209 – 227. doi: 10. 1177/ 0021886391272004

Robson, C. (2011). *Real world research: A resource for users of social research methods in applied settings*. Wiley Chichester.

Roome, N., & Wijen, F. (2006). Stakeholder power and organizational learning in corporate environmental management. *Organization Studies*, 27 (2), 235 – 263. doi: 10. 1177/0170840605057669

Rowley, T. J. (1997). Moving beyond dyadic ties: A network theory of stakeholder influences. *Academy of Management Review*, 22(4), 887 – 910. doi: 10. 2307/259248

Ruan, X., Ochieng, E. G., Price, A. D. F., & Egbu, C. (2013). Time for a real shift to relations: Appraisal of social network analysis applications in the UK construction industry. 13(1), 14. doi:10. 2139/ssrn. 2623032

Sacconi, L. (2004). Corporate Social Responsibility (CSR) as a model of "extend" corporate governance: An explanation based on the economic theories of social contract, reputation and reciprocal conformism. *LIUC, Ethics, Law and Economics*, no. 142.

Saez-Moran, O. , Navarro, G. , & Saez, P. (2008). Towards a standardized social responsibility balance sheet. *Transparency, Information and Communication Technology: Social Responsibility and Accountability in Business and Education*, 131 - 138.

Sardinha, I. D. , Reijnders, L. , & Antunes, P. (2011). Using corporate social responsibility benchmarking framework to identify and assess corporate social responsibility trends of real estate companies owning and developing shopping centres. *Journal of Cleaner Production*, 19(13), 1486 - 1493. doi: 10. 1016/j. jclepro. 2011. 04. 011

Savage, G. , Bunn, M. , Gray, B. , Xiao, Q. , Wang, S. , Wilson, E. , & Williams, E. (2010). Stakeholder collaboration: Implications for stakeholder theory and practice. *Journal of Business Ethics*, 96(1), 21 - 26. doi: 10. 1007/s10551 - 011 - 0939 - 1

Savage, G. T. , Nix, T. W. , Whitehead, C. J. , & Blair, J. D. (1991). Strategies for assessing and managing organizational stakeholders. *The Executive*, 5(2), 61 - 75. doi: 10. 5465/ame. 1991. 4274682

Scholes, K. , & Johnson, G. (2002). *Exploring corporate strategy*. Prentice Hall International.

Schultz, F. , Castello, I. , & Morsing, M. (2013). The construction of corporate social responsibility in network societies: A communication view. *Journal of Business Ethics*, 115(4), 681 - 692. doi: 10. 1007/s10551 -013 - 1826 - 8

Schwartz, M. S. , & Carroll, A. B. (2003). Corporate social responsibility: A three-domain approach. *Business Ethics Quarterly*, 13(4), 503–530.

Sethi, S. P. (1975). Dimensions of corporate social performance: An analytical framework. *California Management Review*, 17(3), 58–64.

Sharma, S., & Henriques, I. (2005). Stakeholder influences on sustainability practices in the Canadian forest products industry. *Strategic Management Journal*, 26(2), 159–180. doi: 10.1002/smj.439

Sheehy, B. (2015). Defining CSR: Problems and solutions. *Journal of Business Ethics*, 131(3), 625–648. doi: 10.1007/s10551–014–2281–x

Shen, L.-Y., Tam, V. W. Y., Tam, L., & Ji, Y.-B. (2010). Project feasibility study: The key to successful implementation of sustainable and socially responsible construction management practice. *Journal of Cleaner Production*, 18(3), 254–259. doi: 10.1016/j.jclepro.2009.10.014

Shen, L. Y., Hao, J. L., Wing, V., Tam, Y., Yao, H., Shen, L.-Y., & Tam, V. W.-Y. (2010). A checklist for assessing sustainability performance of construction projects. *Journal of Civil Engineering and Management*, 13(4), 273–281.

Smith, A. E., & Humphreys, M. S. (2006). Evaluation of unsupervised semantic mapping of natural language with Leximancer concept mapping. *Behavior Research Methods*, 38(2), 262–279. doi: 10.3758/bf03192778

Snyder, C. M. (1996). A dynamic theory of countervailing power. *Rand Journal of Economics*, 27(4), 747–769. doi: 10.2307/2555880

Somech, A., & Drach-Zahavy, A. (2002). Relative power and influence strategy: The effects of agent/target organizational power on superiors' choices of influence strategies. *Journal of Organizational Behavior*, 23(2), 167–179. doi: 10.1002/job.133

Sotiriadou, P., Brouwers, J., & Le, T.-A. (2014). Choosing a qualitative data analysis tool: A comparison of NVivo and Leximancer. *Annals of Leisure Research*, 17(2), 218–234. doi: 10.1080/11745398.2014.902292

Spena, T. R. , & Chiara, A. d. (2012). CSR, innovation strategy and supply chain management: Toward an integrated perspective. *International Journal of Technology Management*, 58, 83 – 108.

Spencer, B. A. , & Taylor, G. S. (1987). A within and between analysis of the relationship between corporate social responsibility and financial performance. *Akron Business and Economic Review*, 18(3), 7 – 18.

Spiller, R. (2000). Ethical business and investment: A model for business and society. *Journal of Business Ethics*, 27(1), 149 – 160.

Steurer, R. (2010). The role of governments in corporate social responsibility: Characterising public policies on CSR in Europe. *Policy Sciences*, 43(1), 49 – 72. doi: 10. 1007/s11077 – 009 – 9084 – 4

Sturdivant, F. D. , & Ginter, J. L. (1977). Corporate social responsiveness: Management attitudes and economic performance. *California Management Review*, 19(3), 30 – 39.

Sudman, S. , & Bradburn, N. M. (1982). *Asking questions: A practical guide to questionnaire design*. Jossey-Bass Publishers.

Sutterfield, J. S. , Friday-Stroud, S. S. , & Shivers-Blackwell, S. L. (2006). A case study of project and stakeholder management failures: Lessons learned. *Project Management Quarterly*, 37(5), 26.

Tang, Z. , Hull, C. E. , & Rothenberg, S. (2012). How corporate social responsibility engagement strategy moderates the CSR-financial performance relationship. *Journal of Management Studies*, 49(7), 1274 – 1303. doi: 10. 1111/j. 1467 – 6486. 2012. 01068. x

Teoh, H. Y. , & Shiu, G. Y. (1990). Attitudes towards corporate social responsibility and perceived importance of social responsibility information characteristics in a decision context. *Journal of Business Ethics*, 9(1), 71 – 77. doi: 10. 1007/bf00382566

Thijssens, T. , Bollen, L. , & Hassink, H. (2015). Secondary stakeholder influence on CSR disclosure: An application of stakeholder salience theory. *Journal of Business Ethics*, 132(4), 873 – 891. doi: 10. 1007/s10551 – 015 – 2623 – 3

Thomas, R. M. (2003). *Blending qualitative and quantitative research methods in theses and dissertations*. Corwin Press.

Thornton, T. , & Leahy, J. (2011). Changes in social capital and networks: A study of community-based environmental management through a school-centered research program. *Journal of Science Education and Technology*, 21(1), 167 – 182. doi: 10. 1007/s10956 – 011 – 9296 – 1

Tievino, L. K. , & Blown, M. E. (2004). Managing to be ethical : Debunking five business ethics myths. *Academy of Management Executive*, 18(2), 69 – 81.

Tong, X. S. , & Wu, Y. (2008). The construction of corporate social responsibility index system and the method of evaluation. Paper presented at the 2008 International Workshop on Strategy and Marketing, Proceedings, London, UK. ⟨Go to ISI⟩://WOS:000264978700006

Trigos, O. B. (2007). An investigation of green supply chain management in the construction industry in the UK. Master of Science, University of East Anglia.

Trost, J. E. (1986). Statistically nonrepresentative stratified sampling: A sampling technique for qualitative studies. *Qualitative Sociology*, 9(1), 54 – 57. doi: 10. 1007/bf00988249

Tsai, P. C. F. , Yeh, C. R. , Wu, S. -L. , & Huang, I. -C. (2005). An empirical test of stakeholder influence strategy models: Evidence from business downsizing in Taiwan. *The International Journal of Human Resource Management*, 16(10), 1862 – 1885. doi: 10. 1080/09585190500298479

Turner, J. C. (2005). Explaining the nature of power: A three-process theory. *European Journal of Social Psychology*, 35(1), 1 – 22. doi: 10. 1002/ejsp.

244

Valackiene, A. , & Miceviciene, D. (2011). Methodological framework analysing a social phenomenon: Stakeholder orientation implementing balanced corporate social responsibility. *Inzinerine Ekonomika-Engineering Economics*, 22(3), 300 – 308.

Valentine, M. (2014). How strong and weak forms of collective responsibility shape team processes. *Academy of Management Proceedings*, 2014(1), 11382. doi: 10. 5465/AMBPP. 2014. 11382abstract

Valentine, M. , & Edmondson, A. C. (2014). Team scaffolds: How meso-level structures support role-based coordination in temporary groups. *Harvard Business School Technology & Operations Mgt. Unit Working Paper* (12 – 062).

Van Aken, J. E. (2004). Management research based on the paradigm of the design sciences: The quest for field-tested and grounded technological rules. *Journal of Management Studies*, 41(2), 219 – 246. doi: 10. 1111/j. 1467 – 6486. 2004. 00430. x

Van Aken, J. E. (2005). Management research as a design science: Articulating the research products of mode 2 knowledge production in management. *British Journal of Management*, 16(1), 19 – 36. doi: 10. 1111/j. 1467 – 8551. 2005. 00437. x

Van Marrewijk, M. (2003). Concepts and definitions of CSR and corporate sustainability: Between agency and communion. *Journal of Business Ethics*, 44(2 – 3), 95 – 105. doi: 10. 1023/A:1023331212247

Van Offenbeek, M. A. G. , & Vos, J. F. J. (2016). An integrative framework for managing project issues across stakeholder groups. *International Journal of Project Management*, 34(1), 44 – 57. doi: http://dx. doi. org/ 10. 1016/j. ijproman. 2015. 09. 006

Van Strien, P. J. (1997). Towards a methodology of psychological practice:

The regulative cycle. *Theory & Psychology*, 7(5), 683 - 700. doi: 10. 1177/0959354397075006

Vance-Borland, K. , & Holley, J. (2011). Conservation stakeholder network mapping, analysis, and weaving. *Conservation Letters*, 4(4), 278 - 288. doi: 10. 1111/j. 1755 - 263X. 2011. 00176. x

Vilanova, M. , Lozano, J. M. , & Arenas, D. (2008). Exploring the nature of the relationship between CSR and competitiveness. *Journal of Business Ethics*, 87(S1), 57 - 69. doi: 10. 1007/s10551 - 008 - 9812 - 2

Wang, K. , Zheng, R. Y. , & Jianlin, L. (2008). Corporate social responsibility for construction enterprises. Paper presented at the Proceedings of 2008 International Conference on Construction & Real Estate Management, Vols 1 and 2, Beijing, China. 〈Go to ISI〉://WOS:000262502700154

Wang, K. , Zheng, R. Y. , Zhu, K. W. , & Jiang, J. L. (2009). Application study of CSR in the crisis management of construction enterprises. Paper presented at the Proceedings of 2009 International Conference on Construction & Real Estate Management, Vols 1 and 2, Beijing, China. 〈Go to ISI〉://WOS:000277467500127

Wartick, S. L. , & Cochran, P. L. (1985). The evolution of the corporate social performance model. *Academy of Management Review*, 10(4), 758 - 769. doi: 10. 5465/AMR. 1985. 4279099

Weber, J. , & Marley, K. A. (2012). In search of stakeholder salience: Exploring corporate social and sustainability reports. *Business & Society*, 51(4), 626 - 649. doi: 10. 1177/0007650309353061

Webster, J. , & Watson, R. T. (2002). Analyzing the past to prepare for the future: Writing a literature review. *Management Information Systems Quarterly*, 26(2), xiii - xxiii.

Whittemore, R. (2005). Combining evidence in nursing research: Methods and implications. *Nursing research*, 54(1), 56 - 62.

Whittemore, R. , & Knafl, K. (2005). The integrative review: Updated methodology. *Journal of advanced nursing*, 52(5), 546 – 553. doi: 10. 1111/j. 1365 – 2648. 2005. 03621. x

Wicks, A. C. , & Freeman, R. E. (1998). Organization studies and the new pragmatism: Positivism, anti-positivism, and the search for ethics. *Organization Science*, 9(2), 123 – 140.

Wilburn, K. , & Wilburn, R. (2014). Demonstrating a commitment to corporate social responsibility not simply shared value. *Business and Professional Ethics Journal*, 33(1), 1 – 15.

Winch, G. , & Bonke, S. (2002). Project stakeholder mapping: Analyzing the interests of project stakeholders. In D. P. Slevin, D. I. Cleland & J. K. Pinto (Eds.), *The frontiers of project management research*. Project Management Institute. (pp. 385 – 403).

Windsor, D. (2006). Corporate social responsibility: Three key approaches. *Journal of Management Studies*, 43(1), 93 – 114.

Wood, D. J. (1991a). Corporate social performance revisited. *The Academy of Management Review*, 16(4), 691 – 691. doi: 10. 2307/258977

Wood, D. J. (1991b). Social issues in management: Theory and research in corporate social performance. *Journal of Management*, 17(2), 383 – 406.

Xun, J. Y. (2013). Corporate social responsibility in China: A preferential stakeholder model and effects. *Business Strategy and the Environment*, 22(7), 471 – 483. doi: 10. 1002/bse. 1757

Yang, J. , Shen, Q. , & Ho, M. F. (2008). A framework for stakeholder management in construction projects I: Theoretical foundation. Paper presented at the Proceedings of 2008 International Conference on Construction & Real Estate Management, Vols 1 and 2, Beijing, China. ⟨Go to ISI⟩://WOS:000262502700026

Yao, H. , Shen, L. , Tan, Y. , & Hao, J. (2011). Simulating the impacts of policy scenarios on the sustainability performance of infrastructure projects. *Automation in Construction*, 20(8), 1060 – 1069. doi: 10. 1016/j. autcon. 2011. 04. 007

Ye, K. H. , & Xiong, B. (2011). *Corporate social performance of construction contractors in China: Evidences from major firms.* Paper presented at the Proceedings of the 16th International Symposium on Advancement of Construction Management and Real Estate, Kowloon, Hong Kong, China. ⟨Go to ISI⟩://WOS:000304017000027

Zahra, S. A. , & Latour, M. S. (1987). Corporate social responsibility and organizational effectiveness—a multivariate approach. *Journal of Business Ethics*, 6(6), 459 – 467. doi: 10. 1007/bf00383288

Zeng, S. X. , Ma, H. Y. , Lin, H. , Zeng, R. C. , & Tam, V. W. Y. (2015). Social responsibility of major infrastructure projects in China. *International Journal of Project Management*, 33(3), 537 – 548. doi: 10. 1016/j. ijproman. 2014. 07. 007

Zhao, Z. -Y. , Zhao, X. -J. , Davidson, K. , & Zuo, J. (2012a). A corporate social responsibility indicator system for construction enterprises. *Journal of Cleaner Production*, 29 – 30, 277 – 289. doi: 10. 1016/j. jclepro. 2011. 12. 036

Zhao, Z. Y. , Zhao, X. J. , Davidson, K. , & Zuo, J. (2012b). A corporate social responsibility indicator system for construction enterprises. *Journal of Cleaner Production*, 29 – 30, 277 – 289. doi: 10. 1016/j. jclepro. 2011. 12. 036

Zhao, Z. Y. , Zhao, X. J. , & Zuo, J. (2011). Study of corporate social responsibility framework for construction companies. Paper presented at the Proceedings of the 16th International Symposium on Advancement of Construction Management and Real Estate, Kowloon, Hong Kong, China. ⟨Go to ISI⟩://WOS:000304017000114

Zhuang, C. , & Wheale, P. (2004). Creating sustainable corporate value: A case study of stakeholder relationship management in China. *Business & Society Review*, 109(4), 507 – 547. doi: 10. 1111/j. 0045 – 3609. 2004. 00208. x

Zietsma, C. , & Winn, M. I. (2007). Building chains and directing flows: Strategies and tactics of mutual influence in stakeholder conflicts. *Business & Society*, 47(1), 68 – 101. doi: 10. 1177/0007650307306641

Zwetsloot, G. I. J. M. (2003). From management systems to corporate social responsibility. *Journal of Business Ethics*, 44, 201 – 208.